THOMAS GRAY.

THE

POETICAL WORKS

OF

COLLINS,

GRAY, AND BEATTIE.

WITH A MEMOIR OF EACH.

BOSTON:
PHILLIPS, SAMPSON, AND COMPANY,
110 Washington Street.
1852.

CONTENTS

TO COLLINS'S POEMS.

CONTENTS

TO GRAY'S POEMS.

CONTENTS

TO BEATTIE'S POEMS.

CONTENTS.

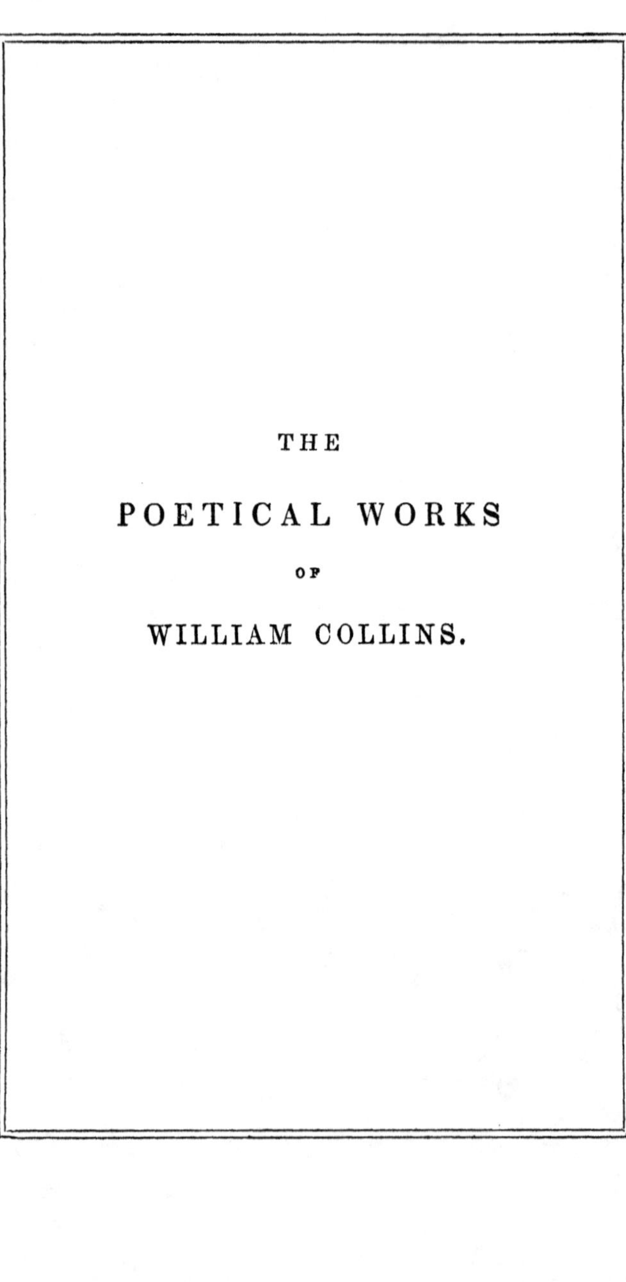

THE

POETICAL WORKS

OF

WILLIAM COLLINS.

LIFE OF COLLINS.

WILLIAM COLLINS was born at Chichester, on the 25th of December, about 1720. His father was a hatter, of good reputation. He was, in 1733, as Dr. Warton has kindly informed me, admitted scholar of Winchester College, where he was educated by Dr. Burton. His English exercises were better than his Latin.

He first courted the notice of the public by some verses to a 'Lady weeping,' published in the Gentleman's Magazine.

In 1740, he stood first in the list of the Scholars to be received in succession at New College; but unhappily there was no vacancy. This was the original misfortune of his life. He became a Commoner of Queen's College, probably with a scanty maintenance; but was in about half a year elected a demy of Magdalen College, where he continued till he had taken a bachelor's degree, and then suddenly left the university; for what reason I know not that he told.

He now (about 1744) came to London a literary adventurer, with many projects in his head, and very little money in his pocket. He designed many works; but his great fault was irresolution, or the frequent calls of immediate necessity broke his schemes, and suffered him to pursue no settled purpose. A man, doubtful of his dinner, or trembling at a creditor, is not much disposed to abstracted meditation, or remote inquiries. He published proposals for a History of the Revival of Learning; and I have heard him speak with great kindness of Leo the Tenth, and with keen resentment of his tasteless successor. But probably not a page of the History was ever written. He planned several tragedies, but he only planned them. He wrote, now-and-then, odes and other poems, and did something, however little.

About this time I fell into his company. His appearance was decent and manly; his knowledge considerable, his views extensive, his conversation elegant, and his disposition cheerful. By degrees I gained his confidence; and one day was admitted to him when he was immured by a bailiff, that was prowling in the street. On this occasion recourse was had to the booksellers, who, on the credit of a translation of Aristotle's Poetics, which he engaged to write with a large commentary, advanced as much money as enabled him to escape into the country. He shewed me the guineas safe in his hand. Soon afterward his uncle, Mr. Martin, a lieutenant-colonel, left him about two thousand pounds; a sum which Collins could scarcely think exhaustible, and which he did not live to exhaust. The guineas were then repaid, and the translation neglected.

But man is not born for happiness: Collins, who, while he *studied to live*, felt no evil but poverty, no sooner *lived to study* than his life was assailed by more dreadful calamities, disease and insanity.

Having formerly written his character, while perhaps it was yet more distinctly impressed upon my memory, I shall insert it here.

'Mr. Collins was a man of extensive literature, and of vigorous faculties. He was acquainted not only with the learned tongues, but with the Italian, French, and Spanish languages. He had employed his mind chiefly upon works of fiction, and subjects of fancy; and, by indulging some peculiar habits of thought, was eminently delighted with those flights of imagination which pass the bounds of nature, and to which the mind is reconciled only by a passive acquiescence in popular traditions. He loved fairies, genii, giants, and monsters; he delighted to rove through the meanders of enchantment, to gaze on the magnificence of golden palaces, to repose by the waterfalls of Elysian gardens.

'This was, however, the character rather of his inclination than his genius; the grandeur of wildness, and the novelty of extravagance, were always desired by him, but were not always attained. Yet as diligence is never wholly lost, if his efforts sometimes caused harshness and obscurity, they likewise produced in happier moments sublimity and splendor. This idea which he had formed of excellence, led him to oriental fictions and allegorical imagery: and, perhaps, while he was intent upon description, he did not sufficiently cultivate sentiment. His poems are the productions of a mind not deficient in fire, nor unfurnished with knowledge either of books or life, but somewhat obstructed in its progress by deviation in quest of mistaken beauties.

'His morals were pure, and his opinions pious; in a long continuance of poverty, and long habits of dissipation, it cannot be expected that any character should be exactly uniform. There is a degree of want by which the freedom of agency is almost destroyed: and long association with fortuitous companions will at last relax the strictness of truth and abate the fervor of sincerity. That this man, wise and virtuous as he was, passed always unentangled through the snares of life, it would be prejudice and temerity to affirm; but it may be said that at least he preserved the source of action unpollated, that his principles were never shaken, that his distinctions of right and wrong were never confounded, and that his faults had nothing of malignity or design, but proceeded from some unexpected pressure, or casual temptation.

'The latter part of his life cannot be remembered but with pity and sadness. He languished some years under that depression of mind which unchains the faculties without destroying them, and leaves reason the knowledge of right, without the power of pursuing it. these clouds which he perceived gathering on his intellects, he endeavored to disperse by travel, and passed into France: but found himself constrained to yield to his malady, and returned. He was for some time confined in a house for lunatics, and afterward retired to the care of his sister in Chichester, where death, in 1756, came to his relief.

'After his return from France, the writer of his character paid him a visit at Islington, where he was waiting for his sister, whom he had directed to meet him. there was then nothing of disorder discernible in his mind by any but himself; but he had withdrawn from study, and travelled with no other book than an English Testament, such as children carry to the school: when his friend took it into his hand, out of curiosity to see what companion a man of letters had chosen, "I have but one book," said Collins, "but that is the best."

'Such was the fate of Collins, with whom I once delighted to converse, and whom I yet remember with tenderness.

'He was visited at Chichester, in his last illness, by his learned friends Dr. Warton and his brother; to whom he spoke with disapprobation of his Oriental Eclogues, as not sufficiently expressive of Asiatic manners, and called them his Irish Eclogues. He shewed them, at the same time, an ode inscribed to Mr. John Hume, on the Superstitions of the Highlands; which they thought superior to his other works.

'His disorder was not alienation of mind, but general laxity and feebleness, a deficiency rather of his vital than intellectual powers. What he spoke wanted neither judgment nor spirit; but a few minutes exhausted him, so that he was forced to rest upon the couch, till a short cessation restored his powers, and he was again able to talk with his former vigour.

'The approaches of this dreadful malady he began to feel soon after his uncle's death; and, with the usual weakness of men so diseased, eagerly snatched that temporary relief with which the table and the bottle flatter and seduce. But his health continually declined, and he grew more and more burthensome to himself.

'To what I have formerly said of his writings may be added, that his diction was often harsh, unskilfully laboured, and injudiciously selected. He affected the obsolete when it was not worthy of revival; and he puts his words out of the common order, seeming to think, with some later candidates for fame, that not to write prose is certainly to write poetry. His lines commonly are of slow motion, clogged and impeded with clusters of consonants. As men are often esteemed who cannot be loved, so the poetry of Collins may sometimes extort praise, when it gives little pleasure.'

Mr. Collins's first production is added here from the 'Poetical Calendar.'

TO MISS AURELIA C—R.

On her weeping at her Sister's Wedding.

Cease, fair Aurelia, cease to mourn;
Lament not Hannah's happy state:
You may be happy in your turn,
And seize the treasure you regret.

With Love united Hymen stands,
And softly whispers to your charms,—
'Meet but your lover in my bands,
You'll find your sister in his arms.'

A monument has been erected by public subscription to Collins. He is represented as just recovered from a wild fit of phrensy, to which he was subject, and in a calm and reclining posture, seeking refuge from his misfortunes in the consolations of the Gospel, while his lyre and one of the first of his poems lie neglected on the ground, &c. The whole was executed by Flaxman, at that time lately returned from Rome: the following most excellent epitaph was written by Mr. Hayley.

Ye who the merits of the dead revere,
Who hold misfortune's sacred genius dear,
Regard this tomb, where Collins, hapless name,
Solicits kindness with a double claim.
Though Nature gave him, and though Science taught
The fire of Fancy, and the reach of thought,
Severely doom'd to Penury's extreme,
He pass'd in madd'ning pain life's fev'rish dream,
While rays of genius only served to shew
The thick'ning horror, and exalt his woe.
Ye walls, that echo'd to his frantic moan,
Guard the due records of this grateful stone;
Strangers to him, enamour'd of his lays,
This fond memorial to his talents raise.
For this the ashes of the bard require,
Who touch'd the tend'rest notes of Pity's lyre;
Who join'd pure faith to strong poetic powers,
Who, in reviving Reason's lucid hours,
Sought on one book his troubled mind to rest,
And rightly deem'd the book of God the best.

STANZAS,

Written by Scott, of Amwell, on his return from Chichester, where he had in vain attempted to find the burial-place of Collins.

To view the beauties of my native land,
  O'er many a pleasing, distant scene, I rove;
Now climb the rock, or wander on the strand,
  Or trace the rill, or penetrate the grove.

From Baia's hills, from Portsea's spreading wave,
  To fair Cicestria's lonely walls I stray;
To her famed Poet's venerated grave
  Anxious my tribute of respect to pay.

O'er the dim pavement of the solemn fane,
  Midst the rude stones that croud th' adjoining space,
The sacred spot I seek: but seek in vain—
  In vain I ask—for none can point the place.

What boots the eye whose quick observant glance
  Marks every nobler, every fairer form?
What, the skill'd ear that sound's sweet charms entrance,
  And the fond breast with generous passion warm?

What boots the power each image to portray,
  The power with force each feeling to express?
How vain the hope that through life's little day,
  The soul with thought of future fame can bless.

While Folly frequent boasts th' insculptured tomb,
  By flattery's pen inscribed with purchased praise;
While rustic Labour's undistinguish'd doom
  Fond Friendship's hand records in humble phrase;

Of Genius oft and Learning worse the lot,
  For them no care, to them no honour shewn:
Alive neglected, and when dead forgot,
  E'en COLLINS slumbers in a grave unknown.

POEMS.

ORIENTAL ECLOGUES

ECLOGUE I.

SELIM; OR, THE SHEPHERD'S MORAL.

Scene—A Valley near Bagdat. *Time*—The Morning.

'Ye Persian maids! attend your poet's lays,
And hear how shepherds pass their golden days.
Not all are blest, whom Fortune's hand sustains
With wealth in courts; nor all that haunt the plains:
Well may your hearts believe the truths I tell;
'Tis virtue makes the bliss where'er we dwell.'

Thus Selim sung, by sacred Truth inspired;
Nor praise, but such as Truth bestow'd, desired:
Wise in himself, his meaning songs convey'd
Informing morals to the shepherd maid;
Or taught the swains that surest bliss to find,
What groves nor streams bestow—a virtuous mind.

When sweet and blushing, like a virgin bride,
The radiant morn resumed her orient pride;
When wanton gales along the valleys play,
Breathe on each flower, and bear their sweets away,
By Tigris' wand'ring waves he sat, and sung
This useful lesson for the fair and young:

'Ye Persian dames, he said, to you belong—
Well may they please—the morals of my song:
No fairer maids, I trust, than you are found,
Graced with soft arts, the peopled world around!
The morn that lights you, to your love supplies
Each gentler ray delicious to your eyes:

b

For you those flowers her fragrant hands bestow,
And yours the love that kings delight to know.
Yet think not these, all beauteous as they are,
The best kind blessings Heaven can grant the fair!
Who trust alone in Beauty's feeble ray,
Boast but the worth Bassora's pearls display;
Drawn from the deep, we own their surface bright,
But, dark within, they drink no lustrous light:
Such are the maids, and such the charms they boast,
By sense unaided, or to virtue lost.
Self-flattering sex! your hearts believe in vain
That Love shall blind, when once he fires the swain;
Or hope a lover by your faults to win,
As spots on ermine beautify the skin:
Who seeks secure to rule, be first her care
Each softer virtue that adorns the fair;
Each tender passion man delights to find,
The loved perfections of a female mind!
'Blest were the days when Wisdom held her reign,
And shepherds sought her on the silent plain;
With Truth she wedded in the secret grove,
Immortal Truth! and daughters bless'd their love.
'O haste, fair maids! ye Virtues, come away,
Sweet Peace and Plenty lead you on your way!
The balmy shrub for you shall love our shore,
By Ind excell'd, or Araby, no more.
'Lost to our fields, for so the Fates ordain,
The dear deserters shall return again.
Come thou, whose thoughts as limpid springs are clear,
To lead the train, sweet Modesty, appear:
Here make thy court amidst our rural scene,
And shepherd-girls shall own thee for their queen:
With thee be Chastity, of all afraid,
Distrusting all, a wise, suspicious maid;
But man the most—not more the mountain doe
Holds the swift falcon for her deadly foe.

Cold is her breast, like flowers that drink the dew;
A silken veil conceals her from the view.
No wild desires amidst thy train be known,
But Faith, whose heart is fix'd on one alone:
Desponding Meekness, with her downcast eyes,
And friendly Pity, full of tender sighs:
And Love, the last: by these your hearts approve,
These are the virtues that must lead to love.'

Thus sung the swain; and ancient legends say,
The maids of Bagdat verified the lay:
Dear to the plains, the Virtues came along,
The shepherds loved, and Selim bless'd his song.

ECLOGUE II.

HASSAN; OR, THE CAMEL-DRIVER.

Scene—The Desert. *Time*—Mid-day.

IN silent horror, o'er the boundless waste
The driver Hassan with his camels past;
One cruse of water on his back he bore,
And his light scrip contain'd a scanty store;
A fan of painted feathers in his hand,
To guard his shaded face from scorching sand.
The sultry sun had gain'd the middle sky,
And not a tree, and not an herb was nigh;
The beasts, with pain, their dusty way pursue,
Shrill roar'd the winds, and dreary was the view!
With desperate sorrow wild, th' affrighted man
Thrice sigh'd, thrice struck his breast, and thus began.
'Sad was the hour, and luckless was the day,
When first from Schiraz' walls I bent my way!

'Ah! little thought I of the blasting wind,
The thirst or pinching hunger that I find

Bethink thee, Hassan, where shall thirst assuage,
When fails this cruse, his unrelenting rage?
Soon shall this scrip its precious load resign;
Then what but tears and hunger shall be thine?
'Ye mute companions of my toils, that bear
In all my griefs a more than equal share!
Here, where no springs in murmurs break away,
Or moss-crown'd fountains mitigate the day,
In vain ye hope the dear delights to know,
Which plains more blest, or verdant vales bestow:
Here rocks alone and tasteless sands are found,
And faint and sickly winds for ever howl around.
Sad was the hour, and luckless was the day,
When first from Schiraz' walls I bent my way!
'Curst be the gold and silver which persuade
Weak men to follow far fatiguing trade!
The lily peace outshines the silver store,
And life is dearer than the golden ore:
Yet money tempts us o'er the desert brown,
To every distant mart and wealthy town.
Full oft we tempt the land, and oft the sea;
And are we only yet repaid by thee?
Ah! why was ruin so attractive made?
Or why fond man so easily betray'd?
Why heed we not, while mad we haste along,
The gentle voice of Peace, or Pleasure's song?
Or wherefore think the flowery mountain's side,
The fountain's murmurs, and the valley's pride,
Why think we these less pleasing to behold
Than dreary deserts, if they lead to gold?
Sad was the hour, and luckless was the day,
When first from Schiraz' walls I bent my way!
'Oh cease, my fears!—all frantic as I go,
When thought creates unnumber'd scenes of woe;
What if the lion in his rage I meet!—
Oft in the dust I view his printed feet;

And, fearful! oft, when day's declining light
Yields her pale empire to the mourner night,
By hunger roused, he scours the groaning plain,
Gaunt wolves and sullen tigers in his train:
Before them Death with shrieks directs their way,
Fills the wild yell, and leads them to their prey.
Sad was the hour, and luckless was the day,
When first from Schiraz' walls I bent my way!

'At that dread hour the silent asp shall creep,
If aught of rest I find, upon my sleep:
Or some swoln serpent twist his scales around,
And wake to anguish with a burning wound.
Thrice happy they, the wise contented poor,
From lust of wealth, and dread of death secure!
They tempt no deserts, and no griefs they find;
Peace rules the day where reason rules the mind.
Sad was the hour, and luckless was the day,
When first from Schiraz' walls I bent my way!

'O hapless youth!—for she thy love hath won,
The tender Zara will be most undone!
Big swell'd my heart, and own'd the powerful maid,
When fast she dropt her tears, as thus she said:
"Farewell the youth whom sighs could not detain,
Whom Zara's breaking heart implored in vain!
Yet as thou go'st may every blast arise
Weak and unfelt, as these rejected sighs!
Safe o'er the wild, no perils may'st thou see,
No griefs endure, nor weep, false youth, like me!
O let me safely to the fair return,
Say, with a kiss, she must not, shall not mourn;
O! let me teach my heart to lose its fears,
Recall'd by Wisdom's voice, and Zara's tears!'

He said; and call'd on Heaven to bless the day
When back to Schiraz' walls he bent his way.

ECLOGUE III.

ABRA; OR, THE GEORGIAN SULTANA.

Scene—A Forest. *Time*—The Evening.

IN Georgia's land, where Teflis' towers are seen,
In distant view, along the level green,
While evening dews enrich the glittering glade,
And the tall forests cast a longer shade,
What time 'tis sweet o'er fields of rice to stray,
Or scent the breathing maize at setting day;
Amidst the maids of Zagen's peaceful grove,
Emyra sung the pleasing cares of love.
Of Abra first began the tender strain,
Who led her youth with flocks upon the plain:
At morn she came her willing flocks to lead,
Where lilies rear them in the watery mead;
From early dawn the live-long hours she told,
Till late at silent eve she penn'd the fold.
Deep in the grove, beneath the secret shade,
A various wreath of odorous flowers she made:
*Gay-motley'd pinks and sweet jonquils she chose,
The violet blue that on the moss-bank grows;
All sweet to sense, the flaunting rose was there:
The finish'd chaplet well adorn'd her hair.

Great Abbas chanced that fated morn to stray,
By Love conducted from the chase away;
Among the vocal vales he heard her song,
And sought, the vales and echoing groves among:
At length he found, and woo'd the rural maid;
She knew the monarch, and with fear obey'd.
'Be every youth like royal Abbas moved,
And every Georgian maid like Abra loved!'

* These flowers are found in very great abundance in some of the provinces of Persia.

The royal lover bore her from the plain;
Yet still her crook and bleating flock remain:
Oft, as she went, she backward turn'd her view,
And bade that crook and bleating flock adieu.
Fair, happy maid! to other scenes remove,
To richer scenes of golden power and love!
Go, leave the simple pipe, and shepherd's strain;
With love delight thee, and with Abbas reign.
'Be every youth like royal Abbas moved,
And every Georgian maid like Abra loved!'

Yet, midst the blaze of courts she fix'd her love
On the cool fountain, or the shady grove;
Still with the shepherd's innocence her mind
To the sweet vale and flowery mead inclined;
And oft as Spring renew'd the plains with flowers,
Breathed his soft gales, and led the fragrant hours,
With sure return she sought the sylvan scene,
The breezy mountains, and the forests green.
Her maids around her mov'd, a duteous band!
Each bore a crook all rural in her hand:
Some simple lay, of flocks and herds they sung:
With joy the mountain and the forest rung.
'Be every youth like royal Abbas moved,
And every Georgian maid like Abra loved!'

And oft the royal lover left the care
And thorns of state, attendant on the fair;
Oft to the shades and low-roof'd cots retired,
Or sought the vale where first his heart was fired:
A russet mantle, like a swain, he wore,
And thought of crowns and busy courts no more.
'Be every youth like royal Abbas moved,
And every Georgian maid like Abra loved!'

Blest was the life that royal Abbas led:
Sweet was his love, and innocent his bed.
What if in wealth the noble maid excel;
The simple shepherd girl can love as well.

Let those who rule on Persia's jewell'd throne
Be famed for love, and gentlest love alone;
Or wreath, like Abbas, full of fair renown,
The lover's myrtle with the warrior's crown.
O happy days! the maids around her say;
O haste, profuse of blessings, haste away!
'Be every youth like royal Abbas moved,
And every Georgian maid like Abra loved!'

ECLOGUE IV.

AGIB AND SECANDER; OR, THE FUGITIVES.

Scene—A Mountain in Circassia. *Time*—Midnight.

In fair Circassia, where, to love inclined,
Each swain was blest, for every maid was kind;
At that still hour, when awful midnight reigns,
And none but wretches haunt the twilight plains;
What time the Moon had hung her lamp on high
And past in radiance through the cloudless sky;
Sad o'er the dews two brother shepherds fled,
Where wildering fear and desperate sorrow led:
Fast as they prest their flight, behind them lay
Wild ravaged plains, and valleys stole away.
Along the mountain's bending sides they ran,
Till, faint and weak, Secander thus began:

Secander.

'Oh, stay thee, Agib, for my feet deny,
No longer friendly to my life, to fly.
Friend of my heart! Oh turn thee and survey,
Trace our long flight through all its length of way!
And first review that long-extended plain,
And yon wide groves, already past with pain!
Yon ragged cliff, whose dangerous path we tried!
And, last, this lofty mountain's weary side!'

Agib.

'Weak as thou art, yet hapless must thou know
The toils of flight, or some severer woe!
Still as I haste, the Tartar shouts behind,
And shrieks and sorrows load the saddening wind:
In rage of heart, with ruin in his hand,
He blasts our harvests, and deforms our land.
Yon citron grove, whence first in fear we came,
Droops its fair honours to the conquering flame:
Far fly the swains, like us, in deep despair,
And leave to ruffian bands their fleecy care.'

Secander.

'Unhappy land! whose blessings tempt the sword,
In vain, unheard, thou call'st thy Persian lord!
In vain thou court'st him, helpless, to thine aid,
To shield the shepherd, and protect the maid!
Far off, in thoughtless indolence resign'd,
Soft dreams of love and pleasure soothe his mind;
Midst fair sultanas lost in idle joy,
No wars alarm him, and no fears annoy.'

Agib.

'Yet these green hills, in summer's sultry heat
Have lent the monarch oft a cool retreat.
Sweet to the sight is Zabran's flowery plain,
And once by maids and shepherds loved in vain!
No more the virgins shall delight to rove
By Sargis' banks, or Irwan's shady grove;
On Tarkie's mountains catch the cooling gale,
Or breathe the sweets of Aly's flowery vale:
Fair scenes! but, ah! no more with peace possest,
With ease alluring, and with plenty blest!
No more the shepherds' whitening tents appear,
Nor the kind products of a bounteous year;
No more the date, with snowy blossoms crown'd!
But Ruin spreads her baleful fires around.'

Secander.

'In vain Circassia boasts her spicy groves,
For ever famed for pure and happy loves:
In vain she boasts her fairest of the fair,
Their eyes' blue languish, and their golden hair.
Those eyes in tears their fruitless grief must send;
Those hairs the Tartar's cruel hand shall rend.'

Agib.

'Ye Georgian swains, that piteous learn from far
Circassia's ruin, and the waste of war:
Some weightier arms than crooks and staffs prepare,
To shield your harvests, and defend your fair:
The Turk and Tartar like designs pursue,
Fix'd to destroy, and steadfast to undo.
Wild as his land, in native deserts bred,
By lust incited, or by malice led,
The villain Arab, as he prowls for prey,
Oft marks with blood and wasting flames the way;
Yet none so cruel as the Tartar foe,
To death inured, and nursed in scenes of woe.'

He said: when loud along the vale was heard
A shriller shriek, and nearer fires appear'd.
Th' affrighted shepherds through the dews of night,
Wide o'er the moonlight hills renew'd their flight.

ODES,

DESCRIPTIVE AND ALLEGORICAL.

TO PITY.

O THOU! the friend of man, assign'd
With balmy hands his wounds to bind,
  And charm his frantic woe,
When first Distress, with dagger keen,
Broke forth to waste his destined scene,
  His wild unsated foe!

By Pella's* bard, a magic name,
By all the griefs his thought could frame,
  Receive my humble mite
Long, Pity, let the nations view
Thy sky-worn robes of tenderest blue,
  And eyes of dewy light!

But wherefore need I wander wide
To old Ilissus' distant side,
  Deserted stream, and mute?
Wild Arun† too has heard thy strains,
And Echo, midst my native plains,
  Been soothed by Pity's lute.

There first the wren thy myrtles shed
On gentlest Otway's infant head,
  To him thy cell was shewn;
And while he sung the female heart,
With youth's soft notes unspoil'd by art,
  Thy turtles mix'd their own.

* Euripides. † A river in Sussex.

Come, Pity! come; by Fancy's aid,
Ev'n now my thoughts, relenting maid,
  Thy temple's pride design:
Its southern site, its truth complete,
Shall raise a wild enthusiast heat
  In all who view the shrine.

There Picture's toil shall well relate,
How chance, or hard involving fate,
  O'er mortal bliss prevail:
The buskin'd Muse shall near her stand,
And sighing prompt her tender hand,
  With each disastrous tale.

There let me oft, retired by day,
In dreams of passion melt away,
  Allow'd with thee to dwell:
There waste the mournful lamp of night,
Till, Virgin, thou again delight
  To hear a British shell!

TO FEAR.

THOU, to whom the world unknown,
With all its shadowy shapes, is shewn;
Who see'st appall'd th' unreal scene,
While Fancy lifts the veil between;
    Ah Fear! ah, frantic Fear!
    I see, I see thee near.
I know thy hurried step, thy haggard eye!
Like thee I start, like thee disorder'd fly,
    For, lo! what monsters in thy train appear!
Danger, whose limbs of giant mould
What mortal eye can fix'd behold?
Who stalks his round, an hideous form,
Howling amidst the midnight storm;

Or throws him on the ridgy steep
Of some loose hanging rock to sleep:
And with him thousand phantoms join'd,
Who prompt to deeds accursed the mind:
And those, the fiends, who near allied,
O'er Nature's wounds, and wrecks preside;
While Vengeance, in the lurid air,
Lifts her red arm, exposed and bare:
On whom that ravening* brood of Fate,
Who lap the blood of Sorrow, wait;
Who, Fear, this ghastly train can see,
And look not madly wild like thee!

Epode.

In earliest Greece, to thee, with partial choice,
The grief-full Muse addrest her infant tongue;
The maids and matrons, on her awful voice,
Silent and pale, in wild amazement hung.

Yet he, the bard† who first invoked thy name,
Disdain'd in Marathon its power to feel:
For not alone he nursed the poet's flame,
But reach'd from Virtue's hand the patriot's steel.

But who is he, whom later garlands grace,
Who left awhile o'er Hybla's dews to rove,
With trembling eyes thy dreary steps to trace,
Where thou and furies shared the baleful grove?

Wrapt in thy cloudy veil th' incestuous queen‡
Sigh'd the sad call her son and husband heard,
When once alone it broke the silent scene,
And he the wretch of Thebes no more appear'd.

O Fear! I know thee by my throbbing heart,
Thy withering power inspired each mournful line,
Though gentle Pity claim her mingled part,
Yet all the thunders of the scene are thine!

* Sophocles' Electra. † Æschylus. ‡ Jocasta.

Antistrophe.

Thou who such weary lengths hast past,
Where wilt thou rest, mad nymph, at last?
Say, wilt thou shroud in haunted cell,
Where gloomy Rape and Murder dwell?
  Or in some hallow'd seat,
  'Gainst which the big waves beat,
Hear drowning seamen's cries in tempests brought.
Dark Power! with shuddering, meek, submitted thought,
Be mine to read the visions old,
Which thy awakening bards have told

  And, lest thou meet my blasted view,
Hold each strange tale devoutly true;
Ne'er be I found, by thee o'er-awed,
In that thrice-hallow'd eve abroad,
When ghosts, as cottage-maids believe,
Their pebbled beds permitted leave,
And goblins haunt, from fire, or fen,
Or mine, or flood, the walks of men!

  O thou, whose spirit most possest
The sacred seat of Shakspeare's breast?
By all that from thy prophet broke,
In thy divine emotions spoke!
Hither again thy fury deal,
Teach me but once like him to feel:
His cypress wreath my meed decree,
And I, O Fear, will dwell with thee.

TO SIMPLICITY.

O Thou, by Nature taught
To breathe her genuine thought,
In numbers warmly pure, and sweetly strong:
Who first on mountains wild,
In Fancy, loveliest child,
Thy babe, and Pleasure's, nursed the powers of song!

Thou, who with hermit heart
Disdain'st the wealth of art,
And gauds, and pageant weeds, and trailing pall:
But com'st a decent maid,
In Attic robe array'd,
O chaste, unboastful nymph! to thee I call!

By all the honey'd store
On Hybla's thymy shore,
By all her blooms, and mingled murmurs dear,
By her whose love-lorn woe,
In evening musings slow,
Soothed, sweetly sad, Electra's poet's ear:

By old Cephisus' deep,
Who spread his wavy sweep
In warbled wanderings round thy green retreat,
On whose enamell'd side,
When holy Freedom died,
No equal haunt allured thy future feet.

O sister meek of Truth,
To my admiring youth
Thy sober aid and native charms infuse!
The flowers that sweetest breathe,
Though beauty cull'd the wreath,
Still ask thy hand to range their order'd hues.

While Rome could none esteem
But virtue's patriot theme,
You loved her hills, and led her laureate band;
But staid to sing alone
To one distinguish'd throne,
And turn'd thy face, and fled her alter'd land.

No more, in hall or bower,
The passions own thy power,
Love, only Love, her forceless numbers mean;
For thou hast left her shrine,
Nor olive more, nor vine,
Shall gain thy feet to bless the servile scene.

Though taste, though genius, bless
To some divine excess,
Faint's the cold work till thou inspire the whole:
What each, what all supply,
May court, may charm our eye,
Thou! only thou canst raise the meeting soul!

Of these let others ask,
To aid some mighty task,
I only seek to find thy temperate vale:
Where oft my reed might sound
To maids and shepherds round,
And all thy sons, O Nature! learn my tale.

ON THE POETICAL CHARACTER.

As once, if not with light regard,
I read aright that gifted bard
(Him whose school above the rest
His loveliest Elfin queen has blest),
One, only one, unrivall'd fair,*
Might hope the magic girdle wear,

* Florimel. See Spenser, Leg. 4th.

At solemn turney hung on high,
The wish of each love-darting eye.

Lo! to each other nymph in turn applied,
  As if, in air unseen, some hovering hand,
Some chaste and angel-friend to virgin-fame,
  With whisper'd spell had burst the starting band,
It left unblest her loathed dishonour'd side;
    Happier, hopeless fair, if never
    Her baffled hand with vain endeavour
Had touch'd that fatal zone to her denied!

Young Fancy thus, to me divinest name,
  To whom, prepared and bathed in heaven,
  The cest of amplest power is given,
  To few the god-like gift assigns,
  To gird their blest prophetic loins,
And gaze her visions wild, and feel unmix'd her flame,
  The band, as fairy legends say,
  Was wove on that creating day,
When He, who call'd with thought to birth
Yon tented sky, this laughing earth,
And drest with springs, and forests tall,
And pour'd the main engirting all,
Long by the loved enthusiast woo'd,
Himself in some diviner mood,
Retiring, sat with her alone,
And placed her on his sapphire throne,
The whiles, the vaulted shrine around,
Seraphic wires were heard to sound,
Now sublimest triumph swelling,
Now on love and mercy dwelling;
And she, from out the veiling cloud,
Breathed her magic notes aloud:
And thou, thou rich-hair'd youth of morn,
And all thy subject life was born!

The dangerous passions kept aloof,
Far from the sainted growing woof;
But near it sat ecstatic Wonder,
Listening the deep applauding thunder:
And Truth, in sunny vest array'd,
By whose the Tarsel's eyes were made;
And the shadowy tribes of Mind,
In braided dance their murmurs join'd,
And all the bright uncounted powers
Who feed on heaven's ambrosial flowers.
—Where is the bard whose soul can now
Its high presuming hopes avow?
Where he who thinks, with rapture blind,
This hallow'd work for him design'd?
High on some cliff, to heaven up-piled,
Of rude access, of prospect wild,
Where, tangled round the jealous steep,
Strange shades o'erbrow the valleys deep,
And holy Genii guard the rock,
Its glooms embrown, its springs unlock,
  While on its rich ambitious head
  An Eden, like his own, lies spread,
I view that oak, the fancied glades among,
By which, as Milton lay, his evening ear,
From many a cloud that dropp'd ethereal dew,
Night sphered in heaven its native strains could hear;
On which that ancient trump he reach'd was hung:
  Thither oft his glory greeting,
  From Waller's myrtle shades retreating,
With many a vow from Hope's aspiring tongue,
My trembling feet his guiding step pursue;
  In vain—Such bliss to one alone,
  Of all the sons of soul, was known,
And Heaven, and Fancy, kindred powers,
Have now o'erturn'd th' inspiring bowers,
Or curtain'd close such scenes from every future view,

ODE,

WRITTEN IN THE YEAR MDCCXLVI.

How sleep the brave, who sink to rest,
By all their country's wishes blest!
When Spring, with dewy fingers cold,
Returns to deck their hallow'd mould,
She there shall dress a sweeter sod
Than Fancy's feet have ever trod

By fairy hands their knell is rung,
By forms unseen their dirge is sung:
There Honour comes, a pilgrim gray,
To bless the turf that wraps their clay,
And Freedom shall awhile repair,
To dwell a weeping hermit there!

TO MERCY.

Strophe.

O THOU! who sitt'st a smiling bride,
By Valour's arm'd and awful side,
Gentlest of sky-born forms, and best adored:
Who oft, with songs, divine to hear,
Winn'st from his fatal grasp the spear,
And hidest in wreaths of flowers his bloodless sword!
Thou who, amidst the deathful field,
By godlike chiefs alone beheld,
Oft with thy bosom bare art found,
Pleading for him, the youth who sinks to ground:
See, Mercy, see! with pure and loaded hands,
Before thy shrine my country's Genius stands,
And decks thy altar still, though pierced with many a wound!

Antistrophe.

When he whom even our joys provoke,
The fiend of Nature, join'd his yoke,
And rushed in wrath to make our isle his prey:
Thy form, from out thy sweet abode,
O'ertook him on his blasted road,
And stopp'd his wheels, and look'd his rage away.
I see recoil his sable steeds,
That bore him swift to savage deeds,
Thy tender melting eyes they own:
O maid! for all thy love in Britain shewn,
Where Justice bars her iron tower,
To thee we build a roseate bower,
Thou, thou shalt rule our queen, and share our monarch's throne!

TO LIBERTY.

Strophe.

Who shall awake the Spartan fife,
And call in solemn sounds to life
The youths, whose locks divinely spreading,
Like vernal hyacinths in sullen hue,
At once the breath of fear and virtue shedding,
Applauding Freedom loved of old to view?
What new Alcæus, fancy-blest,
Shall sing the sword, in myrtles drest,
At Wisdom's shrine awhile its flame concealing,
(What place so fit to seal a deed renown'd?)
Till she her brightest lightnings round revealing,
It leap'd in glory forth, and dealt her prompted wound?
O Goddess! in that feeling hour,
When most its sounds would court thy ears,
Let not my shell's misguided power
E'er draw thy sad, thy mindful tears.

No, Freedom! no, I will not tell
How Rome, before thy weeping face,
With heaviest sound, a giant statue, fell,
Push'd by a wild and artless race
From off its wide ambitious base,
When Time his northern sons of spoil awoke,
And all the blended work of strength and grace,
With many a rude repeated stroke,
And many a barbarous yell, to thousand fragments broke!

Epode I.

Yet e'en, where'er the least appear'd,
Th' admiring world thy hand revered:
Still, 'midst the scatter'd states around,
Some remnants of her strength were found:
They saw, by what escaped the storm,
How wondrous rose her perfect form,
How in the great, the labour'd whole,
Each mighty master pour'd his soul!
For sunny Florence, seat of art,
Beneath her vines preserved a part,
Till they, whom Science loved to name,
(Oh! who could fear it?) quench'd her flame.
And lo, an humbler relic laid
In jealous Pisa's olive shade!
See small Marino joins the theme,
Though least, not last in thy esteem;
Strike, louder strike, th' ennobling strings
To those, whose merchant-sons were kings;
To him who deck'd with pearly pride,
In Adria weds his green-hair'd bride:
Hail, port of glory, wealth, and pleasure!
Ne'er let me change this Lydian measure;
Nor e'er her former pride relate,
To sad Liguria's bleeding state.

Ah, no! more pleased thy haunts I seek,
On wild Helvetia's mountains bleak:
(Where, when the favour'd of thy choice,
The daring archer heard thy voice;
Forth from his eyrie roused in dread,
The ravening eagle northward fled.)
Or dwell in willow'd meads more near,
With those * to whom thy stork is dear:
Those whom the rod of Alva bruised,
Whose crown a British queen refused.
The magic works, thou feel'st the strains,
One holier name alone remains:
The perfect spell shall then avail,
Hail, nymph! adored by Britain, hail!

Antistrophe.

Beyond the measure vast of thought,
The works, the wizard Time has wrought!
The Gaul, 'tis held of antique story,
Saw Britain link'd to his now adverse strand,†
No sea between, nor cliffs sublime and hoary,
He pass'd with unwet feet through all our land.
To the blown Baltic then, they say,
The wild waves found another way,
Where Orcas howls, his wolfish mountains rounding;
Till all the banded west at once 'gan rise,
A wide wild storm even Nature's self confounding,
Withering her giant sons with strange uncouth
surprise.

* The Dutch, amongst whom there are very severe penalties for those who are convicted of killing this bird. They are kept tame in almost all their towns, and particularly at the Hague: of the arms of which they make a part. The common people of Holland are said to entertain a superstitious sentiment, that if the whole species of them should become extinct, they should lose their liberties.

† This tradition is mentioned by several of our old historians. Some naturalists too have endeavoured to support the probability of the fact, by arguments drawn from the correspondent disposition of the two opposite coasts.

This pillar'd earth, so firm and wide,
By winds and inward labours torn.
In thunders dread was push'd aside,
And down the shouldering billows borne.
And see like gems her laughing train,
The little isles on every side;
Mona,* once hid from those who search the main,
Where thousand elfin shapes abide,
And Wight, who checks the westering tide,
For thee consenting Heaven has each bestow'd,
A fair attendant on her sovereign pride:
To thee this blest divorce she owed,
For thou hast made her vales thy loved, thy last abode

Epode II.

Then, too, 'tis said, an hoary pile
'Midst the green navel of our isle,
Thy shrine in some religious wood,
O soul enforcing Goddess! stood;
There oft the painted native's feet
Were wont thy form celestial meet;
Though now with hopeless toil we trace
Time's backward rolls, to find its place;
Whether the fiery-tressed Dane,
Or Roman's self, o'erturned the fane:
Or in what heaven left age it fell;
'Twere hard for modern song to tell.
Yet still, if Truth those beams infuse,
Which guide at once, and charm the Muse,

* There is a tradition in the Isle of Man, that a mermaid becoming enamoured of a young man of extraordinary beauty, took an opportunity of meeting him one day as he walked on the shore, and opened her passion to him, but was received with a coldness, occasioned by his horror and surprise at her appearance. This, however, was so misconstrued by the sea-lady, that in revenge for his treatment of her she punished the whole island, by covering it with a mist, so that all who attempted to carry on any commerce with it, either never arrived at it, but wandered up and down the sea, or were upon a sudden wrecked upon its cliffs.

Beyond yon braided clouds that lie,
Paving the light embroider'd sky,
Amidst the bright pavilion'd plains
The beauteous model still remains.
There happier than in islands blest,
Or bowers by Spring or Hebe drest,
The chiefs who fill our Albion's story,
In warlike weeds, retired in glory,
Hear their consorted Druids sing
Their triumphs to th' immortal string.
How may the poet now unfold
What never tongue or numbers told?
How learn, delighted and amazed,
What hands unknown that fabric raised?
E'en now, before his favour'd eyes,
In Gothic pride it seems to rise!
Yet Grecia's graceful orders join,
Majestic through the mix'd design:
The secret builder knew to choose
Each sphere-found gem of richest hues:
Whate'er heaven's purer mould contains,
When nearer suns emblaze its veins;
There on the walls the Patriot's sight
May ever hang with fresh delight,
And, graved with some prophetic rage,
Read Albion's fame through every age.
Ye forms divine, ye laureate band,
That near her inmost altar stand!
Now soothe her, to her blissful train
Blithe Concord's social form to gain:
Concord, whose myrtle wand can steep
E'en Anger's blood shot eyes in sleep:
Before whose breathing bosom's balm,
Rage drops his steel, and storms grow calm
Here let our sires and matrons hoar
Welcome to Britain's ravaged shore;

Our youths, enamour'd of the fair,
Play with the tangles of her hair,
Till, in one loud applauding sound,
The nations shout to her around,
'Oh how supremely art thou blest!
Thou, lady—thou shalt rule the West!'

TO A LADY,

On the Death of Colonel Charles Ross, in the Action at Fontenoy

Written May, 1745.

WHILE, lost to all his former mirth,
Britannia's genius bends to earth,
And mourns the fatal day;
While stain'd with blood he strives to tear.
Unseemly, from his sea green hair
The wreaths of cheerful May:

The thoughts which musing Pity pays,
And fond Remembrance loves to raise,
Your faithful hours attend:
Still Fancy, to herself unkind,
Awakes to grief the soften'd mind,
And points the bleeding friend.

By rapid Scheldt's descending wave
His country's vows shall bless the grave
Where'er the youth is laid:
That sacred spot the village hind
With every sweetest turf shall bind,
And Peace protect the shade.

O'er him, whose doom thy virtues grieve,
Aërial forms shall sit at eve,
And bend the pensive head!

And, fall'n to save his injured land,
Imperial Honour's awful hand
Shall point his lonely bed!

The warlike dead of every age,
Who fill the fair recording page,
Shall leave their sainted rest;
And, half reclining on his spear,
Each wondering chief by turns appear,
To hail the blooming guest.

Old Edward's sons, unknown to yield,
Shall crowd from Cressy's laurell'd field,
And gaze with fix'd delight:
Again for Britain's wrongs they feel,
Again they snatch the gleamy steel,
And wish th' avenging fight.

But lo, where, sunk in deep despair,
Her garments torn, her bosom bare,
Impatient Freedom lies!
Her matted tresses madly spread,
To every sod which wraps the dead
She turns her joyless eyes.

Ne'er shall she leave that lowly ground
Till notes of triumph bursting round
Proclaim her reign restored:
Till William seek the sad retreat,
And bleeding at her sacred feet,
Present the sated sword.

If, weak to soothe so soft a heart,
These pictured glories nought impart,
To dry thy constant tear:
If yet, in Sorrow's distant eye,
Exposed and pale thou see'st him lie,
Wild War insulting near ·

Where'er from time thou court'st relief,
The Muse shall still, with social grief,
Her gentlest promise keep:
E'en humble Harting's cottaged vale
Shall learn the sad repeated tale,
And bid her shepherds weep.

TO EVENING.

If aught of oaten stop, or pastoral song,
May hope, chaste Eve, to soothe thy modest ear
Like thy own solemn springs,
Thy springs, and dying gales;

O nymph reserved! while now the bright-hair'd sun
Sits in yon western tent, whose cloudy skirts,
With brede ethereal wove,
O'erhang his wavy bed:—

Now air is hush'd, save where the weak-eyed bat
With short shrill shriek flits by on leathern wing;
Or where the beetle winds
His small but sullen horn,

As oft he rises 'midst the twilight path,
Against the pilgrim borne in heedless hum:
Now teach me, maid composed,
To breathe some soften'd strain.

Whose numbers, stealing through thy dark'ning vale,
May not unseemly with its stillness suit,
As, musing slow, I hail
Thy genial loved return!

For when thy folding-star arising shews
His paly circlet, at his warning lamp
The fragrant hours, and elves
Who slept in buds the day,

And many a nymph who wreathes her brows with sedge,
And sheds the freshening dew, and, lovelier still,
The pensive Pleasures sweet,
Prepare thy shadowy car.

Then let me rove some wild and heathy scene,
Or find some ruin 'midst its dreary dells,
Whose walls more awful nod
By thy religious gleams.

Or, if chill blust'ring winds, or driving rain,
Prevent my willing feet, be mine the hut,
That, from the mountain's side,
Views wilds and swelling floods,

And hamlets brown, and dim-discover'd spires,
And hears their simple bell, and marks o'er all
Thy dewy fingers draw
The gradual dusky veil.

While Spring shall pour his showers, as oft he wont,
And bathe thy breathing tresses, meekest Eve!
While Summer loves to sport
Beneath thy lingering light:

While sallow Autumn fills thy lap with leaves;
Or Winter, yelling through the troublous air,
Affrights thy shrinking train,
And rudely rends thy robes:

So long, regardful of thy quiet rule,
Shall Fancy, Friendship, Science, smiling Peace,
Thy gentlest influence own,
And love thy favourite name!

TO PEACE.

O THOU! who badest thy turtles bear
Swift from his grasp thy golden hair,
And sought'st thy native skies;

When War, by vultures drawn from far,
To Britain bent his iron car,
And bade his storms arise!

Tired of his rude tyrannic sway,
Our youth shall fix some festive day,
His sullen shrines to burn:
But thou, who hear'st the turning spheres,
What sounds may charm thy partial ears,
And gain thy blest return!

O Peace! thy injur'd robes up-bind?
O rise, and leave not one behind
Of all thy beamy train:
The British lion, goddess sweet,
Lies stretch'd on earth to kiss thy feet,
And own thy holier reign.

Let others court thy transient smile,
But come to grace thy western isle,
By warlike Honour led;
And, while around her ports rejoice,
While all her sons adore thy choice,
With him for ever wed!

THE MANNERS.

FAREWELL, for clearer ken design'd,
The dim-discover'd tracts of mind;
Truths which, from action's paths retired,
My silent search in vain required!
No more my sail that deep explores,
No more I search those magic shores,
What regions part the world of soul,
Or whence thy streams, Opinion, roll:

If e'er I round such fairy field,
Some power impart the spear and shield,
At which the wizard Passions fly,
By which the giant Follies die!

Farewell the porch, whose roof is seen,
Arch'd with th' enlivening olive's green:
Where Science, prank'd in tissued vest,
By Reason, Pride, and Fancy drest,
Comes like a bride, so trim array'd,
To wed with Doubt in Plato's shade!

Youth of the quick uncheated sight,
Thy walks, Observance, more invite!
O thou, who lov'st that ampler range,
Where life's wide prospects round thee change,
And, with her mingled sons allied,
Throw'st the prattling page aside,
To me in converse sweet impart,
To read in man the native heart,
To learn, where Science sure is found,
From Nature as she lives around:
And, gazing oft her mirror true,
By turns each shifting image view!
Till meddling Art's officious lore
Reverse the lessons taught before;
Alluring from a safer rule,
To dream in her enchanted school;
Thou, Heav'n, whate'er of great we boast,
Hast blest this social science most.

Retiring hence to thoughtful cell,
As Fancy breathes her potent spell,
Not vain she finds the charmful task,
In pageant quaint, in motley mask;
Behold, before her musing eyes
The countless Manners round her rise;

While, ever varying as they pass,
To some Contempt applies her glass:
With these the white-rob'd maids combine,
And those the laughing Satyrs join!
But who is he whom now she views,
In robe of wild contending hues?
Thou by the Passions nursed; I greet
The comic sock that binds thy feet!
O Humour, thou whose name is known
To Britain's favour'd isle alone:
Me too amidst thy band admit;
There where the young eyed healthful Wit
(Whose jewels in his crisped hair
Are placed each other's beams to share),
Whom no delights from thee divide
In laughter loosed, attends thy side!

By old Miletus,* who so long
Has ceased his love-inwoven song;
By all you taught the Tuscan maids,
In changed Italia's modern shades;
By him,† whose knight's distinguish'd name,
Refin'd a nation's lust of fame;
Whose tales e'en now, with echoes sweet,
Castilia's Moorish hills repeat:
Or him,‡ whom Seine's blue nymphs deplore,
In watchet weeds, on Gallia's shore;
Who drew the sad Sicilian maid,
By virtues in her sire betray'd:

O Nature boon, from whom proceed
Each forceful thought, each prompted deed;
If but from thee I hope to feel,
On all my heart imprint thy seal!

* Alluding to the Milesian Tales, some of the earliest romances.

† Cervantes.

‡ Monsieur Le Sage, author of the incomparable Adventures of Gil Blas de Santillane, who died in Paris in the year 1745.

Let some retreating Cynic find
Those oft-turn'd scrolls I leave behind;
The Sports and I this hour agree,
To rove thy scene-full world with thee!

THE PASSIONS.

AN ODE FOR MUSIC.

WHEN Music, heavenly maid, was young,
While yet in early Greece she sung,
The Passions oft, to hear her shell,
Throng'd around her magic cell,
Exulting, trembling, raging, fainting,
Possest beyond the Muse's painting;
By turns they felt the glowing mind
Disturb'd, delighted, raised, refined:
'Till once, 'tis said, when all were fired,
Fill'd with fury, rapt, inspired,
From the supporting myrtles round
They snatch'd her instruments of sound,
And, as they oft had heard apart
Sweet lessons of her forceful art,
Each, for Madness ruled the hour,
Would prove his own expressive power.

First Fear his hand, its skill to try,
  Amid the chords bewilder'd laid,
And back recoil'd, he knew not why,
  E'en at the sound himself had made.

Next Anger rush'd, his eyes on fire,
  In lightnings own'd his secret stings;
In one rude clash he struck the lyre,
  And swept with hurried hand the strings.

With woeful measures wan Despair—
Low solemn sounds his grief beguiled,
A sullen, strange, and mingled air,
'Twas sad by fits, by starts 'twas wild.

But thou, O Hope! with eyes so fair,
What was thy delighted measure?
Still it whisper'd promised pleasure,
And bade the lovely scenes at distance hail!
Still would her touch the strain prolong,
And from the rocks, the woods, the vale,
She call'd on Echo still through all the song;
And where her sweetest theme she chose,
A soft responsive voice was heard at every close,
And Hope enchanted smiled, and waved her golden hair.

And longer had she sung,—but, with a frown,
Revenge impatient rose;
He threw his blood-stain'd sword in thunder down;
And, with a withering look,
The war-denouncing trumpet took,
And blew a blast so loud and dread,
Were ne'er prophetic sounds so full of woe!
And ever and anon he beat
The doubling drum with furious heat;
And though sometimes, each dreary pause between,
Dejected Pity, at his side,
Her soul-subduing voice applied,
Yet still he kept his wild unalter'd mien,
While each strain'd ball of sight seem'd bursting from his head.

Thy numbers, Jealousy, to nought were fix'd,
Sad proof of thy distressful state!
Of differing themes the veering song was mix'd,
And now it courted Love, now raving call'd on Hate.

With eyes upraised, as one inspired,
Pale Melancholy sat retired;
And from her wild sequester'd seat,
In notes by distance made more sweet,
Pour'd through the mellow horn her pensive soul:
And, dashing soft from rocks around,
Bubbling runnels join'd the sound;
Through glades and glooms the mingled measure stole,
Or o'er some haunted streams with fond delay,
Round an holy calm diffusing,
Love of peace and lonely musing,
In hollow murmurs died away.

But O! how alter'd was its sprightlier tone!
When Cheerfulness, a nymph of healthiest hue,
Her bow across her shoulders flung,
Her buskins gemm'd with morning dew,
Blew an inspiring air that dale and thicket rung,
The hunter's call, to Faun and Dryad known.
The oak-crown'd Sisters, and their chaste-eyed Queen
Satyrs and Sylvan boys were seen,
Peeping from forth their alleys green;
Brown Exercise rejoiced to hear,
And Sport leapt up, and seized his beechen spear

Last came Joy's ecstatic trial;
He with vain crown advancing,
First to the lively pipe his hand addrest;
But soon he saw the brisk awakening viol,
Whose sweet entrancing voice he loved the best.
They would have thought who heard the strain,
They saw in Tempe's vale her native maids,
Amidst the festal sounding shades,
To some unwearied minstrel dancing;
While, as his flying fingers kiss'd the strings,
Love framed with Mirth a gay fantastic round;
Loose were her tresses seen, her zone unbound;

And he, amidst his frolic play,
As if he would the charming air repay,
Shook thousand odours from his dewy wings.

O Music! sphere-descended maid,
Friend of Pleasure, Wisdom's aid!
Why, goddess, why, to us denied,
Lay'st thou thy ancient lyre aside?
As, in that loved Athenian bower,
You learn'd an all-commanding power,
Thy mimic soul, O nymph endear'd!
Can well recall what then it heard.
Where is thy native simple heart,
Devote to Virtue, Fancy, Art?
Arise, as in that elder time,
Warm, energetic, chaste, sublime!
Thy wonders, in that god-like age,
Fill thy recording Sister's page—
'Tis said, and I believe the tale,
Thy humblest reed could more prevail,
Had more of strength, diviner rage,
Than all which charms this laggard age;
E'en all at once together found
Cecilia's mingled world of sound—
O bid our vain endeavours cease,
Revive the just designs of Greece:
Return in all thy simple state!
Confirm the tales her sons relate!

AN EPISTLE,

ADDRESSED TO SIR THOMAS HANMER,

On his Edition of Shakspeare's Works.

WHILE, born to bring the Muse's happier days,
A patriot's hand protects a poet's lays,

While nursed by you she sees her myrtles bloom
Green and unwither'd o'er his honour'd tomb;
Excuse her doubts, if yet she fears to tell
What secret transports in her bosom swell:
With conscious awe she hears the critic's fame,
And blushing hides her wreath at Shakspeare's name.
Hard was the lot those injured strains endured,
Unown'd by Science, and by years obscured:
Fair Fancy wept; and echoing sighs confess'd
A fixt despair in every tuneful breast.
Not with more grief th' afflicted swains appear,
When wintry winds deform the plenteous year;
When lingering frosts the ruin'd seats invade,
Where Peace resorted, and the Graces play'd.

Each rising art by just gradation moves,
Toil builds on toil, and age on age improves:
The Muse alone unequal dealt her rage,
And graced with noblest pomp her earliest stage.
Preserved through time, the speaking scenes impart
Each changeful wish of Phædra's tortured heart:
Or paint the curse that mark'd the *Theban's reign,
A bed incestuous, and a father slain.
With kind concern our pitying eyes o'erflow,
Trace the sad tale, and own another's woe.

To Rome removed, with wit secure to please,
The comic sisters kept their native ease:
With jealous fear declining Greece beheld
Her own Menander's art almost excell'd!
But every Muse essay'd to raise in vain
Some labour'd rival of her tragic strain;
Ilyssus' laurels, though transferr'd with toil,
Droop'd their fair leaves, nor knew th' unfriendly soil.

As Arts expired, resistless Dulness rose;
Goths, priests, or Vandals,—all were Learning's foes.

* The Œdipus of Sophocles.

Till* Julius first recall'd each exiled maid,
And Cosmo own'd them in th' Etrurian shade:
Then deeply skill'd in Love's engaging theme,
The soft Provençal pass'd to Arno's stream:
With graceful ease the wanton lyre he strung,
Sweet flow'd the lays—but love was all he sung.
The gay description could not fail to move;
For, led by Nature, all are friends to love.

But Heaven, still various in its works, decreed
The perfect boast of time should last succeed.
The beauteous union must appear at length,
Of Tuscan fancy, and Athenian strength:
One greater Muse Eliza's reign adorn,
And e'en a Shakspeare to her fame be born!

Yet, ah! so bright her morning's opening ray,
In vain our Britain hoped an equal day!
No second growth the western isle could bear,
At once exhausted with too rich a year.
Too nicely Jonson knew the critic's part;
Nature in him was almost lost in art.
Of softer mould the gentle Fletcher came,
The next in order, as the next in name.
With pleas'd attention 'midst his scenes we find
Each glowing thought that warms the female mind;
Each melting sigh, and every tender tear,
The lover's wishes, and the virgin's fear.
His† every strain the Smiles and Graces own:
But stronger Shakspeare felt for man alone:
Drawn by his pen, our ruder passions stand
Th' unrivall'd picture of his early hand.

‡With gradual steps, and slow, exacter France
Saw Art's fair empire o'er her shores advance:

* Julius II. the immediate predecessor of Leo X.
† Their characters are thus distinguished by Mr. Dryden.
‡ About the time of Shakspeare, the poet Hardy was in great repute in France. He wrote, according to Fontenelle, six hundred plays.

By length of toil a bright perfection knew,
Correctly bold, and just in all she drew;
Till late Corneille, with *Lucan's spirit fired,
Breathed the free strain, as Rome and he inspired:
And classic Judgment gain'd to sweet Racine
The temperate strength of Maro's chaster line.

But wilder far the British laurel spread,
And wreaths less artful crown our poet's head.
Yet he alone to every scene could give
Th' historian's truth, and bid the manners live.
Waked at his call, I view with glad surprise
Majestic forms of mighty monarchs rise.
There Henry's trumpets spread their loud alarms,
And laurell'd Conquest waits her hero's arms.
Here gentle Edward claims a pitying sigh,
Scarce born to honours, and so soon to die!
Yet shall thy throne, unhappy infant! bring
No beam of comfort to the guilty king:
The† time shall come, when Glo'ster's heart shall bleed
In life's last hours, with horror of the deed:
When dreary visions shall at last present
Thy vengeful image in the midnight tent;
Thy hand unseen the secret death shall bear,
Blunt the weak sword, and break th' oppressive spear.

Where'er we turn, by Fancy charm'd, we find
Some sweet illusion of the cheated mind.
Oft, wild of wing, she calls the soul to rove
With humbler Nature in the rural grove;
Where swains contented own the quiet scene,
And twilight fairies tread the circled green:
Dress'd by her hand the woods and valleys smile,
And spring diffusive decks th' enchanted isle.

The French poets after him applied themselves in general to the correct improvement of the stage, which was almost totally disregarded by those of our own country, Jonson excepted.

* The favourite author of the elder Corneille.

† Tempus erit Turno, magno cùm optaverit emptum
Intactum Pallanta, &c.

O more than all in powerful genius blest,
Come, take thine empire o'er the willing breast!
Whate'er the wounds this youthful heart shall feel,
Thy songs support me, and thy morals heal!
There every thought the poet's warmth may raise,
There native music dwells in all the lays.
Oh, might some verse with happiest skill persuade
Expressive Picture to adopt thine aid!
What wondrous draughts might rise from every page
What other Raphaels charm a distant age!

Methinks e'en now I view some free design,
Where breathing Nature lives in every line:
Chaste and subdued the modest lights decay,
Steal into shades, and mildly melt away.
—And see, where *Antony, in tears approved,
Guards the pale relics of the chief he loved:
O'er the cold corse the warrior seems to bend,
Deep sunk in grief, and mourns his murder'd friend!
Still as they press he calls on all around,
Lifts the torn robe, and points the bleeding wound.

But who †is he, whose brows exalted bear
A wrath impatient, and a fiercer air?
Awake to all that injured worth can feel,
On his own Rome he turns th' avenging steel:
Yet shall not war's insatiate fury fall
(So Heaven ordains it) on the destin'd wall.
See the fond mother, 'midst the plaintive train,
Hang on his knees, and prostrate on the plain!
Touch'd to the soul, in vain he strives to hide
The son's affection in the Roman's pride:
O'er all the man conflicting passions rise,
Rage grasps the sword, while Pity melts the eyes.

Thus, generous Critic, as thy bard inspires,
The sister Arts shall nurse their drooping fires;

* See the tragedy of Julius Cæsar.
† Coriolanus. See Mr. Spence's dialogue on the Odyssey.

Each from his scenes her stores alternate bring,
Blend the fair tints, or wake the vocal string:
Those Sibyl-leaves, the sport of every wind
(For poets ever were a careless kind),
By thee disposed, no farther toil demand,
But, just to Nature, own thy forming hand.

So spread o'er Greece, th' harmonious whole unknown,
Even Homer's numbers charm'd by parts alone.
Their own Ulysses scarce had wander'd more,
By winds and waters cast on every shore:
When, rais'd by Fate, some former Hanmer join'd
Each beauteous image of the boundless mind:
And bade, like thee, his Athens ever claim
A fond alliance with the Poet's name

DIRGE IN CYMBELINE.

Sung by Guiderus and Arviragus over Fidele, supposed to be dead.

To fair Fidele's grassy tomb
Soft maids and village hinds shall bring
Each opening sweet, of earliest bloom,
And rifle all the breathing Spring.

No wailing ghost shall dare appear
To vex with shrieks this quiet grove;
But shepherd lads assemble here,
And melting virgins own their love.

No wither'd witch shall here be seen,
No goblins lead their nightly crew;
The female fays shall haunt the green,
And dress thy grave with pearly dew!

The red-breast oft at evening hours
  Shall kindly lend his little aid,
With hoary moss, and gather'd flowers,
  To deck the ground where thou art laid.

When howling winds, and beating rain,
  In tempests shake the sylvan cell;
Or midst the chase, on every plain,
  The tender thought on thee shall dwell:

Each lonely scene shall thee restore;
  For thee the tear be duly shed;
Beloved, till life can charm no more;
  And mourn'd, till Pity's self be dead.

ODE

ON

THE DEATH OF MR. THOMSON.

The Scene of the following Stanzas is supposed to lie on the Thames, near Richmond.

I.

In yonder grave a Druid lies,
  Where slowly winds the stealing wave!
The year's best sweets shall duteous rise,
  To deck its poet's sylvan grave!

II.

In yon deep bed of whisp'ring reeds,
  His airy harp* shall now be laid;
That he, whose heart in sorrow bleeds,
  May love through life the soothing shade.

* The harp of Æolus, of which see a description in the Castle of Indolence.

III.

Then maids and youths shall linger here
  And while its sounds at distance swell,
Shall sadly seem in Pity's ear
  To hear the woodland pilgrim's knell.

IV.

Remembrance oft shall haunt the shore
  When Thames in summer wreaths is drest;
And oft suspend the dashing oar
  To bid his gentle spirit rest!

V.

And oft as Ease and Health retire
  To breezy lawn, or forest deep,
The friend shall view yon whitening† spire,
  And 'mid the varied landscape weep.

VI.

But thou, who own'st that earthly bed,
  Ah! what will every dirge avail!
Or tears which Love and Pity shed,
  That mourn beneath the gliding sail!

VII.

Yet lives there one, whose heedless eye
  Shall scorn thy pale shrine glimm'ring near;
With him, sweet bard, may Fancy die,
  And Joy desert the blooming year.

VIII.

But thou, lorn stream, whose sullen tide
  No sedge-crown'd sisters now attend,
Now waft me from the green hill's side,
  Whose cold turf hides the buried friend!

† Richmond Church.

IX.

And see, the fairy valleys fade,
 Dun Night has veil'd the solemn view!
Yet once again, dear parted shade,
 Meek Nature's child, again adieu!

X.

*The genial meads, assign'd to bless
 Thy life, shall mourn thy early doom!
There hinds and shepherd girls shall dress
 With simple hands thy rural tomb.

XI.

Long, long, thy stone and pointed clay
 Shall melt the musing Briton's eyes:
'O vales, and wild woods!' shall he say,
 'In yonder grave your Druid lies!'

VERSES

Written on a Paper which contained a Piece of Bride-cake.

Ye curious hands, that, hid from vulgar eyes,
 By search profane shall find this hallow'd cake,
With virtue's awe forbear the sacred prize,
 Nor dare a theft for love and pity's sake.

This precious relic, form'd by magic power,
 Beneath the shepherd's haunted pillow laid,
Was meant by love to charm the silent hour,
 The secret present of a matchless maid.

The Cyprian queen, at Hymen's fond request,
 Each nice ingredient chose with happiest art;
Fears, sighs, and wishes of th' enamour'd breast,
 And pains that please, are mixt in every part.

* Mr. Thomson resided in the neighbourhood of Richmond some time before his death.

With rosy hand the spicy fruit she brought,
  From Paphian hills, and fair Cytherea's isle;
And temper'd sweet with these the melting thought,
  The kiss ambrosial, and the yielding smile.

Ambiguous looks, that scorn and yet relent,
  Denials mild, and firm unalter'd truth;
Reluctant pride, and amorous faint consent,
  And meeting ardours, and exulting youth.

Sleep, wayward god! hath sworn, while these remain,
  With flattering dreams to dry his nightly tear,
And cheerful Hope, so oft invoked in vain,
  With fairy songs shall sooth his pensive ear.

If, bound by vows to Friendship's gentle side
  And fond of soul, thou hop'st an equal grace,
If youth or maid thy joys and griefs divide,
  O, much entreated, leave this fatal place!

Sweet Peace, who long hath shunn'd my plaintive lay,
  Consents at length to bring me short delight;
Thy careless steps may scare her doves away,
  And grief with raven note usurp the night,

AN ODE

ON THE POPULAR SUPERSTITIONS OF THE HIGHLANDS OF SCOTLAND.

I.

HOME! thou return'st from Thames, whose Naiads long
  Have seen thee ling'ring with a fond delay,
  Mid those soft friends, whose hearts some future day
Shall melt, perhaps, to hear thy tragic song.

Go, not unmindful of that cordial youth,*
  Whom, long endear'd, thou leav'st by Lavant's side;
Together let us wish him lasting truth,
  And joy untainted, with his destin'd bride.
Go! nor regardless, while these numbers boast
  My short-lived bliss, forget my social name;
But think, far off, how, on the southern coast,
  I met thy friendship with an equal flame!
Fresh to that soil thou turn'st, where ev'ry vale
  Shall prompt the poet, and his song demand:
To thee thy copious subjects ne'er shall fail;
  Thou need'st but take thy pencil to thy hand,
  And paint what all believe, who own thy genial land

II.

There must thou wake perforce thy Doric quill;
  'Tis Fancy's land to which thou sett'st thy feet;
  Where still, 'tis said, the fairy people meet,
Beneath each birken shade, on mead or hill.
There each trim lass, that skims the milky store,
  To the swart tribes their creamy bowls allots;
By night they sip it round the cottage-door,
  While airy minstrels warble jocund notes.
There, every herd, by sad experience, knows
  How, wing'd with Fate, their elf-shot arrows fly,
When the sick ewe her summer food foregoes,
  Or, stretch'd on earth, the heart-smit heifers lie.
Such airy beings awe th' untutor'd swain: [neglect:
  Nor thou, though learn'd, his homelier thoughts
Let thy sweet muse the rural faith sustain;
  These are the themes of simple, sure effect,
That add new conquests to her boundless reign,
And fill, with double force, her heart-commanding
  strain.

* A gentleman of the name of Barrow, who introduced Home to Collins.

III.

E'en yet preserved, how often may'st thou hear,
Where to the pole the Boreal mountains run,
Taught by the father to his list'ning son,
Strange lays, whose power had charm'd a Spenser's ear
At ev'ry pause, before thy mind possest,
Old Runic bards shall seem to rise around,
With uncouth lyres, in many-colour'd vest,
Their matted hair with boughs fantastic crown'd:
Whether thou bidd'st the well-taught hind repeat
The choral dirge, that mourns some chieftain brave,
When ev'ry shrieking maid her bosom beat,
And strew'd with choicest herbs his scented grave;
Or whether, sitting in the shepherd's shiel,*
Thou hear'st some sounding tale of war's alarms;
When at the bugle's call, with fire and steel,
The sturdy clans pour'd forth their brawny swarms,
And hostile brothers met to prove each others' arms.

IV.

'Tis thine, to sing, how, framing hideous spells,
In Sky's lone isle, the gifted wizard-seer,
Lodged in the wintry cave, with Fate's fell spear
Or in the depth of Uist's dark forest dwells:
How they, whose sight such dreary dreams engross,
With their own visions oft astonish'd droop'd,
When, o'er the wat'ry strath or quaggy moss,
They see the gliding ghosts' unbodied troop;
Or, if in sports, or on the festive green,
Their destined glance some fated youth descry,
Who now, perhaps, in lusty vigour seen,
And rosy health, shall soon lamented die.

* A summer hut, built in the high part of the mountains, to tend their flocks in the warm season, when the pasture is fine.

For them the viewless forms of air obey,
Their bidding heed, and at their beck repair:
They know what spirit brews the stormful day,
And heartless, oft like moody madness, stare
To see the phantom train their secret work prepare.

V.

'Or on some bellying rock that shades the deep,
'They view the lurid signs that cross the sky,
'Where, in the west, the brooding tempests lie:
'And hear their first, faint, rustling pennons sweep.
'Or in the arched cave, where deep and dark
'The broad, unbroken billows heave and swell,
'In horrid musings wrapt, they sit to mark
'The lab'ring moon; or list the nightly yell
'Of that dread spirit, whose gigantic form
'The seer's entranced eye can well survey,
'Through the dim air who guides the driving storm,
'And points the wretched bark its destined prey.
'Or him who hovers on his flagging wing
'O'er the dire whirlpool, that, in ocean's waste,
'Draws instant down whate'er devoted thing
'The failing breeze within its reach hath placed—
'The distant seaman hears, and flies with trembling haste.

VI.

'Or, if on land the fiend exerts his sway,
'Silent he broods o'er quicksand, bog, or fen,
'Far from the shelt'ring roof and haunts of men,
'When witched darkness shuts the eye of day,
'And shrouds each star that wont to cheer the night;
'Or, if the drifted snow perplex the way,
'With treach'rous gleam he lures the fated wight,
'And leads him flound'ring on and quite astray.'

VII.

To monarchs dear, some hundred miles astray,
Oft have they seen Fate give the fatal blow!
The Seer, in Sky, shriek'd as the blood did flow,
When headless Charles warm on the scaffold lay!
As Boreas threw her young Aurora forth,
In the first year of the first George's reign,
And battles raged in welkin of the North,
They mourn'd in air, fell, fell rebellion slain!
And as, of late, they joy'd in Preston's fight,
Saw, at sad Falkirk, all their hopes near crown'd!
They raved! divining, through their second sight,
Pale, red Culloden, where these hopes were drown'd!
Illustrious William! Britain's guardian name!
One William saved us from a Tyrant's stroke;
He, for a sceptre, gain'd heroic fame,
But thou, more glorious, Slavery's chain hast broke,
To reign a private man, and bow to Freedom's yoke!

VIII.

These, too, thou'lt sing! for well thy magic muse
Can to the topmost heaven of grandeur soar;
Or stoop to wail the swain that is no more!
Ah, homely swains! your homeward steps ne'er lose;
Let not dank Will mislead you to the heath;
Dancing in murky night, o'er fen and lake,
He glows, to draw you downward to your death,
In his bewitch'd, low, marshy, willow brake!
What though far off, from some dark dell espied,
His glimmering mazes cheer th' excursive sight,
Yet turn, ye wanderers, turn your steps aside,
Nor trust the guidance of that faithless light;
For watchful, lurking, mid th' unrustling reed,
At those murk hours the wily monster lies,
And listens oft to hear the passing steed,
And frequent round him rolls his sullen eyes, [prise.
If chance his savage wrath may some weak wretch sur

IX.

Ah, luckless swain! o'er all unblest, indeed!
Whom late bewilder'd in the dank, dark fen,
Far from his flocks, and smoking hamlet, then
To that sad spot where hums the sedgy weed:
On him, enraged, the fiend, in angry mood,
Shall never look with pity's kind concern,
But instant, furious, raise the whelming flood
O'er its drown'd banks, forbidding all return!
Or, if he meditate his wish'd escape,
To some dim hill that seems uprising near,
To his faint eye, the grim and grisly shape,
In all his terrors clad, shall wild appear.
Meantime the wat'ry surge shall round him rise,
Pour'd sudden forth from ev'ry swelling source!
What now remains but tears and hopeless sighs?
His fear-shook limbs have lost their youthful force,
And down the waves he floats, a pale and breathless corse!

X.

For him in vain his anxious wife shall wait,
Or wander forth to meet him on his way;
For him in vain at to-fall of the day,
His babes shall linger at th' unclosing gate!
Ah, ne'er shall he return! Alone, if night,
Her travell'd limbs in broken slumbers steep!
With drooping willows drest, his mournful sprite
Shall visit sad, perchance, her silent sleep:
Then he, perhaps, with moist and wat'ry hand
Shall fondly seem to press her shudd'ring cheek,
And with his blue-swoln face before her stand,
And, shiv'ring cold, these piteous accents speak:
'Pursue, dear wife, thy daily toils, pursue,
At dawn or dusk, industrious as before;
Nor e'er of me one helpless thought renew,

While I lie welt'ring on the osier'd shore, [more!
Drown'd by the Kelpie's* wrath, nor e'er shall aid thee

XI.

Unbounded is thy range; with varied skill [spring
Thy Muse may, like those feath'ry tribes which
From their rude rocks, extend her skirting wing
Round the moist marge of each cold Hebrid isle,
To that hoar pile† which still its ruin shews:
In whose small vaults a pigmy-folk is found,
Whose bones the delver with his spade upthrows,
And culls them, wond'ring, from the hallow'd ground!
Or thither,‡ where beneath the show'ry west,
The mighty kings of three fair realms are laid:
Once foes, perhaps, together now they rest,
No slaves revere them, and no wars invade:
Yet frequent now, at midnight's solemn hour,
The rifted mounds their yawning cells unfold,
And forth the monarchs stalk with sov'reign pow'r,
In pageant robes, and wreath'd with sheeny gold,
And on their twilight tombs aërial council hold.

XII.

But, oh! o'er all, forget not Kilda's race,
On whose bleak rocks, which brave the wasting tides
Fair Nature's daughter, Virtue, yet abides.
Go! just as they, their blameless manners trace!
Then to my ear transmit some gentle song,
Of those whose lives are yet sincere and plain,
Their bounded walks the rugged cliffs along,
And all their prospect but the wintry main.

* The water-fiend.

† One of the Hebrides is called The Isle of Pigmies, where, it is reported, that several miniature bones of the human species have been dug up in the ruins of the chapel there.

‡ Icolmkill, one of the Hebrides, where near sixty of the ancient Scottish, Irish, and Norwegian kings are interred.

With sparing temp'rance at the needful time,
They drain the scented spring: or, hunger-prest,
Along th' Atlantic rock, undreading, climb,
And of its eggs despoil the solan's* nest.
Thus, blest in primal innocence they live,
Sufficed, and happy with that frugal fare
Which tasteful toil and hourly danger give.
Hard is their shallow soil, and bleak and bare;
Nor ever vernal bee was heard to murmur there!

XIII.

Nor need'st thou blush that such false themes engage
Thy gentle mind, of fairer stores possest;
For not alone they touch the village breast,
But fill'd, in elder time, th' historic page.
There, Shakspeare's self, with ev'ry garland crown'd,
Flew to those fairy climes his fancy sheen,
In musing hour; his wayward sisters found,
And with their terrors drest the magic scene.
From them he sung, when, 'mid his bold design,
Before the Scot, afflicted and aghast!
The shadowy kings of Banquo's fated line
Through the dark cave in gleamy pageant past.
Proceed! nor quit the tales which, simply told,
Could once so well my answ'ring bosom pierce;
Proceed, in forceful sounds, and colour bold,
The native legends of thy land rehearse:
To such adapt thy lyre, and suit thy powerful verse.

XIV.

In scenes like these, which, daring to depart
From sober truth, are still to Nature true,
And call forth fresh delight to Fancy's view,
Th' heroic Muse employ'd her Tasso's art!

* An aquatic bird, on the eggs of which the inhabitants of St. Kilda another of the Hebrides, chiefly subsist.

• F

How have I trembled, when, at Tancred's stroke,
Its gushing blood the gaping cypress pour'd!
When each live plant with mortal accents spoke,
And the wild blast upheav'd the vanish'd sword!
How have I sat, when piped the pensive wind,
To hear his harp by British Fairfax strung!
Prevailing poet! whose undoubting mind
Believ'd the magic wonders which he sung!
Hence, at each sound, imagination glows!
Hence, at each picture, vivid life starts here!
Hence his warm lay with softest sweetness flows!
Melting it flows, pure, murm'ring, strong and clear,
And fills th'impassion'd heart, and wins th'harmonious ear!

XV.

All hail! ye scenes, that o'er my soul prevail!
Ye splendid friths and lakes, which, far away,
Are by smooth Annan* fill'd, or past'ral Tay,†
Or Don's‡ romantic springs, at distance, hail!
The time shall come, when I, perhaps, may tread
Your lowly glens, o'erhung with spreading broom;
Or o'er your stretching heaths, by Fancy led;
Or o'er your mountains creep in awful gloom?
Then will I dress once more the faded bower,
Where Jonson§ sat in Drummond's classic shade;
Or crop, from Tiviotdale, each lyric flower,
And mourn, on Yarrow's banks, where Willy's laid!
Meantime, ye pow'rs that on the plains which bore
The cordial youth, on Lothian's plains, attend!—
Where'er Home dwells, on hill, or lowly moor,
To him I love your kind protection lend,
And, touch'd with love like mine, preserve my absent friend!

* † ‡ Three rivers in Scotland.
§ Ben Jonson paid a visit on foot, in 1619, to the Scotch poet Drummond, at his seat of Hawthornden, within four miles of Edinburgh.

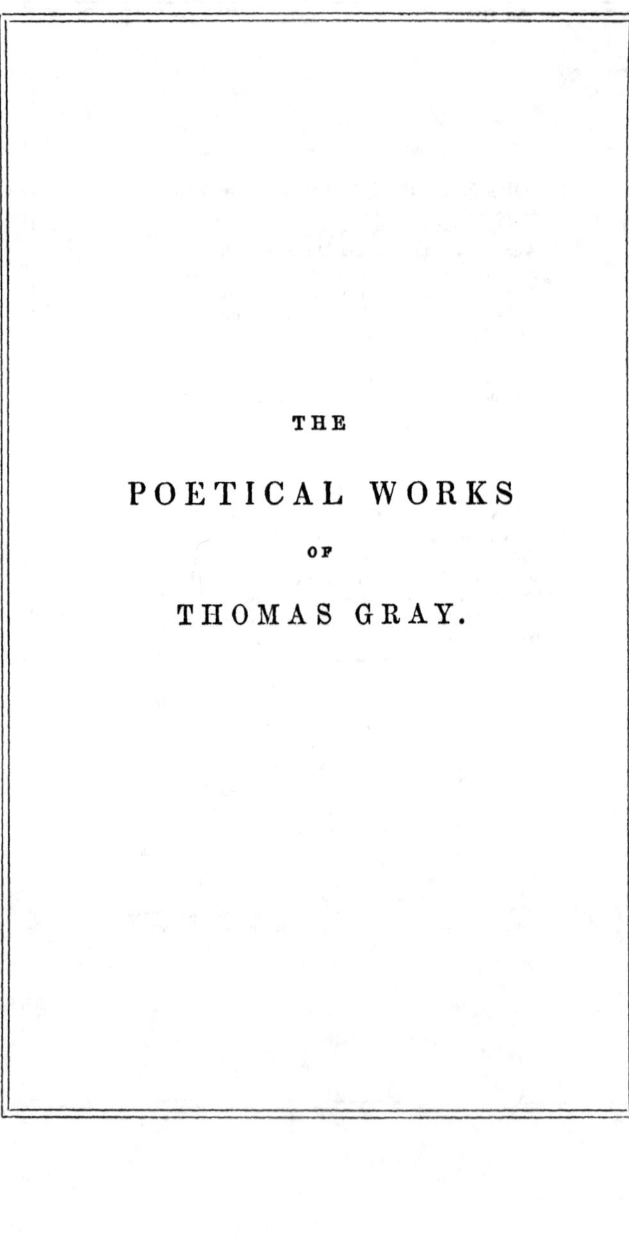

THE

POETICAL WORKS

OF

THOMAS GRAY.

THE LIFE

OF

THOMAS GRAY.

THOMAS GRAY, the son of Mr. Philip Gray, a scrivener of London, was born in Cornhill, November 26, 1716. His grammatical education he received at Eton under the care of Mr. Antrobus, his mother's brother, then assistant to Dr. George; and when he left school, in 1734, entered a pensioner at Peterhouse in Cambridge.

The transition from the school to the college is, to most young scholars, the time from which they date their years of manhood, liberty, and happiness; but Gray seems to have been very little delighted with academical qualifications; he liked at Cambridge neither the mode of life nor the fashion of study, and lived sullenly on to the time when his attendance on lectures was no longer required. As he intended to profess the common law, he took no degree.

When he had been at Cambridge about five years, Mr. Horace Walpole, whose friendship he had gained at Eton, invited him to travel with him as his companion. They wandered through France into Italy; and Gray's 'Letters' contain a very pleasing account of many parts of their journey. But unequal friendships are easily dissolved: at Florence they quarrelled, and parted; and Mr. Walpole is now content to have it told that it was by his fault. If we look, however, without prejudice on the world, we shall find that men, whose consciousness of their own merit sets them above the compliances of servility, are apt enough in their association with superiors to watch their own dignity with troublesome and punctilious jealousy, and in the fervour of independence to exact that attention which they refuse to pay. Part they did, whatever was the quarrel; and the rest of their travels was doubtless more unpleasant to them both. Gray continued his journey in a manner suitable to his own little fortune, with only an occasional servant.

He returned to England in September, 1741, and in about two months afterwards buried his father, who had, by an injudicious waste of money upon a new house, so much lessened his fortune, that Gray thought himself to poor to study the law. He, therefore, retired to Cambridge, where he soon after became bachelor of civil law, and where, without liking the place or its inhabitants, or professing to like them, he passed, except a short residence at London, the rest of his life.

About this time he was deprived of Mr. West, the son of a chancellor of Ireland, a friend on whom he appears to have set a high value, and who deserved his esteem by the powers which he shows in his letters, and in the 'Ode to May,' which Mr. Mason has preserved, as well as by the sincerity with which, when Gray sent him part of 'Agrippina, a tragedy that he had just begun, he gave an opinion which probably intercepted the progress of the work, and which the judgment of every reader will confirm. It was certainly no loss to the English stage that 'Agrippina' was never finished.

In this year (1742) Gray seems to have applied himself seriously to poetry; for in this year were produced the 'Ode to Spring,' his 'Prospect of Eton,' and his 'Ode to Adversity.' He began likewise a Latin Poem, 'De Principiis Cogitandi.

It may be collected from the narrative of Mr. Mason, that his first ambition was to have excelled in Latin poetry: perhaps it were reasonable to wish that he had prosecuted his design; for, though there is at present some embarrassment in his phrase, and some harshness in his lyric numbers, his copiousness of language is such as very few possess; and his lines, even when imperfect, discover a writer whom practice would have made skilful.

He now lived on at Peterhouse, very little solicitous what others did or thought, and cultivated his mind and enlarged his views without any other purpose than of improving and amusing himself; when Mr. Mason, being elected fellow of Pembroke Hall, brought him a companion who was afterwards to be his editor, and whose fondness and fidelity has kindled in him a zeal of admiration which cannot be reasonably expected from the neutrality of a stranger, and the coldness of a critic.

In his retirement he wrote (1747) an ode on the 'Death of Mr. Walpole's Cat;' and the year afterwards attempted a poem, of more importance, on 'Government and Education,' of which the fragments which remain have many excellent lines.

His next production (1750) was his far-famed 'Elegy in the Church-yard,' which, finding its way into a magazine, first, I believe, made him known to the public.

An invitation from Lady Cobham about this time gave occasion to an odd composition called 'A Long Story,' which adds little to Gray's character.

Several of his pieces were published (1753) with designs by Mr. Bentley: and that they might in some form or other make a book, only one side of each leaf was printed. I believe the poems and the plates recommended each other so well, that the whole impression was soon bought. This year he lost his mother.

Some time afterwards (1756) some young men of the college, whose chambers were near his, diverted themselves with disturbing him by frequent and troublesome noises, and, as is said, by pranks yet more offensive and contemptuous. This insolence, having endured it awhile, he represented to the governors of the society, among whom, perhaps, he had no friends; and, finding his complaint little regarded, removed himself to Pembroke Hall.

In 1757, he published 'The Progress of Poetry, and 'The Bard,' two compositions at which the readers of poetry were at first content to gaze in mute amazement.

Some that tried them confessed their inability to understand them, though Warburton said they were understood as well as 'the works of Milton and Shakspeare, which it is the fashion to admire. Garrick wrote a few lines in their praise. Some hardy champions undertook to rescue them from neglect; and in a short time many were content to be shewn beauties which they could not see.

Gray's reputation was now so high, that after the death of Cibber, he had the honour of refusing the laurel, which was then bestowed on Mr. Whitehead.

His curiosity, not long after, drew him away from Cambridge to a lodging near the Museum, where he resided near three years, reading and transcribing; and, so far as can be discovered, very little affected by two odes on 'Oblivion' and 'Obscurity,' in which his lyric performances were ridiculed with much contempt and much ingenuity.

When the professor of modern history at Cambridge died, he was, as he says, 'cockered and spirited up,' till he asked it of Lord Bute, who sent him a civil refusal; and the place was given to Mr. Brocket, the tutor of Sir James Lowther.

His constitution was weak, and, believing that his health was promoted by exercise and change of place, he undertook (1765) a journey into Scotland, of which his account, so far as it extends, is very curious and elegant: for, as his comprehension was ample, his curiosity extended to all the works of art, all the appearances of nature, and all the monuments of past events. He naturally contracted a friendship with Dr. Beattie, whom he found a poet, a philosopher, and a good man. The Mareschal College at Aberdeen offered him the degree of doctor of laws, which, having omitted to take it at Cambridge, he thought it decent to refuse.

What he had formerly solicited in vain was at last given him without solicitation. The professorship of history became again vacant, and he received (1768) an offer of it from the Duke of Grafton. He accepted and retained it to his death: always designing lectures, but never appearing reading them; uneasy at his neglect of duty, and appeasing his uneasiness with designs of reformation, and with a resolution which he believed himself to have made of resigning the office, if he found himself unable to discharge it.

Ill health made another journey necessary, and he visited (1769) Westmoreland and Cumberland. He that reads his epistolary narration, wishes, that to travel, and to tell his travels, had been more of his employment; but it is by studying at home that we must obtain the ability of travelling with intelligence and improvement.

His travels and his studies were now near their end. The gout, of which he had sustained many weak attacks, fell upon his stomach, and, yielding to no medicines, produced strong convulsions, which (July 30, 1771) terminated in death.

His character I am willing to adopt, as Mr. Mason has done, from a letter written to my friend Mr. Boswell by the Rev. Mr. Temple, rector of St. Gluvias in Cornwall; and am as willing as his warmest well-wisher to believe it true.

'Perhaps he was the most learned man in Europe He was equally acquainted with the elegant and profound parts of science, and that not superficially, but thoroughly. He knew every branch of history, both natural and civil; had read all the original historians of England, France, and Italy; and was a great antiquarian. Criticism, metaphysics, morals, politics, made a principal part of his study; voyages and travels of all sorts were his favourite amusements; and he had a fine taste in painting, prints, architecture, and gardening. With such a fund of knowledge, his conversation must have been equally instructing and entertaining; but he was also a good man, a man of virtue and humanity. There is no character without some speck, some imperfection; and I think the greatest defect in his was an affectation in delicacy, or rather effeminacy, and a visible fastidiousness, or contempt and disdain of his inferiors in science. He also had, in some degree, that weakness which disgusted Voltaire so much in Mr Congreve; though he seemed to value others chiefly according to the progress that they had made in know ledge, yet he could not bear to be considered merely as a man of letters; and, though without birth, or fortune, or station, his desire was to be looked upon as a private independent gentleman, who read for his amusement. Perhaps it may be said, What signifies so much knowledge, when it produced so little? Is it worth taking so much pains to leave no memorials but a few poems? But let it be considered that Mr. Gray was to others at least innocently employed; to himself certainly beneficially. His time passed agreeably: he was every day making some new acquisition in science; his mind was enlarged, his heart softened, his virtue strengthened; the world and mankind were shewn to him without a mask; and he was taught to consider every thing as trifling, and unworthy of the attention of a wise man, except the pursuit of knowledge and practice of virtue, in that state wherein God hath placed us.'

To this character Mr. Mason has added a more particular account of Gray's skill in zoology. He has remarked that Gray's effeminacy was affected most 'before those whom he did not wish to please;' and that he is unjustly charged with making knowledge his sole reason of preference, as he paid his esteem to none whom he did not likewise believe to be good.

What has occurred to me from the slight inspection of his Letters in which my undertaking has engaged me is, that his mind had a large grasp; that his curiosity was unlimited, and his judgment cultivated; that he was a man likely to love much where he loved at all; but that he was fastidious and hard to please. His contempt, however, is often employed where I hope it will be approved, upon scepticism and infidelity. His short account of Shaftesbury I will insert.

'You say you cannot conceive how Lord Shaftesbury came to be a philosopher in vogue; I will tell you; first, he was a lord; secondly, he was as vain as any of his readers; thirdly, men are very prone to believe what they do not understand; fourthly, they will believe any thing at all, provided they are under no obligation to believe it; fifthly, they love to take a new road, even when that road leads no where; sixthly, he was reckoned a fine writer, and seems always to mean more than he said. Would you have any more reasons? An interval of above forty years has pretty well destroyed the charm. A dead lord ranks with commoners· vanity is no longer interested in the matter; for a new road has become an old one.'

Mr. Mason has added, from his own knowledge, that, though Gray was poor, he was not eager of money; and that out of the little that he had, he was very willing to help the necessitous.

As a writer he had this peculiarity, that he did not write his pieces first rudely, and then correct them, but laboured every line as it arose in the train of composition; and he had a notion not very peculiar, that he could not write but at certain times, or at happy moments; a fantastic foppery, to which my kindness for a man of learning and virtue wishes him to have been superior.

Gray's poetry is now to be considered; and I hope not to be looked on as an enemy to his name, if I confess that I contemplate it with less pleasure than his life.

His ode 'On Spring' has something poetical, both in the language and the thought; but the language is too luxuriant, and the thoughts have nothing new. There has of late arisen a practice of giving to adjectives derived from substantives the termination of participles; such as the *cultured* plain, the *daisied* bank; but I was sorry to see, in the lines of a scholar like Gray, the *honied* Spring. The morality is natural, but too stale; the conclusion is pretty.

The poem 'On the Cat' was doubtless by its Author considered as a trifle; but it is not a happy trifle. In the first stanza, 'the azure flowers *that* blow' shew resolutely a rhyme is sometimes made when it cannot easily be found. Selima, the Cat, is called a nymph, with some violence both to language and sense; but there is no good use made of it when it is done, for of the two lines,

> What female heart can gold despise?
> What cat's averse to fish?

the first relates merely to the nymph, and the second only to the cat. The sixth stanza contains a melancholy truth, that 'a favourite has no friend;' but the last ends in a pointed sentence of no relation to the purpose; if *what glistered* had been *gold*, the cat would not have gone into the water; and, if she had, would not less have been drowned.

The 'Prospect of Eton College' suggests nothing to Gray which every beholder does not equally think and feel. His supplication to father Thames, to tell him who drives the hoop or tosses the ball, is useless and puerile. Father Thames has no better means of knowing than himself. His epithet 'buxom health' is not elegant; he seems not to understand the word. Gray thought his language more poetical as it was more remote from common use; finding in Dryden 'honey redolent of spring,' an expression that reaches the utmost limits of our language, Gray drove it a little more beyond common apprehension, by making 'gales' to be 'redolent of joy and youth.'

Of the 'Ode on Adversity' the hint was at first taken from 'O Diva, gratum quæ regis Antium:' but Gray has excelled his original by the variety of his sentiments, and by their moral application. Of this piece, at once poetical and rational, I will not, by slight objections, violate the dignity.

My process has now brought me to the *wonderful* 'Wonder of Wonders,' the two Sister Odes, by which, though either vulgar ignorance or common sense at first universally rejected them, many have been since persuaded to think themselves delighted. I am one of those that are willing to be pleased, and therefore would gladly find the meaning of the first stanza of 'The Progress of Poetry.'

Gray seems in his rapture to confound the images of 'spreading sound and running water.' A 'stream of music' may be allowed; but where does 'music,' however 'smooth and strong,' after having visited the 'verdant vales, roll down the steep amain,' so as that 'rocks and nodding groves rebellow to the roar?' If this be said of music, it is nonsense; if it be said of water, it is nothing to the purpose.

The second stanza, exhibiting Mars' car and Jove's eagle, is unworthy of further notice. Criticism disdains to chase a school-boy to his common places.

To the third it may likewise be objected, that it is drawn from mythology, though such as may be more easily assimilated to real life. Idalia's 'velvet green' has something of cant. An epithet or metaphor drawn from Nature enobles Art; an epithet or metaphor drawn from Art degrades Nature. Gray is too fond of words arbitrarily compounded. 'Many-twinkling' was formerly censured as not analogical; we may say 'many-spotted,' but scarcely 'many-spotting.' This stanza, however, has something pleasing.

Of the second ternary of stanzas, the first endeavours to tell something, and would have told it, had it not been crossed by Hyperion: the second describes well enough the universal prevalence of poetry; but I am afraid that the conclusion will not arise from the premises. The caverns of the north and the plains of Chili are not the residences of 'glory and generous shame.' But that Poetry and Virtue go always together is an opinion so pleasing, that I can forgive him who resolves to think it true.

The third stanza sounds big with 'Delphi,' and 'Egean,' and 'Ilissus,' and 'Meander,' and 'hallowed fountains,' and 'solemn sound;' but in all Gray's odes there is a kind of cumbrous splendour which we wish away. His position is at last false: in the time of Dante and Petrarch, from whom we derive our first school of Poetry, Italy was overrun by 'tyrant power,' and 'coward vice;' nor was our state much better when we first borrowed the Italian arts.

Of the third ternary, the first gives a mythological birth of Shakspeare. What is said of that mighty genius is true; but it is not said happily: the real effects of this poetical power are put out of sight by the pomp of the machinery. Where truth is sufficient to fill the mind, fiction is worse than useless; the counterfeit debases the genuine.

His account of Milton's blindness, if we suppose it caused by study in the formation of his poem, a supposition surely allowable, is poetically true, and happily imagined. But the *car* of Dryden, with his *two coursers*, has nothing in it peculiar; it is a car in which any other rider may be placed.

'The Bard' appears, at the first view, to be, as Algarotti and others have remarked, an imitation of the prophecy of Nereus. Algarotti thinks it superior to its original; and, if preference depends only on the imagery and animation of the two poems, his judgment is right. There is in 'The Bard' more force, more thought, and more variety. But to copy is less than to invent, and the copy has been unhappily produced at a wrong time. The fiction of Horace was to the Romans credible; but its revival disgusts us with apparent and unconquerable falsehood. *Incredulus odi.*

To select a singular event, and swell it to a giant's bulk by fabulous appendages of spectres and predictions, has little difficulty; for he that forsakes the probable may always find the marvellous. And it has little use; we are affected only as we believe; we are improved only as we find something to be imitated or declined. I do not see that 'The Bard' promotes any truth, moral or political.

His stanzas are too long, especially his epodes; the ode is finished before the ear has learned its measures, and consequently before it can receive pleasure from their consonance and recurrence.

Of the first stanza the abrupt beginning has been celebrated: but technical beauties can give praise only to the inventor. It is in the power of any man to rush abruptly upon his subject, that has read the ballad of 'Johnny Armstrong,'

Is there ever a man in all Scotland—

The initial resemblances or alliterations, 'ruin, ruthless, helm, or hauberk,' are below the grandeur of a poem that endeavours at sublimity.

In the second stanza the Bard is well described; but in the third we have the puerilities of obsolete mythology. When we are told that 'Cadwallo hush'd the stormy main,' and that 'Modred made huge Plinlimmon bow his cloud topp'd head,' attention recoils from the repetition of a tale that, even when it was first heard, was heard with scorn.

The *weaving* of the *winding-sheet* he borrowed, as he owns, from the Northern Bards: but their texture, however, was very properly the work of female powers, as the act of spinning the thread of life is another mythology. Theft is always dangerous; Gray has made weavers of slaughtered bards by a fiction outrageous and incongruous. They are then called upon to 'Weave the warp, and weave the woof,' perhaps with no great propriety; for it is by crossing the *woof* with the *warp* that men weave the *web* or piece; and the first line was dearly bought by the admission of its wretched correspondent, 'Give ample room and verge enough.'* He has, however, no other line as bad.

The third stanza of the second ternary is commended, I think, beyond its merit. The personification is indistinct. *Thirst* and *Hunger* are not alike; and their features, to make the imagery perfect should have been discriminated. We are told, in the same stanza, how 'towers are fed.' But I will no longer look for particular faults; yet let it be observed that the ode might have been concluded with an action of better example, but suicide is always to be had, without expense of thought.

These odes are marked by glittering accumulations of ungraceful ornaments; they strike, rather than please; the images are magnified by affectation; the language is laboured into harshness. The mind of the writer seems to work with unnatural violence. 'Double, double, toil and trouble.' He has a kind of strutting dignity, and is tall by walking on tiptoe. His art and his struggle are too visible, and there is too little appearance of ease and nature.

To say that he had no beauties would be unjust; a man like him, of great learning and great industry, could not but produce something valuable. When he pleases least, it can only be said that a good design was ill directed.

His translations of Northern and Welsh Poetry deserve praise; the imagery is preserved, perhaps often improved; but the language is unlike the language of other poets.

* 'I have a soul, that like an *ample* shield
Can take in all; and *verge enough* for more.'
Dryden's Sebastian.

In the character of his Elegy I rejoice to concur with the common reader; for by the common sense of readers, uncorrupted with literary prejudices, after all the refinements of subtilty and the dogmatism of learning, must be finally decided all claim to poetical honours. The 'Church yard' abounds with images which find a mirror in every mind, and with sentiments to which every bosom returns an echo. The four stanzas, beginning 'Yet even these bones,' are to me original: I have never seen the notions in any other place; yet he that reads them here persuades himself that he has always felt them. Had Gray written often thus, it had been vain to blame, and useless to praise him.

POEMS.

ODES.

I. ON THE SPRING.

Lo! where the rosy-bosom'd Hours,
Fair Venus' train, appear,
Disclose the long-expected flowers,
And wake the purple year!
The Attic warbler pours her throat,
Responsive to the cuckoo's note,
The untaught harmony of spring:
While, whisp'ring pleasure as they fly,
Cool Zephyrs through the clear blue sky
Their gather'd fragrance fling.

Where'er the oak's thick branches stretch
A broader, browner shade;
Where'er the rude and moss-grown beech
O'er-canopies the glade,
Beside some water's rushy brink
With me the Muse shall sit, and think
(At ease reclined in rustic state)
How vain the ardour of the crowd,
How low, how little are the proud,
How indigent the great!
Still is the toiling hand of Care:
The panting herds repose:
Yet hark, how through the peopled air
The busy murmur glows!
The insect youth are on the wing,
Eager to taste the honied spring,

And float amid the liquid noon:
  Some lightly o'er the current skim,
  Some shew their gaily-gilded trim,
Quick-glancing to the sun.

To Contemplation's sober eye
  Such is the race of man:
And they that creep, and they that fly,
  Shall end where they began.
    Alike the busy and the gay
    But flutter through life's little day,
    In fortune's varying colours drest:
      Brush'd by the hand of rough Mischance,
      Or chill'd by Age, their airy dance
    They leave, in dust to rest.

    Methinks I hear in accents low
      The sportive kind reply:
    'Poor moralist! and what art thou?
      A solitary fly!
    Thy joys no glittering female meets,
    No hive hast thou of hoarded sweets,
    No painted plumage to display:
      On hasty wings thy youth is flown;
      Thy sun is set, thy spring is gone—
    We frolic, while 'tis May.'

II. ON THE DEATH OF A FAVOURITE CAT,

Drowned in a Tub of Gold Fishes.

'Twas on a lofty vase's side,
Where China's gayest art had dyed
The azure flowers, that blow;
  Demurest of the tabby kind,
  The pensive Selima reclined,
Gazed on the lake below.

Her conscious tail her joy declared;
The fair round face, the snowy beard,
The velvet of her paws,
  Her coat, that with the tortoise vies,
  Her ears of jet, and emerald eyes,
She saw; and purr'd applause.

Still had she gazed; but 'midst the tide
Two angel forms were seen to glide,
The Genii of the stream:
  Their scaly armour's Tyrian hue
  Through richest purple to the view
Betray'd a golden gleam.

The hapless Nymph with wonder saw:
A whisker first, and then a claw,
With many an ardent wish,
  She stretch'd in vain to reach the prize.
  What female heart can gold despise?
What Cat's averse to fish?

Presumptuous Maid! with looks intent
Again she stretch'd, again she bent,
Nor knew the gulf between.
  (Malignant Fate sate by, and smiled)
  The slipp'ry verge her feet beguiled,
She tumbled headlong in.

Eight times emerging from the flood,
She mew'd to ev'ry wat'ry God,
Some speedy aid to send.
  No Dolphin came, no Nereid stirr'd:
  Nor cruel Tom, nor Susan heard—
A fav'rite has no friend!

From hence, ye beauties, undeceived,
Know, one false step is ne'er retrieved
  And be with caution bold.
Not all that tempts your wand'ring eyes
And heedless hearts, is lawful prize
  Nor all, that glisters, gold

III. ON A DISTANT PROSPECT OF ETON COLLEGE.

Ἄνθρωπος ἱκανὴ πρόφασις εἰς τὸ δυστυχεῖν.
Menander.

Ye distant spires, ye antique towers,
That crown the wat'ry glade,
Where grateful Science still adores
Her Henry's* holy shade;
And ye, that from the stately brow
Of Windsor's heights th' expanse below
Of grove, of lawn, of mead survey;
Whose turf, whose shade, whose flowers among
Wanders the hoary Thames along
His silver-winding way!

Ah happy hills! ah pleasing shade!
Ah fields beloved in vain,
Where once my careless childhood stray'd
A stranger yet to pain!
I feel the gales that from ye blow
A momentary bliss bestow,
As waving fresh their gladsome wing,
My weary soul they seem to sooth,
And, redolent of joy and youth,
To breathe a second spring.

Say, Father Thames, for thou hast seen
Full many a sprightly race,
Disporting on thy margent green,
The paths of pleasure trace,
Who foremost now delight to cleave
With pliant arm thy glassy wave?
The captive linnet which enthral?
What idle progeny succeed
To chase the rolling circle's speed,
Or urge the flying ball?

* King Henry the Sixth, founder of the College.

While some on earnest business bent
  Their murm'ring labours ply
'Gainst graver hours, that bring constraint
  To sweeten liberty:
Some bold adventurers disdain
The limits of their little reign,
And unknown regions dare descry:
  Still as they run they look behind,
  They hear a voice in every wind,
And snatch a fearful joy.

Gay hope is theirs, by fancy fed,
  Less pleasing when possest;
The tear forgot as soon as shed,
  The sunshine of the breast:
Theirs buxom health of rosy hue,
Wild wit, invention ever new,
And lively cheer of vigour born;
  The thoughtless day, the easy night,
  The spirits pure, the slumbers light,
That fly th' approach of morn.

Alas! regardless of their doom,
  The little victims play!
No sense have they of ills to come,
  Nor care beyond to-day:
Yet see how all around 'em wait
The ministers of human fate,
And black Misfortune's baleful train:
  Ah, shew them where in ambush stand,
  To seize their prey, the murth'rous band
Ah, tell them they are men!

These shall the fury Passions tear,
  The vultures of the mind,
Disdainful Anger, pallid Fear,
  And Shame that sculks behind;
Or pining Love shall waste their youth,
Or Jealousy with rankling tooth,

That inly gnaws the secret heart,
And Envy wan, and faded Care,
Grim-visaged comfortless Despair,
And Sorrow's piercing dart.

Ambition this shall tempt to rise,
Then whirl the wretch from high,
To bitter Scorn a sacrifice,
And grinning Infamy.
The stings of Falsehood those shall try,
And hard Unkindness' alter'd eye,
That mocks the tear it forced to flow;
And keen Remorse with blood defiled,
And moody Madness laughing wild
Amid severest woe.

Lo, in the vale of years beneath
A griesly troop are seen,
The painful family of Death,
More hideous than their queen:
This racks the joints, this fires the veins,
That every labouring sinew strains,
Those in the deeper vitals rage:
Lo, Poverty, to fill the band,
That numbs the soul with icy hand,
And slow-consuming Age.

To each his suff'rings: all are men,
Condemn'd alike to groan;
The tender for another's pain,
Th' unfeeling for his own.
Yet ah! why should they know their fate,
Since sorrow never comes too late,
And happiness too swiftly flies?
Thought would destroy their paradise.
No more; where ignorance is bliss,
'Tis folly to be wise

IV. TO ADVERSITY.

Ζῆνα——
Τὸν φρονεῖν βροτοὺς ὁδώ-
σαντα, τῷ πάθει μαθὰν
Θέντα κυρίως ἔχειν.
Æschylus, in Agamemnon.

DAUGHTER of Jove, relentless power,
Thou tamer of the human breast,
Whose iron scourge and tort'ring hour
The Bad affright, afflict the Best!
Bound in thy adamantine chain
The proud are taught to taste of pain,
And purple tyrants vainly groan
With pangs unfelt before, unpitied and alone

When first thy sire to send on earth
Virtue, his darling child, design'd,
To thee he gave the heav'nly birth,
And bade to form her inf nt mind.
Stern rugged Nurse! thy rigid lore
With patience many a year she bore:
What sorrow was, thou bad'st her know,
And from her own she learn'd to melt at others' woe.

Scared at thy frown terrific, fly
Self-pleasing Folly's idle brood,
Wild Laughter, Noise, and thoughtless Joy
And leave us leisure to be good.
Light they disperse, and with them go
The summer Friend, the flattering Foe;
By vain Prosperity received,
To her they vow their truth, and are again believed.

Wisdom in sable garb array'd,
Immersed in rapt'rous thought profound,
And Melancholy, silent maid,
With leaden eye, that loves the ground,

Still on thy solemn steps attend :
Warm Charity, the general friend,
With Justice, to herself severe,
And Pity, dropping soft the sadly-pleasing tear.

Oh, gently on thy suppliant's head,
  Dread Goddess, lay thy chast'ning hand!
Not in thy Gorgon terrors clad,
  Nor circled with the vengeful band
(As by the impious thou art seen)
With thund'ring voice, and threat'ning mien,
With screaming Horror's funeral cry,
Despair, and fell Disease, and ghastly Poverty.

Thy form benign, oh, Goddess, wear,
  Thy milder influence impart,
Thy philosophic train be there
  To soften, not to wound my heart.
The generous spark extinct revive,
Teach me to love and to forgive,
Exact my own defects to scan,
What others are to feel, and know myself a Man.

V. THE PROGRESS OF POESY.

*Pindaric.**

Φωνᾶντα συνετοῖσιν· ἐς
Δὲ Χατίζει τὸ πὰν, ἑρμηνέων.
Pindar, Olymp. II.

I. 1.

AWAKE, Æolian lyre, awake,
And give to rapture all thy trembling strings.
†From Helicon's harmonious springs,
A thousand rills their mazy progress take:
The laughing flowers, that round them blow,
Drink life and fragrance as they flow.
Now the rich stream of music winds along
Deep, majestic, smooth, and strong,
Through verdant vales, and Ceres' golden reign:
Now rolling down the steep amain,
Headlong, impetuous, see it pour:
The rocks, and nodding groves, rebellow to the roar.

I. 2.

‡Oh! Sov'reign of the willing soul,
Parent of sweet and solemn breathing airs,
Enchanting shell! the sullen Cares,
And frantic Passions, hear thy soft control.
On Thracia's hills the Lord of War
Has curb'd the fury of his car,

* When the author first published this and the following Ode, he was advised, even by his friends, to subjoin some few explanatory notes; but had too much respect for the understanding of his readers to take that liberty.

† The subject and simile, as usual with Pindar, are united. The various sources of poetry, which gives life and lustre to all it touches, are here described, its quiet majestic progress enriching every subject (otherwise dry and barren) with a pomp of diction and luxuriant harmony of numbers; and its more rapid and irresistible course, when swoln and hurried away by the conflict of tumultuous passions

‡ Power of harmony to calm the turbulent sallies of the soul. The thoughts are borrowed from the first Pythian of Pindar.

And dropp'd his thirsty lance at thy command.
Perching on the sceptred hand
Of Jove, thy magic lulls the feather'd king
With ruffled plumes, and flagging wing:
Quench'd in dark clouds of slumber lie
The terror of his beak, and lightnings of his eye.

I. 3.

*Thee the voice, the dance, obey,
Temper'd to thy warbled lay.
O'er Idalia's velvet green
The rosy-crowned Loves are seen,
On Cytherea's day,
With antic Sport, and blue-eyed Pleasures,
Frisking light in frolic measures;
Now pursuing, now retreating,
  Now in circling troops they meet:
To brisk notes in cadence beating
  Glance their many-twinkling feet.
Slow melting strains their Queen's approach declare:
  Where'er she turns the Graces homage pay.
With arms sublime, that float upon the air,
  In gliding state she wins her easy way:
O'er her warm cheek, and rising bosom move
The bloom of young Desire, and purple light of Love

II. 1.

†Man's feeble race what ills await!
  Labour, and Penury, the racks of Pain,
Disease, and Sorrow's weeping train,
  And Death, sad refuge from the storms of Fate!
The fond complaint, my song, disprove,
And justify the laws of Jove.

* Power of harmony to produce all the graces of motion in the body.

† To compensate the real and imaginary ills of life, the Muse was given to mankind by the same Providence that sends the day by its cheerful presence to dispel the gloom and terrors of the night.

Say, has he giv'n in vain the heav'nly Muse?
Night, and all her sickly dews,
Her spectres wan, and birds of boding cry,
He gives to range the dreary sky:
Till down the eastern cliffs afar
Hyperion's march they spy, and glittering shafts of war.

II. 2.

*In climes beyond the solar road,
Where shaggy forms o'er ice-built mountains roam,
The Muse has broke the twilight-gloom
To cheer the shivering native's dull abode.
And oft, beneath the od'rous shade
Of Chili's boundless forests laid,
She deigns to hear the savage youth repeat
In loose numbers wildly sweet
Their feather-cinctured chiefs, and dusky loves.
Her track, where'er the Goddess roves,
Glory pursue, and generous Shame,
Th' unconquerable Mind, and Freedom's holy flame.

II. 3.

†Woods, that wave o'er Delphi's steep,
Isles, that crown th' Ægean deep,
Fields, that cool Ilissus laves,
Or where Mæander's amber waves
In lingering lab'rinths creep,
How do your tuneful Echoes languish,
Mute, but to the voice of Anguish!

* Extensive influence of poetic genius over the remotest and most uncivilized nations: its connexion with liberty, and the virtues that naturally attend on it.—(See the Erse, Norwegian, and Welsh Fragments; the Lapland and American Songs.)

† Progress of poetry from Greece to Italy, and from Italy to England. Chaucer was not unacquainted with the writings of Dante or of Petrarch. The Earl of Surrey and Sir Thomas Wyatt had travelled in Italy, and formed their taste there; Spenser imitated the Italian writers; Milton improved on them; but this school expired soon after the Restoration, and a new one arose on the French model, which has subsisted ever since.

Where each old poetic Mountain
  Inspiration breath'd around;
Ev'ry shade and hallow'd fountain
  Murmur'd deep a hollow sound:
Till the sad Nine in Greece's evil hour
  Left their Parnassus for the Latian plains.
Alike they scorn the pomp of tyrant Power,
  And coward Vice, that revels in her chains,
When Latium had her lofty spirit lost,
They sought, oh Albion! next thy sea-encircled coast.

III. 1.

Far from the sun and summer-gale,
  In thy green lap was Nature's* darling laid,
  What time, where lucid Avon stray'd,
To him the mighty mother did unveil
Her awful face: the dauntless child
Stretch'd forth his little arms, and smiled.
'This pencil take,' she said, 'whose colours clear
Richly paint the vernal year:
Thine too these golden keys, immortal boy!
This can unlock the gates of Joy;
Of Horror that, and thrilling Fears,
Or ope the sacred source of sympathetic Tears.'

III. 2.

Nor second He,† that rode sublime
  Upon the seraph-wings of Ecstasy,
  The secrets of th' abyss to spy.
He pass'd the flaming bounds of space and time:
The living-throne, the sapphire-blaze,
Where angels tremble, while they gaze,
He saw; but blasted with excess of light,
Closed his eyes in endless night.

* Shakspeare. † Milton.

Behold where Dryden's less presumptuous car
Wide o'er the fields of glory bear
Two coursers of ethereal race,
With necks in thunder clothed, and long-resounding
pace.

III. 3.

Hark, his hands the lyre explore!
Bright-eyed Fancy, hovering o'er,
Scatters from her pictured urn
Thoughts, that breathe, and words, that burn.
*But ah! 'tis heard no more——
Oh! lyre divine, what daring Spirit
Wakes thee now? though he inherit
Nor the pride, nor ample pinion,
†That the Theban eagle bear,
Sailing with supreme dominion
Through the azure deep of air:
Yet oft before his infant eyes would run
Such forms, as glitter in the Muse's ray
With orient hues, unborrow'd of the Sun:
Yet shall he mount, and keep his distant way
Beyond the limits of a vulgar fate,
Beneath the Good how far—but far above the Great.

* We have had in our language no other odes of the sublime kind, than that of Dryden on St. Cecilia's day: for Cowley (who had his merit) yet wanted judgment, style, and harmony, for such a task. That of Pope is not worthy of so great a man. Mr. Mason, indeed, of late days, has touched the true chords, and with a masterly hand, in some of his Choruses,—above all in the last of Caractacus;

'Hark! heard ye not yon footstep dread" &c.

† Pindar.

VI. THE BARD.

*Pindaric.**

'RUIN seize thee, ruthless king!
Confusion on thy banners wait!
Though fann'd by conquest's crimson wing,
They mock the air with idle state.
Helm, or hauberk's† twisted mail,
Nor e'en thy virtues, tyrant, shall avail
To save thy secret soul from nightly fears,
From Cambria's curse, from Cambria's tears!'
Such were the sounds, that o'er the crested pride
Of the first Edward scatter'd wild dismay,
As down the steep of Snowdon's‡ shaggy side
He wound with toilsome march his long array.
Stout Glo'ster§ stood aghast in speechless trance;
'To arms!' cried Mortimer,‖ and couch'd his quiv'ring lance.

I. 2.

On a rock, whose haughty brow
Frowns o'er old Conway's foaming flood,
Robed in the sable garb of woe,
With haggard eyes the Poet stood
(Loose his beard, and hoary hair
Stream'd, like a meteor, to the troubled air);

* This Ode is founded on a tradition current in Wales, that Edward the First, when he completed the conquest of that country, ordered all the bards that fell into his hands to be put to death.

† The hauberk was a texture of steel ringlets, or rings interwoven, forming a coat of mail, that sat close to the body, and adapted itself to every motion.

‡ *Snowdon* was a name given by the Saxons to that mountainous tract which the Welsh themselves call *Craigian-eryri*: it included all the highlands of Caernarvonshire and Merionethshire, as far east as the river Conway. R. Hygden, speaking of the Castle of Conway, built by King Edward the First, says, 'Ad ortum amnis Conway ad clivum montis Erery;' and Matthew of Westminster, (ad ann. 1283), 'Apud Aberconway ad pedes montis Snowdoniæ fecit erigi castrum forte.'

§ Gilbert de Clare, surnamed the Red, earl of Gloucester and Hertford, son-in-law to King Edward.

‖ Edmond de Mortimer, lord of Wigmore.

They both were *Lords-Marchers*, whose lands lay on the borders of Wales, and probably accompanied the king in this expedition.

And with a master's hand, and prophet's fire,
Struck the deep sorrows of his lyre.
'Hark, how each giant oak, and desert cave,
  Sighs to the torrent's awful voice beneath!
O'er thee, oh king! their hundred arms they wave,
  Revenge on thee in hoarser murmurs breathe;
Vocal no more, since Cambria's fatal day,
To high-born Hoel's harp, or soft Llewellyn's lay.

I. 3.

'Cold is Cadwallo's tongue,
  That hush'd the stormy main:
Brave Urien, sleeps upon his craggy bed:
  Mountains, ye mourn in vain
Modred, whose magic song
Made huge Plinlimmon bow his cloud-topp'd head.
On dreary Arvon's shore * they lie,
  Smear'd with gore, and ghastly pale:
  Far, far aloof th' affrighted ravens sail;
The famish'd eagle † screams, and passes by.
Dear, lost companions of my tuneful art,
  Dear, as the light that visits these sad eyes,
Dear, as the ruddy drops that warm my heart,
  Ye died amidst your dying country's cries——
No more I weep. They do not sleep.
  On yonder cliffs, a griesly band,
I see them sit; they linger yet,
  Avengers of their native land:
With me in dreadful harmony they join,
And‡ weave with bloody hands the tissue of thy line.'

* The shores of Caernarvonshire opposite to the isle of Anglesey.

† Camden and others observe, that eagles used annually to build their aerie among the rocks of Snowdon, which from thence (as some think) were named by the Welsh *Craigian eryri*, or the crags of the eagles. At this day (I am told) the highest point of Snowdon is called *the eagle's nest*. That bird is certainly no stranger to this island, as the Scots and the people of Cumberland, Westmoreland, &c. can testify: it even has built its nest in the Peak of Derbyshire. (See Willoughby's Ornithol. published by Ray.)

‡ See the Norwegian Ode, that follows.

II. 1.

'Weave the warp, and weave the woof,
The winding-sheet of Edward's race.
Give ample room, and verge enough
The characters of hell to trace.
Mark the year, and mark the night,
*When Severn shall re-echo with affright;
The shrieks of death, through Berkley's roof that ring,
Shrieks of an agonizing king!
†She-wolf of France, with unrelenting fangs,
That tear'st the bowels of thy mangled mate,
‡ From thee be born, who o'er thy country hangs
The scourge of Heav'n! What terrors round him wait!
Amazement in his van, with Flight combined,
And Sorrow's faded form, and Solitude behind.

II. 2.

' Mighty victor, mighty lord,
§ Low on his funeral couch he lies!
No pitying heart, no eye, afford
A tear to grace his obsequies.
Is the sable §Warrior fled?
Thy sun is gone. He rests among the dead.
The swarm, that in thy noon-tide beam were born?
Gone to salute the rising Morn.
‖Fair laughs the Morn, and soft the Zephyr blows,
While proudly riding o'er the azure realm
In gallant trim the gilded vessel goes;
Youth on the prow, and Pleasure at the helm;
Regardless of the sweeping whirlwind's sway,
That, hush'd in grim repose, expects his evening-prey.

* Edward the Second, cruelly butchered in Berkley Castle.
† Isabel of France, Edward the Second's adulterous queen.
‡ Triumphs of Edward the Third in France.
§ Death of that king, abandoned by his children, and even robbed in his last moments by his courtiers and his mistress.
§ Edward the Black Prince, dead some time before his father.
¶ Magnificence of Richard the Second's reign. See Froissard, and other contemporary writers.

II. 3.

* Fill high the sparkling bowl,
The rich repast prepare;
Reft of a crown, he yet may share the feast:
Close by the regal chair
Fell Thirst and Famine scowl
A baleful smile upon their baffled guest.
Heard ye the din of †battle bray,
Lance to lance, and horse to horse?
Long years of havock urge their destin'd course,
And through the kindred squadrons mow their way.
Ye Towers of Julius,‡ London's lasting shame,
With many a foul and midnight murder fed,
Revere his §consort's faith, his father's‖ fame,
And spare the meek¶ usurper's holy head!
Above, below, the **rose of snow,
Twin'd with her blushing foe, we spread:
The bristled ††boar in infant gore
Wallows beneath the thorny shade.
Now, brothers, bending o'er th' accursed loom,
Stamp we our vengeance deep, and ratify his doom.

III. 1.

"Edward, lo! to sudden fate
(Weave we the woof. The thread is spun.)

* Richard the Second (as we are told by Archbishop Scroop and the confederate lords in their manifesto, by Thomas of Walsingham, and all the older writers) was starved to death. The story of his assassination, by Sir Piers, of Exon, is of much later date.

† Ruinous civil wars of York and Lancaster.

‡ Henry the Sixth, George duke of Clarence, Edward the Fifth, Richard duke of York, &c. believed to be murdered secretly in the Tower of London. The oldest part of that structure is vulgarly attributed to Julius Cæsar.

§ Margaret of Anjou, a woman of heroic spirit, who struggled hard to save her husband and her crown.

‖ Henry the Fifth.

¶ Henry the Sixth, very near being canonized. The line of Lancaster had no right of inheritance to the crown.

** The white and red roses, devices of York and Lancaster.

†† The silver boar was the badge of Richard the Third: whence he was usually known, in his own time, by the name of *the Boar*.

*Half of thy heart we consecrate.
  (The web is wove. The work is done.")
'Stay, oh stay! nor thus forlorn
Leave me unbless'd, unpitied, here to mourn:
In yon bright track, that fires the western skies,
They melt, they vanish from my eyes.
But oh! what solemn scenes, on Snowdon's height
  Descending slow, their glittering skirts unroll?
Visions of glory, spare my aching sight,
  Ye unborn ages, crowd not on my soul!
No more our long-lost† Arthur we bewail.
All hail,‡ ye genuine kings! Britannia's issue hail!

III. 2.

'Girt with many a baron bold,
  Sublime their starry fronts they rear;
And gorgeous dames, and statesmen old
  In bearded majesty, appear.
In the midst a form divine!
Her eye proclaims her of the Briton-line;
Her lion-port,§ her awe commanding face,
Attemper'd sweet to virgin-grace.
What strings symphonious tremble in the air,
  What strains of vocal transport round her play!
Hear from the grave, great Taliessin,|| hear!
  They breathe a soul to animate thy clay.
Bright Rapture calls, and soaring, as she sings,
Waves in the eye of Heav'n her many-colour'd wings.

* Eleanor of Castile died a few years after the conquest of Wales. The heroic proof she gave of her affection for her lord is well known. The monuments of his regret and sorrow for the loss of her are still to be seen at Northampton, Geddington, Waltham, and other places.

† It was the common belief of the Welsh nation, that King Arthur was still alive in Fairy-Land, and should return again to reign over Britain.

‡ Both Merlin and Taliessin had prophesied, that the Welsh should regain their sovereignty over this island; which seemed to be accomplished in the House of Tudor.

§ Speed, relating an audience given by Queen Elizabeth to Paul Dzialinski, ambassador of Poland, says, 'And thus she, lion-like rising, daunted the malapert orator no less with her stately port and majestical deporture, than with the tartnesse of her princelie checkes.'

|| Taliessin, chief of the bards, flourished in the sixth century. His works are still preserved, and his memory held in high veneration among his countrymen.

III. 3.

'The verse adorn again
  Fierce War, and faithful Love,
And Truth severe, by fairy Fiction drest.
  In *buskin'd measures move
Pale Grief, and pleasing Pain,
With Horror, tyrant of the throbbing breast.
A †voice as of the cherub choir,
  Gales from blooming Eden bear;
  And ‡distant warblings lessen on my ear,
That lost in long futurity expire.
Fond, impious man, think'st thou yon sanguine cloud,
  Raised by thy breath, hath quench'd the orb of day?
To morrow he repairs the golden flood,
  And warms the nations with redoubled ray.
Enough for me: with joy I see
  The different doom our Fates assign.
Be thine Despair, and sceptred Care;
  To triumph, and to die, are mine.'
He spoke, and headlong from the mountain's height,
Deep in the roaring tide he plung'd to endless night.

VII. FOR MUSIC.§

Irregular.

I.

'HENCE, avaunt ('tis holy ground),
  Comus, and his midnight crew,
And Ignorance with looks profound,
  And dreaming Sloth of pallid hue,

* Shakspeare. † Milton.

‡ The succession of poets after Milton's time.

§ This Ode was performed in the Senate-House at Cambridge, July 1, 1769, at the installation of his grace Augustus Henry Fitzroy, duke of Grafton, chancellor of the University.

Mad Sedition's cry profane,
Servitude that hugs her chain,
Nor in these consecrated bowers
Let painted Flatt'ry hide her serpent-train in flowers,
Nor Envy base, nor creeping Gain
Dare the Muse's walk to stain,
While bright-ey'd Science watches round:
Hence, away, 'tis holy ground!'

II.

From yonder realms of empyrean day
Bursts on my ear th' indignant lay:
There sit the sainted Sage, the Bard divine,
The few, whom Genius gave to shine
Through every unborn age, and undiscover'd clime.
Rapt in celestial transport they,
Yet hither oft a glance from high
They send of tender sympathy
To bless the place, where on their opening soul
First the genuine ardour stole.
'Twas Milton struck the deep-toned shell,
And, as the choral warblings round him swell,
Meek Newton's self bends from his state sublime,
And nods his hoary head, and listens to the rhyme.

III.

'Ye brown o'er-arching groves,
That Contemplation loves,
Where willowy Camus lingers with delight.
  Oft at the blush of dawn
  I trod your level lawn,
Oft woo'd the gleam of Cynthia silver-bright
In cloisters dim, far from the haunts of Folly,
With Freedom by my side, and soft-ey'd Melancholy.'

IV.

But hark! the portals sound, and pacing forth
  With solemn steps and slow,

High potentates, and dames of royal birth,
And mitred fathers in long order go:
Great *Edward, with the lilies on his brow,
From haughty Gallia torn,
And †sad Chatillon, on her bridal morn,
That wept her bleeding Love, and princely‡ Clare,
And §Anjou's heroine, and ‖the paler Rose,
The rival of her crown and of her woes,
And ¶ either Henry there,
The murder'd Saint, and the majestic Lord,
That broke the bonds of Rome.
(Their tears, their little triumphs o'er,
Their human passions now no more,
Save Charity, that glows beyond the tomb)
All that on Granta's fruitful plain
Rich streams of regal bounty pour'd,
And bade these awful fanes and turrets rise,
To hail their Fitzroy's festal morning come·
And thus they speak in soft accord
The liquid language of the skies.

V.

'What is grandeur, what is power?
Heavier toil, superior pain.
What the bright reward we gain?
The grateful memory of the good.

* Edward the Third; who added the *fleur de lys* of France to the arms of England. He founded Trinity College.

† Mary de Valentia, countess of Pembroke, daughter of Guy de Chatillon, comte de St. Paul in France, of whom tradition says, that her husband, Audemar de Valentia, earl of Pembroke, was slain at a tournament on the day of his nuptials. She was the foundress of Pembroke College, or Hall, under the name of Aula Mariæ de Valentia.

‡ Elizabeth de Burg, countess of Clare, was wife of John de Burg, son and heir of the Earl of Ulster, and daughter of Gilbert de Clare, earl of Gloucester, by Joan of Acres, daughter of Edward the First. Hence the poet gives her the epithet of 'princely.' She founded Clare Hall.

§ Margaret of Anjou, wife of Henry the Sixth, foundress of Queen's College. The poet has celebrated her conjugal fidelity in the former Ode: V. Epode 2d, line 13th.

‖ Elizabeth Widville, wife of Edward the Fourth (hence called the paler Rose, as being of the House of York). She added to the foundation of Margaret of Anjou.

¶ Henry the Sixth and Eighth. The former founder of King's, the latter the greatest benefactor to Trinity College.

Sweet is the breath of vernal shower,
The bee's collected treasures sweet,
Sweet Music's melting fall, but sweeter yet
The still small voice of Gratitude.'

VI.

Foremost and leaning from her golden cloud
The *venerable Marg'ret see!
'Welcome, my noble son, (she cries aloud)
To this, thy kindred train, and me:
Pleased in thy lineaments we trace
†A Tudor's fire, a Beaufort's grace.
Thy liberal heart, thy judging eye,
The flower unheeded shall descry,
And bid it round heav'n's altars shed
The fragrance of its blushing head:
Shall raise from earth the latent gem
To glitter on the diadem.

VII.

'Lo, Granta waits to lead her blooming band,
Not obvious, not obtrusive, She
No vulgar praise, no venal incense flings;
Nor dares with courtly tongue refined
Profane thy inborn royalty of mind:
She reveres herself and thee.
With modest pride to grace thy youthful brow
The laureate wreath, that ‡Cecil wore, she brings,
And to thy just, thy gentle hand
Submits the fasces of her sway,
While spirits blest above and men below
Join with glad voice the loud symphonious lay.

* Countess of Richmond and Derby; the mother of Henry the Seventh, foundress of St. John's and Christ's Colleges.

† The countess was a Beaufort, and married to a Tudor: hence the application of this line to the Duke of Grafton, who claims descent from both these families.

‡ Lord Treasurer Burghley was chancellor of the University, in the reign of Queen Elizabeth.

VIII.

'Through the wild waves, as they roar,
  With watchful eye and dauntless mien
Thy steady course of honour keep,
Nor fear the rocks, nor seek the shore:
  The Star of Brunswick smiles serene
And gilds the horrors of the deep.'

VIII. THE FATAL SISTERS.

*From the Norse Tongue.**

Now the storm begins to lower
  (Haste, the loom of Hell prepare),
Iron-sleet of arrowy shower
  Hurtles in the darken'd air.

* To be found in the Orcades of Thormodus Torfæus; Hafniæ, 1697, folio: and also in Bartholinus.

Vitt er orpit fyrir valfalli, &c.

The design of Mr. Gray in writing this and the three following imitative Odes is given in the Memoirs of his Life. For the better understanding the first of these, the reader is to be informed, that in the eleventh century, *Sigurd*, earl of the Orkney Islands, went with a fleet of ships, and a considerable body of troops, into Ireland, to the assistance of *Sictryg with the silken beard*, who was then making war on his father-in-law *Brian*, king of Dublin: the earl and all his forces were cut to pieces, and *Sictryg* was in danger of a total defeat; but the enemy had a greater loss by the death of *Brian*, their king, who fell in the action. On Christmas-day (the day of the battle) a native of *Caithness*, in Scotland, saw at a distance a number of persons on horseback riding full speed towards a hill, and seeming to enter into it. Curiosity led him to follow them, till looking through an opening in the rocks, he saw twelve gigantic figures resembling women: they were all employed about a loom; and as they wove, they sung the following dreadful song; which, when they had finished, they tore the web into twelve pieces, and (each taking her portion) galloped six to the north and as many to the south. These were the *Valkyriur*, female divinities, servants of *Odin* (or *Woden*) in the Gothic Mythology. Their name signifies *Choosers of the slain*. They were mounted on swift horses, with drawn swords in their hands; and in the throng of battle selected such as were destined to slaughter, and conducted them to *Valkalla*, the hall of *Odin*, or paradise of the brave; where they attended the banquet, and served the departed heroes with horns of mead and ale.

Glitt'ring lances are the loom,
Where the dusky warp we strain,
Weaving many a soldier's doom,
Orkney's woe, and Randver's bane.

See the griesly texture grow
('Tis of human entrails made),
And the weights, that play below
Each a gasping warrior's head.

Shafts for shuttles, dipt in gore,
Shoo the trembling cords along.
Sword, that once a monarch bore,
Keeps the tissue close and strong

Mista black, terrific maid,
Sangrida, and Hilda see,
Join the wayward work to aid:
'Tis the woof of victory.

Ere the ruddy sun be set,
Pikes must shiver, javelins sing,
Blade with clattering buckler meet,
Hauberk crash, and helmet ring.

(Weave the crimson web of war)
Let us go, and let us fly,
Where our friends the conflict share,
Where they triumph, where they die.

As the paths of fate we tread,
Wading through th' ensanguined field:
Gondula, and Geira, spread
O'er the youthful king your shield.

We the reins to slaughter give,
Ours to kill, and ours to spare:
Spite of danger he shall live
(Weave the crimson web of war).

They, whom once the desert-beach
  Pent within its bleak domain,
Soon their ample sway shall stretch
  O'er the plenty of the plain.

Low the dauntless earl is laid,
  Gored with many a gaping wound;
Fate demands a nobler head;
  Soon a king shall bite the ground.

Long his loss shall Erin weep,
  Ne'er again his likeness see;
Long her strains in sorrow steep,
  Strains of Immortality!

Horror covers all the heath,
  Clouds of carnage blot the sun.
Sisters, weave the web of death;
  Sisters, cease; the work is done.

Hail the task, and hail the hands!
  Songs of joy and triumph sing!
Joy to the victorious bands;
  Triumph to the younger king.

Mortal, thou that hear'st the tale,
  Learn the tenor of our song.
Scotland, through each winding vale
  Far and wide the notes prolong.

Sisters, hence with spurs of speed:
  Each her thundering falchion wie'
Each bestride her sable steed:
  Hurry, hurry to the field.

IX. THE DESCENT OF ODIN.*

From the Norse-Tongue.

UPROSE the King of Men with speed,
And saddled strait his coal-black steed;
Down the yawning steep he rode,
That leads to †Hela's drear abode.
Him the Dog of Darkness spied,
His shaggy throat he open'd wide,
While from his jaws, with carnage fill'd,
Foam and human gore distill'd:
Hoarse he bays with hideous din,
Eyes that glow, and fangs that grin;
And long pursues, with fruitless yell,
The Father of the powerful spell.
Onward still his way he takes
(The groaning earth beneath him shakes),
Till full before his fearless eyes
The portals nine of hell arise.
Right against the eastern gate,
By the moss-grown pile he sate;
Where long of yore to sleep was laid
The dust of the prophetic Maid.
Facing to the northern clime,
Thrice he traced the Runic rhyme;
Thrice pronounced, in accents dread,
The thrilling verse that wakes the dead;
Till from out the hollow ground
Slowly breathed a solemn sound.

* The original is to be found in Bortholinus, de causis contemnendæ mortis; Hafniæ, 1689, quarto.

Upreis Odinn allda gautr, &c.

† *Niflheimr*, the hell of the Gothic nations, consisted of nine worlds, to which were devoted all such as died of sickness, old age, or by any other means than in battle: over it presided Hela, the Goddess of Death.

Pr. What call unknown, what charms presume
To break the quiet of the tomb?
Who thus afflicts my troubled sprite,
And drags me from the realms of night?
Long on these mould'ring bones have beat
The winter's snow, the summer's heat,
The drenching dews and driving rain!
Let me, let me sleep again.
Who is he, with voice unblest,
That calls me from the bed of rest?

O. A traveller, to thee unknown,
Is he that calls, a Warrior's Son.
Thou the deeds of light shalt know;
Tell me what is done below,
For whom yon glitt'ring board is spread,
Drest for whom yon golden bed.

Pr. Mantling in the goblet see
The pure bev'rage of the bee;
O'er it hangs the shield of gold;
'Tis the drink of Balder bold;
Balder's head to death is giv'n.
Pain can reach the Sons of Heav'n!
Unwilling I my lips unclose:
Leave me, leave me to repose.

O. Once again my call obey,
Prophetess, arise, and say,
What dangers Odin's child await,
Who the author of his fate.

Pr. In Hoder's hand the hero's doom:
His brother sends him to the tomb.
Now my weary lips I close:
Leave me, leave me to repose.

O. Prophetess, my spell obey,
Once again arise, and say,

Who th' avenger of his guilt,
By whom shall Hoder's blood be spilt.

Pr. In the caverns of the west,
By Odin's fierce embrace comprest,
A wond'rous Boy shall Rinda bear,
Who ne'er shall comb his raven-hair,
Nor wash his visage in the stream,
Nor see the sun's departing beam;
Till he on Hoder's corse shall smile
Flaming on the fun'ral pile.
Now my weary lips I close:
Leave me, leave me to repose.

O. Yet awhile my call obey,
Prophetess, awake, and say,
What Virgins these, in speechless woe,
That bend to earth their solemn brow,
That their flaxen tresses tear,
And snowy veils, that float in air.
Tell me whence their sorrows rose:
Then I leave thee to repose.

Pr. Ha! no traveller art thou,
King of Men, I know thee now,
Mightiest of a mighty line——

O. No boding maid of skill divine
Art thou, nor prophetess of good;
But mother of the giant-brood!

Pr. Hie thee hence, and boast at home,
That never shall inquirer come
To break my iron-sleep again;
Till *Lok has burst his tenfold chain.

* *Lok* is the evil Being, who continues in chains till the *Twilight of the Gods* approaches, when he shall break his bonds; the human race, the stars, and sun shall disappear; the earth sink in the seas, and fire consume the skies: even Odin himself and his kindred-deities shall perish. For a farther explanation of this mythology, see 'In-

Never, till substantial Night
Has reassumed her ancient right;
Till wrapp'd in flames, in ruin hurl'd,
Sinks the fabric of the world.

X. THE TRIUMPHS OF OWEN.*

From the Welsh.

OWEN'S praise demands my song,
Owen swift, and Owen strong;
Fairest flower of Roderic's stem,
†Gwyneth's shield, and Britain's gem.
He nor heaps his brooded stores,
Nor on all profusely pours;
Lord of every regal art,
Liberal hand, and open heart.

Big with hosts of mighty name,
Squadrons three against him came;
This the force of Eirin hiding,
Side by side as proudly riding,
On her shadow long and gay
‡Lochlin ploughs the wat'ry way;
There the Norman sails afar
Catch the winds, and join the war:
Black and huge along they sweep,
Burthens of the angry deep.
Dauntless on his native sands
§The Dragon-Son of Mona stands;

troduction à l'Histoire de Dannemarc, par Mons. Mallet,' 1755, quarto; or rather a translation of it, published in 1770, and entitled, 'Northern Antiquities,' in which some mistakes in the original are judiciously corrected.

* From Mr. Evans's Specimens of the Welsh Poetry; London, 1764, quarto. Owen succeeded his father Griffin in the principality of North Wales, A. D. 1120. This battle was fought near forty years afterward.

† North Wales. ‡ Denmark.

§ The red dragon is the device of Cadwallader, which all his descendants bore on their banners.

In glitt'ring arms and glory drest,
High he rears his ruby crest.
There the thund'ring strokes begin,
There the press, and there the din;
Talymalfra's rocky shore
Echoing to the battle's roar.
Check'd by the torrent-tide of blood
Backward Meinai rolls his flood;
While, heap'd his master's feet around,
Prostrate warriors gnaw the ground.
While his glowing eye-balls turn,
Thousand banners round him burn.
Where he points his purple spear,
Hasty, hasty Rout is there,
Marking with indignant eye
Fear to stop, and shame to fly.
There Confusion, Terror's child,
Conflict fierce, and Ruin wild,
Agony, that pants for breath,
Despair and honourable Death.

XI. THE DEATH OF HOEL.

*From the Welsh.**

HAD I but the torrent's might,
With headlong rage and wild affright
Upon Deïra's squadrons hurl'd,
To rush, and sweep them from the world!

Too, too secure in youthful pride,
By them my friend, my Hoel, died,
Great Cian's son: of Madoc old
He ask'd no heaps of hoarded gold;

* Of Aneurim, styled the Monarch of the Bards. He flourished about the time of Taliessin, A. D. 570. This Ode is extracted from the Gododin. (See Mr. Evans's Specimens, p. 71. and 73.)

Alone in Nature's wealth array'd,
He ask'd, and had the lovely Maid.
To Cattraeth's vale in glitt'ring row
Twice two hundred warriors go;
Every warrior's manly neck
Chains of regal honour deck,
Wreath'd in many a golden link:
From the golden cup they drink
Nectar, that the bees produce,
Or the grape's ecstatic juice.
Flush'd with mirth and hope they burn;
But none from Cattraeth's vale return,
Save Aëron brave, and Conan strong,
(Bursting through the bloody throng)
And I, the meanest of them all,
That live to weep, and sing their fall.

SONNET*

ON THE DEATH OF MR. RICHARD WEST

In vain to me the smiling Mornings shine,
  And redd'ning Phœbus lifts his golden fire:
The birds in vain their amorous descant join,
  Or cheerful fields resume their green attire:
These ears, alas! for other notes repine,
  A different object do these eyes require;
My lonely anguish melts no heart but mine,
  And in my breast the imperfect joys expire.
Yet Morning smiles the busy race to cheer,
  And new-born pleasure brings to happier men;
The fields to all their wonted tribute bear;
  To warm their little loves the birds complain:
I fruitless mourn to him that cannot hear,
  And weep the more, because I weep in vain.

* See Memoirs, Sect. 3.

EPITAPH I.

ON MRS. CLARKE.*

Lo! where the silent Marble weeps,
A friend, a wife, a mother sleeps:
A heart, within whose sacred cell
The peaceful Virtues loved to dwell.
Affection warm, and faith sincere,
And soft humanity were there.
In agony, in death resign'd,
She felt the wound she left behind.
Her infant image, here below,
Sits smiling on a father's woe:
Whom what awaits, while yet he strays
Along the lonely vale of days?
A pang, to secret sorrow dear;
A sigh; an unavailing tear;
Till Time shall ev'ry grief remove,
With Life, with Memory, and with Love.

EPITAPH II.†

ON SIR WILLIAM WILLIAMS.

Here, foremost in the dangerous paths of fame,
  Young Williams fought for England's fair renown;
His mind each muse, each grace adorn'd his frame,
  Nor Envy dared to viow him with a frown.

* This lady, the wife of Dr. Clarke, physician at Epsom, died April 27, 1757; and is buried in the church of Beckenham, Kent.

† This epitaph was written at the request of Mr. Frederick Montague, who intended to have inscribed it on a monument at Bellisle, at the siege of which this accomplished youth was killed, 1761; but from some difficulty attending the erection of it, the design was not executed.

At Aix his voluntary sword he drew,
  There first in blood his infant honour seal'd;
From fortune, pleasure, science, love he flew,
  And scorn'd repose when Britain took the field.

With eyes of flame, and cool undaunted breast,
  Victor he stood on Bellisle's rocky steeps——
Ah! gallant youth! this marble tells the rest,
  Where melancholy Friendship bends, and weeps.

ELEGY

WRITTEN IN A COUNTRY CHURCH-YARD.

THE Curfew tolls the knell of parting day,
  The lowing herds wind slowly o'er the lea,
The ploughman homeward plods his weary way,
  And leaves the world to darkness and to me.

Now fades the glimmering landscape on the sight,
  And all the air a solemn stillness holds,
Save where the beetle wheels his droning flight,
  And drowsy tinklings lull the distant folds:

Save that from yonder ivy-mantled tower
  The moping owl does to the moon complain
Of such as, wand'ring near her secret bower,
  Molest her ancient solitary reign.

Beneath those rugged elms, that yew-tree's shade,
  Where heaves the turf in many a mould'ring heap,
Each in his narrow cell for ever laid,
  The rude Forefathers of the Hamlet sleep.

The breezy call of incense-breathing Morn,
  The swallow twitt'ring from the straw-built shed,
The cock's shrill clarion, or the echoing horn,
  No more shall rouse them from their lowly bed

I

For them no more the blazing hearth shall burn,
  Or busy housewife ply her evening care:
No children run to lisp their sire's return,
  Or climb his knees the envied kiss to share.

Oft did the harvest to their sickle yield,
  Their furrow oft the stubborn glebe has broke;
How jocund did they drive their team afield!
  How bow'd the woods beneath their sturdy stroke!

Let not Ambition mock their useful toil,
  Their homely joys, and destiny obscure;
Nor Grandeur hear with a disdainful smile
  The short and simple annals of the poor.

The boast of heraldry, the pomp of power,
  And all that beauty, all that wealth e'er gave,
Await alike th' inevitable hour:—
  The paths of glory lead but to the grave.

Nor you, ye Proud, impute to These the fault,
  If Memory o'er their tomb no trophies raise,
Where through the long-drawn aisle and fretted vault
  The pealing anthem swells the note of praise.

Can storied urn or animated bust
  Back to its mansion call the fleeting breath?
Can Honour's voice provoke the silent dust,
  Or Flatt'ry soothe the dull cold ear of Death?

Perhaps in this neglected spot is laid
  Some heart once pregnant with celestial fire;
Hands, that the rod of empire might have sway'd,
  Or waked to ecstacy the living lyre.

But knowledge to their eyes her ample page
  Rich with the spoils of time did ne'er unroll;
Chill Penury repress'd their noble rage,
  And froze the genial current of the soul.

Full many a gem, of purest ray serene,
  The dark unfathom'd caves of ocean bear:
Full many a flower is born to blush unseen,
  And waste its sweetness on the desert air.

Some village-Hampden, that with dauntless breast
  The little Tyrant of his fields withstood;
Some mute inglorious Milton here may rest,
  Some Cromwell guiltless of his country's blood.

Th' applause of list'ning senates to command,
  The threats of pain and ruin to despise,
To scatter plenty o'er a smiling land,
  And read their history in a nation's eyes,

Their lot forbade: nor circumscribed alone
  Their growing virtues, but their crimes confined;
Forbade to wade through slaughter to a throne,
  And shut the gates of mercy on mankind.

The struggling pangs of conscious truth to hide,
  To quench the blushes of ingenuous shame,
Or heap the shrine of Luxury and Pride
  With incense kindled at the Muse's flame.

Far from the madding crowd's ignoble strife
  Their sober wishes never learn'd to stray;
Along the cool sequester'd vale of life
  They kept the noiseless tenor of their way.

Yet ev'n these bones from insult to protect
  Some frail memorial still erected nigh,
With uncouth rhymes and shapeless sculpture deck'd,
  Implores the passing tribute of a sigh.

Their name, their years, spelt by th' unletter'd muse,
  The place of fame and elegy supply:
And many a holy text around she strews,
  That teach the rustic moralist to die.

For who, to dumb Forgetfulness a prey,
This pleasing anxious being e'er resign'd,
Left the warm precincts of the cheerful day,
Nor cast one longing, lingering look behind?

On some fond breast the parting soul relies,
Some pious drops the closing eye requires;
Ev'n from the tomb the voice of Nature cries,
Ev'n in our ashes live their wonted fires.

For thee, who mindful of th' unhonour'd Dead,
Dost in these lines their artless tale relate;
If chance, by lonely Contemplation led,
Some kindred Spirit shall inquire thy fate,

Haply some hoary-headed Swain may say,
'Oft have we seen him at the peep of dawn
Brushing with hasty steps the dews away,
To meet the sun upon the upland lawn.

'There at the foot of yonder nodding beech
That wreathes its old fantastic roots so high,
His listless length at noontide would he stretch,
And pore upon the brook that babbles by.

'Hard by yon wood, now smiling as in scorn,
Mutt'ring his wayward fancies he would rove;
Now drooping, woeful wan, like one forlorn,
Or crazed with care, or cross'd in hopeless love.

'One morn I miss'd him on the 'custom'd hill,
Along the heath and near his fav'rite tree;
Another came; nor yet beside the rill,
Nor up the lawn, nor at the wood was he;

'The next, with dirges due in sad array
Slow through the church-way path we saw him borne.
Approach and read (for thou canst read) the lay
Graved on the stone beneath yon aged thorn.

THE EPITAPH.

HERE rests his head upon the lap of Earth,
  A Youth, to Fortune and to Fame unknown;
Fair Science frown'd not on his humble birth,
  And Melancholy mark'd him for her own.

Large was his bounty, and his soul sincere,
  Heav'n did a recompense as largely send:
He gave to Mis'ry all he had, a tear,
  He gain'd from Heav'n ('twas all he wish'd) a friend.

No farther seek his merits to disclose,
  Or draw his frailties from their dread abode
(There they alike in trembling hope repose),
  The bosom of his Father and his God.

VERSES
ON
THE MARRIAGE OF HIS ROYAL HIGHNESS THE PRINCE OF WALES.

IGNARÆ nostrûm mentes, et inertia corda,
Dum curas regum, et sortem miseramur iniquam,
Quæ solio affixit, vetuitque calescere flammâ
Dulci, quæ dono divum, gratissima serpit
Viscera per, mollesque animis lene implicat æstus,
Nec teneros sensus, Veneris nec præmia nôrunt,
Eloquiumve oculi, aut facunda silentia linguæ:

Scilicit ignorant lacrymas, sævosque dolores,
Dura rudimenta, et violentiæ exordia flammæ;
Scilicit ignorant, quæ flumine tinxit amaro
Tela Venus, cæcique armamentaria Divi,
Irasque, insidiasque, et tacitum sub pectore vulnus·
Namque sub ingressu, primoque in limine Amoris

Luctus et ultrices posuere cubilia Curæ;
Intus habent dulces Risus, et Gratiæ sedem,
Et roseis resupina toris, roseo ore Voluptas:
Regibus huc faciles aditus; communia spernunt
Ostia, jamque expers duris custodibus istis
Panditur accessus, penetraliaque intima Templi.

Tuque Oh! Angliacis, Princeps, spes optima regnis,
Ne tantum, ne finge metum; quid imagine captus
Hæres, et mentem pictura pascis inani?
Umbram miraris: nec longum tempus, et ipsa
Ibit in amplexus, thalamosque ornabit ovantes.
Ille tamen tabulis inhians longum haurit amorem,
Affatu fruitur tacito, auscultatque tacentem
Immemor artificis calami, risumque, ruboremque
Aspicit in fucis, pictæque in virginis ore:
Tanta Venus potuit; tantus tenet error amantes.

Nascere, magna Dies, qua sese Augusta Britanno
Committat Pelago, patriamque relinquat amœnam;
Cujus in adventum jam nunc tria regna secundos
Attolli in plausus, dulcique accensa furore
Incipiunt agitare modos, et carmina dicunt:
Ipse animo sedenim juvenis comitatur euntem
Explorat ventos, atque auribus aëra captat,
Atque auras, atque astra vocat crudelia; pectus
Intentum exultat, surgitque arrecta cupido;
Incusat spes ægra fretum, solitoque videtur
Latior effundi pontus, fructusque morantes.

Nascere, Lux major, qua sese Augusta Britanno
Committat juveni totam, propriamque dicabit;
At citius (precor) Oh! cedas melioribus astris:
Nox finem pompæ, finemque imponere curis
Possit, et in thalamos furtim deducere nuptam;
Sufficiat requiemque viris, et amantibus umbras;

Adsit Hymen, et subridens cum matre Cupido
Accedant, sternantque toros, ignemque ministrent;
Ilicet haud pictæ incandescit imaginæ formæ
Ulterius juvenis, verumque agnoscit amorem.

Sculptile sicut ebur, faciemque arsisse venustam
Pygmaliona canunt; ante hanc suspiria ducit,
Alloquiturque amens, flammamque et vulnera narrat;
Implorata Venus jussit cum vivere signum,
Fœminæam inspirans animam; quæ gaudia surgunt,
Audiit ut primæ nascentia murmura linguæ,
Luctari in vitam, et paulatim volvere ocellos
Sedulus, aspexitque novâ splendescere flammâ;
Corripit amplexu vivam, jamque oscula jungit
Acria confestim, recipitque rapitque; prioris
Immemor ardoris, Nymphæque oblitus eburnæ.

THO. GRAY, Pet. Coll

SONG.*

THYRSIS, when he left me, swore
In the Spring he would return.
Ah! what means the op'ning flower?
And the bud that decks the thorn?
'Twas the nightingale that sung!
'Twas the lark that upward sprung!

Idle notes! untimely green!
Why such unavailing haste?
Gentle gales and sky serene
Prove not always Winter past.
Cease, my doubts, my fears to move—
Spare the honour of my love.

* At the request of Miss Speed.

*With Beauty, with Pleasure surrounded, to languish—
To weep without knowing the cause of my anguish;
To start from short slumbers, and wish for the morning—
To close my dull eyes when I see it returning;
Sighs sudden and frequent, looks ever dejected—
Words that steal from my tongue, by no meaning
connected!
Ah, say, fellow-swains, how these symptoms befel me
They smile, but reply not—Sure Delia can tell me!

TOPHET:

An Epigram.

[Mr. Etough,† of Cambridge University, was remarkable for his eccentricities and personal appearance. A Mr. Tyson of Bene't College, made an etching of his head, and presented it to Mr. Gray, who wrote under it the following lines.]

Thus Tophet look'd; so grinn'd the brawling fiend,
Whilst frighted prelates bow'd, and call'd him friend.
Our mother-church, with half-averted sight,
Blush'd as she bless'd her grisly proselyte;
Hosannas rung through Hell's tremendous borders,
And Satan's self had thoughts of taking orders.

IMPROMPTU,

Suggested by a View, in 1766, of the Seat and Ruins of a deceased Nobleman, at Kingsgate, Kent.

Old, and abandon'd by each venal friend,
Here H——d form'd the pious resolution
To smuggle a few years, and strive to mend
A broken character and constitution.

* These lines will be found in a note in the second volume of Warton's Edition of Pope's Works.
† Gentleman's Magazine, Vol. LVI. p. 25. 281.

On this congenial spot he fix'd his choice;
  Earl Goodwin trembled for his neighb'ring sand;
Here sea-gulls scream, and cormorants rejoice,
  And mariners, though shipwreck'd, dread to land.

Here reign the blust'ring North and blighting East,
  No tree is heard to whisper, bird to sing;
Yet Nature could not furnish out the feast,
  Art he invokes new horrors still to bring.

Here mould'ring fanes and battlements arise,
  Turrets and arches nodding to their fall;
Unpeopled monast'ries delude our eyes,
  And mimic desolation covers all.

'Ah!' said the sighing peer, 'had B—te been true,
  Nor M—'s, R—'s, B—'s friendship vain,
Far better scenes than these had blest our view,
  And realized the beauties which we feign.

'Purged by the sword, and purified by fire,
  Then had we seen proud London's hated walls;
Owls would have hooted in St. Peter's choir,
  And foxes stunk and litter'd in St. Paul's.'

THE CANDIDATE;

OR, THE CAMBRIDGE COURTSHIP.

Written a short time previous to the election of a High Steward.

WHEN sly Jemmy Twitcher had smugg'd up his face,
With a lick of court white-wash, and pious grimace,
A wooing he went, where three sisters of old
In harmless society guttle and scold.

'Lord! sister,' says Physic to Law, 'I declare,
Such a sheep-biting look, such a pick-pocket air.
Not I for the Indies!—You know I'm no prude,—
But his name is a shame,—and his eyes are so lewd!
Then he shambles and straddles so oddly—I fear—
No—at our time of life 'twould be silly, my dear.'

'I don't know,' says Law, 'but methinks for his look
'Tis just like the picture in Rochester's book;
Then his character, Phizzy,—his morals—his life—
When she died, I can't tell, but he once had a wife.
They say he's no Christian, loves drinking and w——g,
And all the town rings of his swearing and roaring!
His lying and filching, and Newgate-bird tricks;—
Not I—for a coronet, chariot and six.'

Divinity heard, between waking and dozing,
Her sisters denying, and Jemmy proposing:
From table she rose, and with bumper in hand,
She stroked up her belly, and stroked down her band—
'What a pother is here about wenching and roaring!
Why, David loved catches, and Solomon w——g:
Did not Israel filch from th' Egyptians of old
Their jewels of silver and jewels of gold?
The prophet of Bethel, we read, told a lie:
He drinks—so did Noah;—he swears—so do I:
To reject him for such peccadillos, were odd;
Besides, he repents—for he talks about G**;—

[*To* Jemmy.]

Never hang down your head, you poor penitent elf;
Come, buss me—I'll be Mrs. Twitcher myself.

• • • • • • • •
• • • • • • • •

SKETCH

OF HIS OWN CHARACTER.*

Too poor for a bribe, and too proud to impórtune;
He had not the method of making a fortune:
Could love and could hate, so was thought somewhat
odd;
No very great Wit, he believed in a God.
A post or a pension he did not desire,
But left church and state to Charles Townshend and
Squire.†

* Written in 1761, and found in one of his pocket-books.
† Fellow of St. John's College, Cambridge, and afterwards Bishop of St. David's.

POEMS,

ADDRESSED TO, AND IN MEMORY OF

MR. GRAY.

UPON HIS ODES.

By David Garrick, Esq.

REPINE not, Gray, that our weak dazzled eyes
Thy daring heights and brightness shun;
How few can trace the eagle to the skies,
Or, like him, gaze upon the sun!

Each gentle reader loves the gentle Muse,
That little dares and little means;
Who humbly sips her learning from Reviews,
Or flutters in the Magazines.

No longer now from Learning's sacred store
Our minds their health and vigour draw;
Homer and Pindar are revered no more,
No more the Stagyrite is law.

Though nursed by these, in vain thy Muse appears
To breathe her ardours in our souls;
In vain to sightless eyes and deaden'd ears
The lightning gleams, the thunder rolls:

Yet droop not, Gray, nor quit thy heaven-born art;
Again thy wond'rous powers reveal;
Wake slumb'ring Virtue in the Briton's heart,
And rouse us to reflect and feel!

With ancient deeds our long-chill'd bosoms fire,
Those deeds that mark Eliza's reign?
Make Britons Greeks again, then strike the lyre,
And Pindar shall not sing in vain.

ON THE BACKWARDNESS OF SPRING.

By the late Mr. Richard West.

DEAR Gray, that always in my heart
Possessest far the better part,
What mean these sudden blasts that rise
And drive the Zephyrs from the skies?
O join with mine thy tuneful lay,
And invocate the tardy May.

Come, fairest Nymph, resume thy reign!
Bring all the Graces in thy train!
With balmy breath and flowery tread,
Rise from thy soft ambrosial bed;
Where, in Elysian slumber bound,
Embow'ring myrtles veil thee round.

Awake, in all thy glories drest,
Recall the Zephyrs from the west;
Restore the sun, revive the skies,
At mine, and Nature's call, arise!
Great Nature's self upbraids thy stay,
And misses her accustom'd May.

See! all her works demand thy aid;
The labours of Pomona fade:
A plaint is heard from ev'ry tree;
Each budding flow'ret calls for thee;
The birds forget to love and sing;
With storms alone the forests ring.

Come, then, with Pleasure at thy side,
Diffuse thy vernal spirit wide;
Create, where'er thou turn'st thine eye,
Peace, Plenty, Love, and Harmony:
Till ev'ry being share its part,
And Heaven and Earth be glad at heart.

ON THE DEATH OF MR. GRAY.

Me quoque Musarum studium sub nocte silenti
Artibus assuetis sollicitare solet. *Claudian.*

ENOUGH of fabling, and th' unhallow'd haunts
Of Dian' and of Delia, names profane,
Since not Diana nor all Delia's train
Are subjects that befit a serious song;
For who the bards among
May but compare with thee, lamented Gray!
Whose pensive, solemn lay,
Drew all the list'ning shepherds in a ring,
Well pleased to hear thee sing
Thy moving notes, on sunny hill or plain,
And catch new grace from thy immortal strain.

O wood-hung Menaï, and ye sacred groves
Of Delphi, we still venerate your names,
Whose awful shades inspired the Druids' dreams.
Your recess, though imagined, Fancy loves,
And through these long-lost scenes delighted roves:
So future bards perhaps shall sing of Thames,
And as they sing shall say,
'Twas there of old where mused illustrious Gray!
By Isis' banks his tuneful lays would suit,
To Pindar's lofty lyre, or Sappho's Lesbian lute

Oft would he sing, when the still Eve came on,
Till sable Night resumed her ebon throne,
And taught us, in his melancholic mood,
To scorn the great, and love the wise and good;
Told us, 'twas virtue never dies,
And to what ills frail mankind open lies;
How safe through life's tempestuous sea to steer,
Where dang'rous rocks, and shelves and whirlpools, oft
appear.

And when fair Morn arose again to view,
A fairer landscape still he drew,
That blooms like Eden in his charming lays,
The hills and dales, and Heav'n's cerulean blue,
Brighten'd o'er all by Sol's resplendent rays.

The musky gale, in rosy vale,
And gilded clouds on azure hills,
The fragrant bow'rs, and painted flow'rs,
And tinklings of the silver rills;
The very insects, that in sunbeams play,
Turn useful monitors in his grave moral lay.

But ah! sad Melancholy intervenes,
And draws a cloud o'er all these shining scenes
'Tis her, alas! we often find
The troubler of each great unbounded mind,
And, leagued with her associate Fear
Will tremble lest the turning sphere,
And sinking earth, and reeling planets run
In dire disorder with the falling sun.

But now, great Bard, thy life of pain is o'er;
'Tis we must weep, though thou shalt grieve no more.
Through other scenes thou now dost rove,
And clothed with gladness walk'st the courts above
And listen'st to the heavenly choir,
Hymning their God, while seraphs strike the lyre.
Safe with them in those radiant climes of bliss,
Thou now enjoy'st eternal happiness.

ON THE DEATH OF MR GRAY.

By the Earl of Carlisle.

WHAT spirit's that which mounts on high,
Borne on the arms of every tuneful Muse?
His white robes flutter to the gale:
They wing their way to yonder opening sky,
In glorious state through yielding clouds they sail,
And scents of heavenly flowers on earth diffuse.

What avails the poet's art?
What avails his magic hand?
Can he arrest Death's pointed dart,
Or charm to sleep his murderous band?
Well I know thee, gentle shade!
That tuneful voice, that eagle eye—
Quick bring me flowers that ne'er shall fade,
The laurel wreath that ne'er shall die;
With every honour deck his funeral bier,
For he to every Grace and every Muse was dear!

The listening Dryad, with attention still,
On tiptoe oft would near the poet steal,
To hear him sing upon the lonely hill
Of all the wonders of th' expanded vale,

The distant hamlet, and the winding stream,
The steeple shaded by the friendly yew,
Sunk in the wood the sun's departing gleam,
The grey-robed landscape stealing from the view.

*Or wrapt in solemn thought, and pleasing woe,
O'er each low tomb he breathed his pious strain,
A lesson to the village swain,
And taught the tear of rustic grief to flow!—

* Alluding to Mr. Gray's Elegy written in a Country Church-yard.

*But soon with bolder note, and wilder flight,
O'er the loud strings his rapid hand would run:
Mars hath lit his torch of war,
Ranks of heroes fill the sight!
Hark! the carnage is begun!
And see the furies through the fiery air [bear.
O'er Cambria's frighten'd land the screams of horror

†Now, led by playful Fancy's hand,
O'er the white surge he treads with printless feet,
To magic shores he flies, and fairy land,
Imagination's blest retreat.
Here roses paint the crimson way,
No setting sun, eternal May.
Wild as the priestess of the Thracian fane,
When Bacchus leads the madd'ning train,
His bosom glowing with celestial fire,
To harmony he struck the golden lyre;
To harmony each hill and valley rung!
The bird of Jove, as when Apollo sung,
To melting bliss resign'd his furious soul,
With milder rage his eyes began to roll,
The heaving down his thrilling joys confest,
Till by a mortal's hand subdued he sunk to rest.

‡O, guardian angel of our early day,
Henry, thy darling plant must bloom no more!
By thee attended, pensive would he stray, [shore.
Where Thames, soft-murmuring, laves his winding
Thou bad'st him raise the moralizing song,
Through life's new seas the little bark to steer;
The winds are rude and high, the sailor young;
Thoughtless, he spies no furious tempest near,
Till to the poet's hand the helm you gave,
From hidden rocks an infant crew to save!

* The Bard, a Pindaric Ode.
† The Progress of Poetry, a Pindaric Ode.
‡ Ode on a distant Prospect of Eton College.

*Ye fiends who rankle in the human heart,
Delight in woe, and triumph in our tears,
Resume again
Your dreadful reign:
Prepare the iron scourge, prepare the venom'd dart,
Adversity no more with lenient air appears;
The snakes that twine about her head
Again their frothy poison shed;
For who can now her whirlwind flight control,
Her threatening rage beguile?
He who could still the tempest of her soul,
And force her livid lips to smile,
To happier seats is fled!
Now seated by his Thracian sire,
At the full feast of mighty Jove
To heavenly themes attunes his lyre,
And fills with harmony the realms above!

LINES

TO THE MEMORY OF MR. GRAY.

Extracted from the third book of

MASON'S 'ENGLISH GARDEN.

CLOSED is that curious ear by death's cold hand,
That mark'd each error of my careless strain
With kind severity; to whom my muse
Still loved to whisper, what she meant to sing
In louder accent; to whose taste supreme
She first and last appeal'd, nor wish'd for praise,
Save when his smile was herald to her fame.

* Hymn to Adversity.

Yes, thou art gone; yet friendship's falt'ring tongue
Invokes thee still; and still, by fancy soothed,
Fain would she hope her Gray attends the call.
Why then, alas! in this my fav'rite haunt,
Place I the urn, the bust, the sculptured lyre,
Or fix this votive tablet, fair inscribed
With numbers worthy thee, for they are thine?
Why, if thou hear'st me still, these symbols sad
Of fond memorial? Ah! my pensive soul!
He hears me not, nor ever more shall hear
The theme his candour, not his taste, approved.

Oft, 'smiling as in scorn,' oft would he cry,
'Why waste thy numbers on a trivial art,
That ill can mimic ev'n the humblest charms
Of all-majestic Nature?' At the word
His eye would glisten, and his accents glow
With all the Poet's frenzy, 'Sov'reign queen!
Behold, and tremble, while thou view'st her state
Throned on the heights of Skiddaw: call thy art
To build her such a throne; that art will feel
How vain her best pretensions. Trace her march
Amid the purple crags of Borrowdale;
And try like those to pile thy range of rock
In rude tumultuous chaos. See! she mounts
Her Naiad car, and, down Lodore's dread cliff
Falls many a fathom, like the headlong bard
My fabling fancy plunged in Conway's flood;
Yet not like him to sink in endless night:
For, on its boiling bosom, still she guides
Her buoyant shell, and leads the wave along;
Or spreads it broad, a river, or a lake,
As suits her pleasure; will thy boldest song
E'er brace the sinews of enervate art
To such dread daring? will it ev'n direct
Her hand to emulate those softer charms

That deck the banks of Dove, or call to birth
The bare romantic crags, and copses green,
That sidelong grace her circuit, whence the rills,
Bright in their crystal purity, descend
To meet their sparkling queen? around each fount
The hawthorns crowd, and knit their blossom'd sprays
To keep their sources sacred. Here, even here,
Thy art, each active sinew stretch'd in vain,
Would perish in its pride. Far rather thou
Confess her scanty power, correct, control,
Tell her how far, nor farther, she may go!
And rein with reason's curb fantastic taste.'

Yes, I will hear thee, dear lamented shade,
And hold each dictate sacred. What remains
Unsung shall so each leading rule select
As if still guided by thy judgment sage;
While, as still modell'd to thy curious ear,
Flow my melodious numbers; so shall praise,
If aught of praise the verse I weave may claim,
From just posterity reward my song.

FRAGMENT

ON THE DEATH OF MR. GRAY.

* * * * * * * * *

FAIR are the gardens of the Aonian mount,
And sweet those blooming flow'rs
Which paint the Maiden's bow'rs;
And clear the waters of the gurgling fount!
Swift they wind through chequer'd allies;
Huddling down to th' open valleys;
Where the quick ripple in the sunbeams plays,
Turning to endless forms each glance of twinkling blaze.

O'er the gay scene th' enamour'd inmates roam:
And gather fresh ideas as they rise
From Nature's manifold supplies.
Alas! for whom!
Many a gleam of sprightly thought,
Many a sad and sable mood,
Whether from dazzling lustre brought,
Or nursed by shades of darksome wood,
Keep death-like silence on their native shore,
Since he that gave them speech, is heard no more.
Flown is the spirit of Gray,
Like common breath to mingle with the air:
Yet still those Goddesses' peculiar care,
That breathe harmonious lay.
Retired to yonder grassy mound
In leaves of dusky hue encompass'd round,
They bid their plaintive accents fill
The covert hollows of the bosom'd hill:
With liquid voice and magic hand
Calliope informs the band:
Hush'd are the warblers of the grove, attentive to the sound.

'Soft and slow
Let the melting measures flow,
Nor lighter air disturb majestic woe.
And thou, sage Priestess* of our holy fire,
Who saw'st the Poet's flame expire,
Thy precious drops profusely shed
O'er his well-deserving head.
Thou nurtur'dst once a grateful throng,
When Milton pour'd the sweets of song,
On *Lycidas sunk low.*

* Cambridge University, where Gray died.

'Now wake the faithful lyre——mute Dulness reigns:
Your echoes waft no more the friendly theme:
Clogg'd with thick vapours from the neighb'ring plains,
Where old Cam hardly moves his sluggard stream.
But when some public cause
Claims festive song or more melodious tear,
Discordant murmurs grate mine ear.
Ne'er modell'd by Pierian laws,
Then idly glares full many a motley toy,
Anacreontic grief, and creeping strains of joy.

'Far other modes were thine,
Victim of hasty fate,
Whom now the powers of melody deplore;
Whether in lofty state*
Thou bad'st thy train divine
Of raptures on Pindaric pinions soar:
Or hoping from thyself to fly
To *childhood's careless* scenes,†
Thou sent'st a warm refreshing eye
On Nature's faded greens:

'Or when thy calm and steadfast mind
With philosophic reach profound
Self-pleasing vanities resign'd,
Fond of the look, *that loves the ground*; ‡
Discern'd by Reason's equal light,
How gaudy Fortune cheats the sight;
While the coarse maid, innured to pain,
Supports the lab'ring heart, and Virtue's happiest reign

'But most the music of thy plantive moan§
With lengthen'd note detains the list'ning ear,
As lost in thought thou wander'st all alone
Where spirits hover round their mansions drear.

* See Gray's Pindaric Odes.
† Ode on a distant prospect of Eton College.
‡ Hymn to Adversity. § Church-yard Elegy.

'By Contemplation's eye serenely view'd,
Each lowly object wears an awful mien:
'Tis our own blindness veils the latent good:
The works of Nature need but to be seen.
'Thou saw'st her beaming from the hamlet-sires
Beneath those rugged elms, that yew-tree's shade;
Where now, still faithful to *their wonted fires*,*
Thy own dear ashes are *for ever laid*.'

STANZAS

ON THE DEATH OF MR. GRAY.

By a Lady.

WHERE sleeps the Bard who graced Museus' hearse
With fragrant trophies by the Muses wove!
Shall Gray's cold urn in vain demand the verse,
Oh! can his Mason fail in plaintive love?

No; with the Nine inwrapp'd in social woe,
His lyre unstrung, sad vigil he must keep;
With them he mourns, with them his eyes o'erflow,
For such a Bard immortal Maids can weep.

Their early pupil in the heav'nly lore
Of sacred poesy and moral song,
They taught the youth on eagle wing to soar,
And bore him through aërial heights along.

Fancy, obedient to the dread command,
With brilliant Genius, marshall'd forth his way:
They lured his steps to Cambria's once-famed land,
And sleeping Druids felt his magic lay.

But vain the magic lay, the warbling lyre,
Imperious Death! from thy fell grasp to save;
He knew, and told it with a Poet's fire,
'The paths of glory lead but to the grave.'

* Gray was buried at Stoke, the scene of the Elegy.

And shall the Bard, whose sympathizing mind
  Mourn'd o'er the simple rustic's turfy cell,
To strew his tomb no grateful mourner find,
  No village swain to ring one parting knell!

Yes, honour'd shade! the fringed brook I'll trace,
  Green rushes culling thy dank grave to strew;
With mountain flow'rs I'll deck the hallow'd place,
  And fence it round with osiers mix'd with yew.

THE TEARS OF GENIUS:

AN ODE.

By Mr. Taite.

On Cam's fair banks, where Learning's hallow
  Majestic rises on the astonish'd sight,
Where oft the Muse has led the favourite swain
  And warm'd his soul with Heaven's inspiring ig

Beneath the covert of the sylvan shade,
  Where deadly cypress, mix'd with mournful ye
Far o'er the vale a gloomy stillness spread,
  Celestial Genius burst upon the view.

The bloom of youth, the majesty of years,
  The soften'd aspect, innocent and kind,
The sigh of sorrow, and the streaming tears,
  Resistless all, their various pow'r combined.

In her fair hand a silver harp she bore,
  Whose magic notes, soft-warbling from the string,
Give tranquil joy the breast ne'er knew before,
  Or raise the soul on rapture's airy wing.
By grief impell'd, I heard her heave a sigh,
While thus the rapid strain resounded through the sky;

Haste, ye sister powers of song,
  Hasten from the shady grove,
Where the river rolls along,
  Sweetly to the voice of love.

Where, indulging mirthful pleasures,
  Light you press the flow'ry green,
And from Flora's blooming treasures
  Cull the wreaths for Fancy's queen.

Where your gently-flowing numbers,
  Floating on the fragrant breeze,
Sink the soul in pleasing slumbers
  On the downy bed of ease.

For graver strains prepare the plantive lyre,
  That wakes the softest feelings of the soul;
Let lonely Grief the melting verse inspire,
  Let deep'ning Sorrow's solemn accents roll.

Rack'd by the hand of rude Disease
  Behold our fav'rite Poet lies!
While every object form'd to please
  Far from his couch ungrateful flies.

The blissful Muse, whose favouring smile
  So lately warm'd his peaceful breast,
Diffusing heavenly joys the while,
  In Transport's radiant garments drest,
With darksome grandeur and enfeebled blaze,
Sinks in the shades of night, and shuns his eager gaze.

The gaudy train, who wait on Spring,*
  Tinged with the pomp of vernal pride,
The youths who mount on Pleasure's wing,†
  And idly sport on Thames's side,
With cool regard their various arts employ,
Nor rouse the drooping mind, nor give the pause of joy.

* Ode on Spring.
† Ode on the Prospect of Eton College.

Ha! what forms, with port sublime,*
Glide along in sullen mood,
Scorning all the threats of time,
High above Misfortune's flood.

They seize their harps, they strike the lyre
With rapid hand, with freedom's fire.
Obedient Nature hears the lofty sound,
And Snowdon's airy cliffs the heavenly strains resound.

In pomp of state, behold they wait,
With arms outstretch'd, and aspects kind,
To snatch on high to yonder sky,
The child of Fancy left behind:
Forgot the woes of Cambria's fatal day,
By rapture's blaze impell'd, they swell the artless lay.

But ah! in vain they strive to soothe,
With gentle arts, the tort'ring hours;
Adversity,† with rankling tooth,
Her baleful gifts profusely pours.

Behold she comes, the fiend forlorn,
Array'd in Horror's settled gloom;
She strews the briar and prickly thorn,
And triumphs in th' infernal doom.
With frantic fury and insatiate rage
She gnaws the throbbing breast and blasts the glowing page.

No more the soft Æolian flute‡
Breathes through the heart the melting strain:
The powers of Harmony are mute
And leave the once-delightful plain;
With heavy wing, I see them beat the air,
Damp'd by the leaden hand of comfortless Despair.

* The Bard, an Ode.
† Hymn to Adversity.
‡ The Progress of Poesy.

Yet stay, O ! stay, celestial pow'rs,
  And with a hand of kind regard
Dispel the boist'rous storm that lours
  Destructive on the fav'rite bard ;
O watch with me his last expiring breath,
And snatch him from the arms of dark, oblivious death.

Hark ! the Fatal Sisters* join,
  And with Horror's mutt'ring sounds,
Weave the tissue of his line,
  While the dreadful spell resounds.

'Hail, ye midnight sisters, hail !
  Drive the shuttle swift along ;
Let your secret charms prevail
  O'er the valiant and the strong.

'O'er the glory of the land,
  O'er the innocent and gay,
O'er the Muse's tuneful band—
  Weave the fun'ral web of Gray.'

'Tis done, 'tis done—the iron hand of pain,
  With ruthless fury and corrosive force,
Racks every joint, and seizes every vein :
  He sinks, he groans, he falls a lifeless corse.

Thus fades the flow'r nipp'd by the frozen gale,
  Though once so sweet, so lovely to the eye :
Thus the tall oaks, when boist'rous storms assail,
  Torn from the earth, a mighty ruin lie.

Ye sacred sisters of the plaintive verse,
  Now let the stream of fond affection flow ;
O pay your tribute o'er the slow-drawn hearse,
  With all the manly dignity of woe.

* The Fatal Sisters, an Ode.

Oft when the curfew tolls its parting knell
  With solemn pause yon Church-yard's gloom survey,
While Sorrow's sighs and tears of Pity tell
  How just the moral of the Poet's lay.*

O'er his green grave, in Contemplation's guise,
  Oft let the pilgrim drop a silent tear:
Oft let the shepherd's tender accents rise,
  Big with the sweets of each revolving year;
Till prostrate Time adore his deathless name,
Fix'd on the solid base of adamantine fame.

EPITAPH
ON
MR. GRAY'S MONUMENT
IN WESTMINSTER ABBEY.

By Mr. Mason.

No more the Grecian Muse unrivall'd reigns;
  To Britain let the nations homage pay!
She boasts a Homer's fire in Milton's strains,
  A Pindar's rapture in the lyre of Gray.

* Elegy in a Country Church-yard.

THE

POETICAL WORKS

OF

JAMES BEATTIE, L.L.D.

LIFE OF BEATTIE.

THE subject of the present memoir was born in 1735, at Lawrence Kirk in the county of Kincardine. His father seems to have been a person in many respects superior to his rank in life. Though only the tenant of an inconsiderable farm, and consequently filling a station in society very little favourable to the cultivation of a taste for literature, he is said to have possessed a fondness for books, and to have exhibited a decided talent for poetical composition. Young Beattie was not yet ten years old when his father died: but they who know how soon the first impulse is given to the mind; how deeply every early impression is stamped upon the character; and how tenaciously the good and evil of the parent cling about the child, may, perhaps, be inclined to attribute somewhat of the celebrity of the man to the example and the instructions which were presented to the opening [illegible]

After the loss of this invaluable parent, our poet found a kind and fatherly protector in his elder brother; who placed him at a school in his native place, and continued him there, under a tutor of the name of Milne, till, in 1749, he obtained a bursary at the Marischal College, Aberdeen. This exhibition, which is said to have been the best in the university, did not produce him more than five pounds a-year. Beattie was not more distinguished for his diligent attention to the studies of the place, than for the moral propriety of his conduct. In this period of his life he laid the foundation of that various and useful learning which he afterward brought forward so effectively in the course of his literary life. The only science from which he was averse was the mathematics. In this he attained no extraordinary proficiency. He scrupulously performed all that was required of him by the regulations of the college; but it was by an effort of duty, not an impulse of inclination. It presented him with all the labour and none of the sweets of study; and after the appointed task was completed, he returned with redoubled eager ness to subjects which were more in unison with the ardour of his affections and the liveliness of his imagination. His exemplary conduct, and the decided marks of ability that he displayed in the course of his college life, secured to him the favour of the Professors Blackwell and Gerard, under whose instruction he more immediately fell from his situation in the university. In 1750 he obtained the premium for the best Greek analysis of the fourth book of the Odyssey, and, after completing the appointed course of study, he was, in 1753, graduated as Master of Arts, which in the Scotch universities is the first degree conferred.

Immediately on his leaving college he was appointed master of the school of Fordoun, the parish adjoining Lawrence-Kirk. While in this obscure and humble situation, he published in the Scottish Magazine, a few pieces of poetry.

These productions, though marked by very slight indications of the talent which their author subsequently displayed, obtained him some local fame, and were the means of making him known as a meritorious and ingenious young man to Mr. Garden, an eminent Scottish lawyer, and to the celebrated Lord Monboddo. By these his first patrons Beattie was introduced to the tables of the gentry of his immediate neighbourhood, and was received with kindness and consideration in those higher classes of society, to which it is very unusual for the parochial schoolmaster to obtain the honour of admittance.

Beattie had not been master of the school of Fordoun above four years, when he became candidate for the mastership of the high school of Aberdeen; but failed in his application. It is said that his successful competitor was his superior in the minutiæ of the Latin grammar. His reputation for scholarship did not, however, appear to have been in any degree compromised by his defeat; and in the next vacancy he was elected by the magistrates without any second examinations having been required.

This appointment was rather desirable to Beattie, on account of its placing him in the midst of a literary society, and affording him an easy access to books, than from the prospect of its pecuniary emoluments. He had not been long in possession of this situation when he committed his first volume of poems to the press. They were admired by his friends and much praised by the English Reviews; but they did not satisfy the matured taste and judgment of their author. He, indeed, formed a correct estimation of its merits. It was decidedly unworthy his abilities; and was not calculated to increase the reputation, which he had, even in that early period of his life, acquired for talent and accomplishment. With the exception of four short poems, which, after considerable correction, he was induced to admit among the number of his poetical works, he was solicitous to erase every trace of these early effusions from the public mind. He bought up every copy of the volume which he had an opportunity of procuring; and seemed to consider the publication of it as so discreditable a stain on the fair and brilliant page of his literary life, that he is reported never to have informed his children of the existence of this his first, juvenile, and renounced production.

In the same year with the appearance of the above mentioned work, 1761, he was appointed, by the king's patent, professor of philosophy to the university. His department embraced both moral philosophy and logic, and it acquired a peculiar interest in the mind of Beattie, from its conferring on him the task of delivering the last course of instruction which the pupils received in the university, previous to their exchanging the tranquil studies of their college for the active competitions of the world. This preferment was sudden and unexpected; and, at the age of twenty five, he began to deliver to his pupils a course of lectures on those vast, important, and comprehensive subjects, which only the greatest minds are capable of entertaining in all their bearings and relations, and which, of all others, require the greatest vigour, and animation, and liveliness of style to render them striking and attractive. It is evident, however, that these topics had long been familiar with his thoughts, that he brought to the professor's chair a rich store of information, which might readily be wrought and moulded to the required purpose: and such was the diligence of his application, that, in the period of a very few years, he not only completed such a course of lectures on moral philosophy and logic, as most richly answered the splendid expectations which his friends and patrons had formed of his abilities; but prepared those invaluable works by which the name of Beattie would rank among the highest class of prose writers, though it had never been distinguished on the list of poets.

In 1785 he produced a poem entitled 'The Judgment of Paris.' It is found in the 'Scottish Magazine;' and is, perhaps, as well worthy of revival as some of his minor pieces. His friend and biographer, Sir William Forbes, has thought fit not to include this effort of his muse in the collection of his works. The subsequent year was marked by the publication of some lines 'On the Proposal for erecting a Monument to Churchill, in Westminster Abbey.' They have neither beauty nor dignity to recommend them; and are disgraced by an unredeemed bitterness of feeling and expression, which it was not generous to exercise against the dead. Churchill was a bad man, and a dishonour to the church of which he was a minister. If virtue had been essential to securing him a memorial among the distinguished characters whose names live on the venerable walls of Westminster, his advocates would have found themselves destitute of any just pretence for his admission; but that distinction has been conferred on talent, without any reference to morals; to the celebrity of genius, and not to purity of life; and the friends of Churchill might without presumption have conceived that he merited by the force and energy of his verses, an honour merely literary, which had been conferred on many who were as much his inferiors in intellectual power as they surpassed him in profaneness and debauchery. That Beattie should have thought it right to resist the proposition, cannot be considered a matter of surprise. It is well to render the highest honours that the living can bestow upon the dead, as pure in their distribution as they are likely to be eagerly desired, to circumscribe their application, to confer them only upon those who have exhibited the union of talent and virtue; and thus, as it were, by sanctifying the recompenses of ambition, to ensure the wise and salutary direction of those endowments of which the candidates for such distinctions may be possessed. But there were other ways of uttering his remonstrances, besides the satirizing the memory of one who had been sufficiently punished for the intemperance of his life, and the virulence of his writings, in the poverty, the disease, the failure of ability, and the ignominy that awaited his decline of days; and Beattie should not have outraged the gentleness of his own character to libel the libeller; and to imitate one of the weightiest crimes of Churchill, under the pretence of visiting it with chastisement which was its due. These lines were also very wisely rejected by Sir William Forbes; for why retain that which it is not creditable to have written, and not interesting to read?

In 1770, the celebrated 'Essay on Truth,' was first presented to the public. It was written with a view to ascertain the *standard of truth*, and explain its immutability. It was his object to shew that his opinions, however contrary to the genius of scepticism, and inconsistent with the principles and the practice of infidel writers, were agreeable with the genius of true philosophy, and the principles and practice of those who are on all hands acknowledged to have been most successful in the pursuit of truth. He concludes by laying down the rules by which the fallacies of the infidel philosophy may be detected by every person of *common sense*, though he may not possess that acuteness of metaphysical knowledge, which might fit him for the refutation of such errors. This essay met with the highest possible success; it was translated into several foreign languages: its author was presented with an honorary degree of Doctor of Laws from the university of Oxford. He was, on his arrival in England, introduced to the first literary society of the metropolis, and received as the friend of Burke, of Porteus, of Johnson, and of all that renowned fraternity of genius, by which the time was so pre-eminently distinguished. He was honoured by an interview with his sovereign, from whom he received the warmest tribute of admiration, and a pension of two hundred a year; and he was requested by Sir Joshua Reynolds to sit for his portrait, in which that celebrated painter has mingled the highest eulogy of his subject with the most splendid exhibition of his skill as an artist, and represented Beattie surrounded by a group of allegorical figures, among whom the demon of falsehood is discovered as flying before the genius of truth. Perhaps the strongest argument that can be adduced for allowing the unrestrained publication of infidel works, may be derived from effects produced by the publication of Hume's Essays. How few have been really seduced from their dependance on the gospel by those cold and elaborate disquisitions! how many thousands have been confirmed in faith by the 'Evidences' of Paley, and the 'Essay on Truth' of Beattie, which would most probably never have been undertaken but for the publication of them! Beattie has been accused of treating Hume with too much asperity in his writings, and of speaking of the propriety of excluding him from civil society. How far such an expulsion might have been deserved as an act of justice to a man, who, after declaring in one of his Essays that the writer who 'disabused mankind of their reliance on a future state would deserve ill of his country,' composed an elaborate essay against the immortality of the soul, and incurred the reproach which he had himself denounced, I will not take upon myself to decide; but to speak of a man thus acting against his principles, and condemned by his own sentence, without expressing the deepest indignation, argues an excess of complacency that must astonish the characteristic stoicism of philosophy herself. If Beattie has not spoken of the blasphemies of Hume with the gentleness that is thought decorous, it is to be regretted. It is desirable to gain so complete a mastery over every natural affection, as to be even able to discuss the calumnies that falsehood and malevolence may raise against one's parent or one's God, without being conscious of any warmer feeling than a desire of vindicating and asserting the truth; but as long as the human heart is actuated by the warm current of the blood, it will be impossible for any one of an ordinary temperament to observe so frigid and unamiable a composure.

The 'Essay on Truth' was in the same year followed by the first book of the 'Minstrel.' This poem first appeared without the name of its author; but the beauties were immediately and justly appreciated. The second part was not published till 1774. When Gray criticised the Minstrel, he objected to its author, that, after many stanzas, the description went on, and the narrative stopped. Beattie very justly answered to this remark, that he meant the poem for description, not for incident. But he seems to have forgotten this proper apology, when he mentions, in one of his letters, his intention of producing Edwin in some subsequent books, in the character of a warlike bard, inspiring his countrymen to battle, and contributing to repel the invaders. This intention, if he ever seriously entertained it, might have produced some new kind of poem, but would have formed an incongruous counterpart to the piece as it now stands, which, as a picture of tranquil life, and a vehicle of contemplative morality, possesses a charm that is inconsistent with the bold evolutions of heroic narrative. After having pourtrayed his young enthusiast with such advantage in a state of visionary quiet, it would have been too violent a transition to have begun a new book, to surround him with dates of time, and names of places. The interest which we attach to Edwin's character would have been lost in a more ambitious effort to make him a greater, a more important, or a more locally defined being. It is the solitary growth of his genius, and his isolated and mystic abstraction from mankind, that fix our attention on the romantic features of that genius. The simplicity of his fate does not divert us from his mind to his circumstances. A more unworldly air is given to his character, that, instead of being tacked to the fate of kings, he was one "who envied not, who never thought of kings;" and that, instead of mingling with the troubles which deface the creation, he only existed to make his thoughts the mirror of its beauty and magnificence. Another English critic, Dr. Aikin, has blamed Edwin's vision of the fairies as too splendid and artificial for a simple youth; but there is nothing in the situation ascribed to Edwin, as he lived in minstrel days, that necessarily excluded such materials from his fancy. Had he beheld steam engines, or dock yards, in his sleep, the vision might have been pronounced to be too artificial; but he might have heard of fairies, and their dances, and even of tapers, gold, and gems, from the ballads of his native country. In the second book of the poem, there are some fine stanzas; but the author has taken Edwin from the school of nature, and placed him in his own, that of moral philosophy, and hence a degree of languor is experienced by the reader.—The above remarks on the most celebrated of Dr. Beattie's works I have transcribed from the seventh volume of Campbell's British Poets. They convey the sentiments of one of the best poets of the present age, on one of the brightest ornaments of the last.

At the request of several of his friends, Dr. Beattie was induced, in the year 1776, to prepare for the press a new edition of the 'Essay on Truth,' to which he added several original Essays. This work was splendidly printed in quarto, and published by subscription entirely for his own benefit. The price was a guinea, and the list of subscribers, which amounted to four hundred and seventy-six, was enriched with the titles of many persons of the highest rank in the kingdom, and with the names of all the most distinguished literary characters of the time. The number of copies subscribed for amounted to seven hundred and thirty-two. The receipts must therefore have been considerable, and to Beattie a very beneficial supply, who was by no means in affluent circumstances, his pension being only two hundred a-year, and his professorship never being equal to that sum.

On his return to Scotland it was proposed that he should be removed to some situation in the University of Edinburgh; but he had then many personal enemies,—the zealous friends of Hume, whom he was accused of having too severely treated in his writings; and he preferred the kindness of his old friends, and the quiet of Aberdeen, to a more lucrative and conspicuous appointment in the metropolitan university.—In the same generous disregard of temporalities he declined entering holy orders, and accepting a living in the church of England, which had been offered to him through Dr. Porteus, on the part of the Bishop of Winchester. He thought that by continuing a layman, and refusing the emoluments that might accrue to him from his writings in the cause of religion, his arguments would have a more powerful influence on the minds of his readers; than if he had become a clergyman, and thus, as it were, appeared as a retained advocate, rather than the voluntary assertor of the truth.

He again appeared before the public as an Author, in 1776, with a volume of 'Essays,' which was followed by a second in 1783. Of these works Cowper has delivered an opinion, which, coming from so distinguished an author, it would be unpardonable to omit:—'Beattie is the most agreeable and amiable writer I ever met with; the only author I have seen whose critical and philosophical researches are diversified and embellished by a poetical imagination, that makes even the dryest subject, and the leanest, a feast for the epicure in books. He is so much at his ease too, that his own character appears in every page, and, which is very rare, we see not only the writer, but the man; and the man so gentle, so well-tempered, so happy in his religion, and so humane in his philosophy, that it is necessary to love him if one has any sense of what is lovely.'*

In 1786, he printed his 'Evidences of the Christian Religion,' and in 1790, and 1793, he completed his literary course by the publication of a work in two volumes, 'On the Elements of Moral Science.' These contain in a connected and somewhat enlarged form, the abstract of the lectures which he used to dictate to his scholars.

Such is the literary history of this distinguished man. Successful in all that he undertook, and meriting his success by the diligence of his application, by the variety of his knowledge, and by the virtuous ends to which his talents were applied. From his earliest boyhood to the last stage of life he trod onward in a path of excellence, and of brightening celebrity. His learning obtained for him the respect and admiration of his country, and the invaluable qualities of his heart and temper conciliated the most ardent friendship and affection from those by whom it is a distinction to be known, and an honour to be loved. But though renowned, admired, and loved, his life was the re-

* Hayley's Life of Cowper, vol. iii. p. 247.

verse of happy. His sorrows, at the conclusion of his existence, were heavily accumulated upon him; and they struck the heart where it was most keenly and most painfully sensitive. His wife, with whom he had lived long and happily, became deranged, and was obliged to be removed from the house of her husband. His eldest son, a youth of the highest promise, and to whom his father was attached with more than a father's love, for he was joined with him in the professorship, and they had become friends and fellow-students, and the associates of each other's labours, died, after a short illness, in the twenty-second year of his age. The unhappy Beattie had scarcely began to revive from the shock of this severe affliction, when the peace of his home was again mournfully interrupted. His sole surviving child, at the age of eighteen, when beginning to shew the indications of talent and of virtue, not inferior to those which had so tenderly endeared his elder brother to the affection of his father, was suddenly cut off. This misfortune seems to have crushed the spirits, and for a time, to have alienated the mind of Beattie. He no longer mingled in the intercourse of society. He gave up all his literary correspondence. He said that 'he had done with this world,' and he acted as if he felt that there was no longer any thing on earth worth living for to him: all the links which bound him to the enjoyments or the business of this world were snapt, never again to be united. He performed mechanically the duties of his professorship; but he intermitted all the studies in which he had previously occupied himself. Sometimes, indeed, he appeared to struggle for fortitude; and strove to console the agony of his afflictions by the recollection of the severer fate from which his children had been delivered. As he thought on the hereditary disease by which their mother was afflicted, he would endeavour to tranquillize his mind by reflecting on the grievous intellectual malady from which death had saved them; and exclaim 'How could I have borne to see those elegant minds mangled with madness.'

Beattie was struck with palsy in 1799, and after repeated attacks of the same disease, died in 1803.

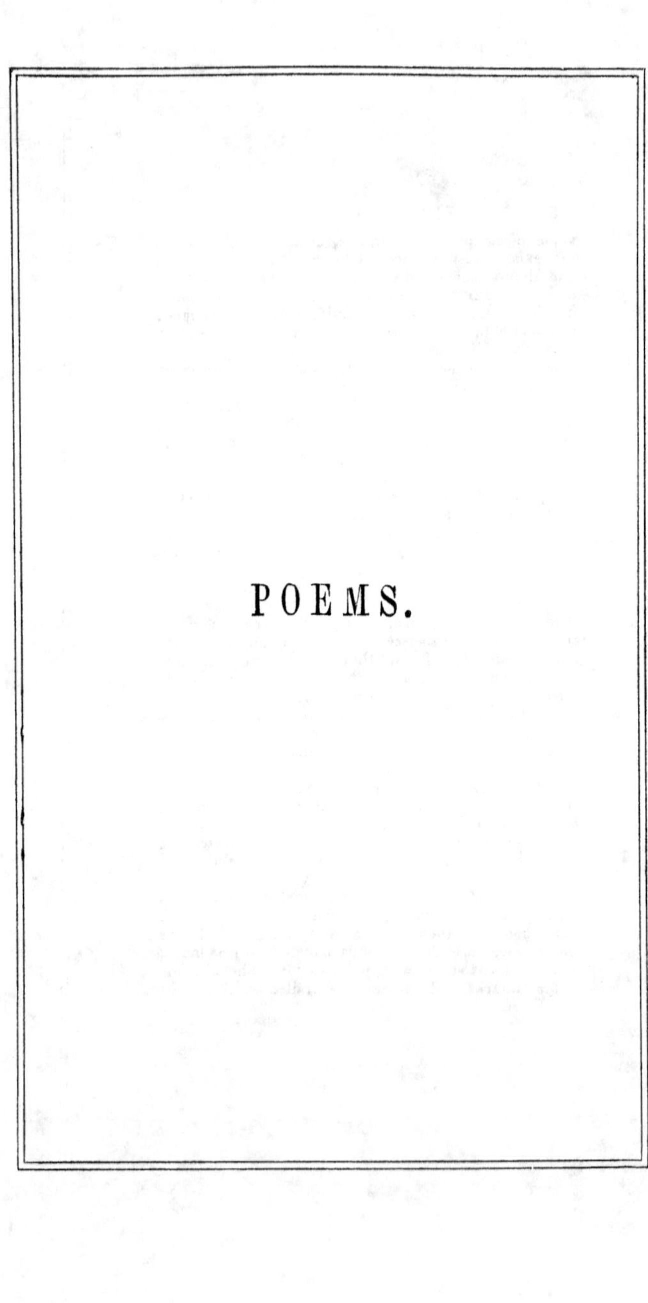

POEMS.

THE MINSTREL:

OR,

THE PROGRESS OF GENIUS.

PREFACE.

THE design was to trace the progress of a poetical genius, born in a rude age, from the first dawning of fancy and reason, till that period at which he may be supposed capable of appearing in the world as a Minstrel, that is, as an itinerant poet and musician;—a character which, according to the notions of our forefathers, was not only respectable, but sacred.

I have endeavoured to imitate Spenser in the measure of his verse, and in the harmony, simplicity, and variety of his composition. Antique expressions I have avoided; admitting, however, some old words, where they seemed to suit the subject: but I hope none will be found that are now obsolete, or in any degree not intelligible to a reader of English poetry.

To those who may be disposed to ask what could induce me to write in so difficult a measure, I can only answer, that it pleases my ear, and seems, from its gothic structure and original, to bear some relation to the subject and spirit of the poem. It admits both simplicity and magnificence of sound and of language, beyond any other stanza that I am acquainted with. It allows the sententiousness of the couplet, as well as the more complex modulation of blank verse. What some critics have remarked, of its uniformity growing at last tiresome to the ear, will be found to hold true only when the poetry is faulty in other respects.

THE MINSTREL.

BOOK I.

AH! who can tell how hard it is to climb
The steep where Fame's proud temple shines afar;
Ah! who can tell how many a soul sublime
Has felt the influence of malignant star,
And waged with Fortune an eternal war;
Check'd by the scoff of Pride, by Envy's frown,
And Poverty's unconquerable bar,
In life's low vale remote has pin'd alone,
Then dropt into the grave, unpitied and unknown!

And yet the languor of inglorious days
Not equally oppressive is to all:
Him, who ne'er listen'd to the voice of praise,
The silence of neglect can ne'er appal.
There are, who, deaf to mad Ambition's call,
Would shrink to hear th' obstreperous trump of Fame;
Supremely blest, if to their portion fall
Health, competence, and peace. Nor higher aim
Had he, whose simple tale these artless lines proclaim.

The rolls of Fame I will not now explore;
Nor need I here describe, in learned lay,
How forth the Minstrel fared in days of yore,
Right glad of heart, though homely in array;
His waving locks and beard all hoary gray:
While from his bending shoulder, decent hung
His harp, the sole companion of his way,
Which to the whistling wind responsive rung:
And ever as he went some merry lay he sung.

Fret not thyself, thou glittering child of pride,
That a poor villager inspires my strain;
With thee let Pageantry and Power abide;
The gentle Muses haunt the sylvan reign;

Where through wild groves at eve the lonely swain
Enraptur'd roams, to gaze on Nature charms.
They hate the sensual, and scorn the vain,
The parasite their influence never warms,
Nor him whose sordid soul the love of gold alarms.

Though richest hues the peacock's plumes adorn,
Yet horror screams from his discordant throat.
Rise, sons of harmony, and hail the morn,
While warbling larks on russet pinions float:
Or seek at noon the woodland scene remote,
Where the gray linnets carol from the hill.
O let them ne'er, with artificial note,
To please a tyrant, strain the little bill,
But sing what Heaven inspires, and wander where they [will.

Liberal, not lavish, is kind Nature's hand;
Nor was perfection made for man below.
Yet all her schemes with nicest art are plann'd,
Good counteracting ill, and gladness woe.
With gold and gems if Chilian mountains glow;
If bleak and barren Scotia's hills arise;
There plague and poison, lust and rapine grow;
Here peaceful are the vales, and pure the skies,
And freedom fires the soul, and sparkles in the eyes

Then grieve not thou, to whom th' indulgent Muse
Vouchsafes a portion of celestial fire:
Nor blame the partial Fates, if they refuse
Th' imperial banquet, and the rich attire.
Know thine own worth, and reverence the lyre.
Wilt thou debase the heart which God refined?
No; let thy heaven-taught soul to Heaven aspire,
To fancy, freedom, harmony, resign'd;
Ambition's groveling crew for ever left behind.

Canst thou forego the pure ethereal soul
In each fine sense so exquisitely keen,
On the dull couch of Luxury to loll,
Stung with disease, and stupified with spleen;

Fain to implore the aid of Flattery's screen,
Even from thyself thy loathsome heart to hide,
(The mansion then no more of joy serene),
Where fear, distrust, malevolence, abide,
And impotent desire, and disappointed pride?

O how canst thou renounce the boundless store
Of charms which Nature to her votary yields?
The warbling woodland, the resounding shore,
The pomp of groves, and garniture of fields;
All that the genial ray of morning gilds,
And all that echoes to the song of even,
And that the mountain's sheltering bosom shields,
And all the dread magnificence of Heaven,
O how canst thou renounce, and hope to be forgiven?

These charms shall work thy soul's eternal health,
And love, and gentleness, and joy, impart.
But these thou must renounce, if lust of wealth
E'er wins its way to thy corrupted heart:
For ah! it poisons like a scorpion's dart;
Prompting th' ungenerous wish, the selfish scheme,
The stern resolve unmoved by pity's smart,
The troublous day, and long distressful dream.
Return, my roving Muse, resume thy purposed theme.

There lived in Gothic days, as legends tell,
A shepherd-swain, a man of low degree;
Whose sires, perchance, in Fairyland might dwell,
Sicilian groves, or vales of Arcady;
But he, I ween, was of the north countrie!*
A nation famed for song, and beauty's charms;
Zealous, yet modest; innocent, though free;
Patient of toil; serene amidst alarms;
Inflexible in faith; invincible in arms.

* There is hardly an ancient ballad or romance, wherein a minstrel or a harper appears, but he is characterised, by way of eminence, to have been 'of the north countrie.' It is probable, that under this appellation were formerly comprehended all the provinces to the north of the Trent. See Percy's Essay on the English Minstrels.

The shepherd-swain of whom I mention made
On Scotia's mountains fed his little flock;
The sickle, scythe, or plough, he never sway'd;
An honest heart was almost all his stock;
His drink the living water from the rock;
The milky dams supplied his board, and lent
Their kindly fleece to baffle winter's shock;
And he, though oft with dust and sweat besprent,
Did guide and guard their wanderings, wheresoe'er
they went.

From labour health, from health contentment springs:
Contentment opes the source of every joy.
He envied not, he never thought of, kings;
Nor from those appetites sustain'd annoy,
That chance may frustrate, or indulgence cloy;
Nor Fate his calm and humble hopes beguiled;
He mourn'd no recreant friend, nor mistress coy,
For on his vows the blameless Phœbe smiled,
And her alone he loved, and loved her from a child

No jealousy their dawn of love o'ercast,
Nor blasted were their wedded days with strife;
Each season look'd delightful as it past,
To the fond husband, and the faithful wife.
Beyond the lowly vale of shepherd life
They never roam'd; secure beneath the storm
Which in Ambition's lofty land is rife,
Where peace and love are canker'd by the worm
Of pride, each bud of joy industrious to deform.

The wight, whose tale these artless lines unfold,
Was all the offspring of this humble pair:
His birth no oracle or seer foretold;
No prodigy appear'd in earth or air,
Nor aught that might a strange event declare.
You guess each circumstance of Edwin's birth
The parent's transport, and the parent's care;

The gossip's prayer for wealth, and wit, and worth;
And one long summer-day of indolence and mirth.

And yet poor Edwin was no vulgar boy,
Deep thought oft seem'd to fix his infant eye.
Dainties he heeded not, nor gaude, nor toy,
Save one short pipe of rudest ministrelsy:
Silent when glad; affectionate, though shy;
And now his look was most demurely sad;
And now he laugh'd aloud, yet none knew why.
The neighbours stared and sigh'd, yet bless'd the lad:
Some deem'd him wondrous wise, and some believed
him mad.

But why should I his childish feats display?
Concourse, and noise, and toil, he ever fled;
Nor cared to mingle in the clamorous fray
Of squabbling imps; but to the forest sped,
Or roam'd at large the lonely mountain's head;
Or, where the maze of some bewilder'd stream
To deep untrodden groves his footsteps led,
There would he wander wild, till Phœbus' beam,
Shot from the western cliff, released the weary team.

Th' exploit of strength, dexterity, or speed,
To him nor vanity nor joy could bring.
His heart, from cruel sport estranged, would bleed
To work the woe of any living thing,
By trap or net, by arrow or by sling;
These he detested; those he scorn'd to wield:
He wish'd to be the guardian, not the king,
Tyrant far less, or traitor of the field.
And sure the sylvan reign unbloody joy might yield.

Lo! where the stripling, wrapt in wonder, roves
Beneath the precipice o'erhung with pine;
And sees, on high, amidst th' encircling groves,
From cliff to cliff the foaming torrents shine:

While waters, woods, and winds, in concert join,
And Echo swells the chorus to the skies.
Would Edwin this majestic scene resign
For aught the huntsman's puny craft supplies?
Ah! no: he better knows great Nature's charms to prize.

And oft he traced the uplands, to survey,
When o'er the sky advanced the kindling dawn,
The crimson cloud, blue main, and mountain gray,
And lake, dim gleaming on the smoky lawn:
Far to the west the long long vale withdrawn,
Where twilight loves to linger for awhile;
And now he faintly kens the bounding fawn,
And villager abroad at early toil.
But lo: the Sun appears. and heaven, earth, ocean, smile.

And oft the craggy cliff he loved to climb,
When all in midst the world below was lost.
What dreadful pleasure! there to stand sublime,
Like shipwreck'd mariner on desert coast,
And view th' enormous waste of vapour, tost
In billows, lengthening to th' horizon round,
Now scoop'd in gulfs, with mountains now emboss'd!
And hear the voice of mirth and song rebound,
Flocks, herds, and waterfalls, along the hoar profound

In truth he was a strange and wayward wight,
Fond of each gentle, and each dreadful scene.
In darkness, and in storm, he found delight:
Nor less, than when on ocean-wave serene
The southern Sun diffused his dazzling shene.
Ev'n sad vicissitude amused his soul:
And if a sigh would sometimes intervene,
And down his cheek a tear of pity roll,
A sigh, a tear, so sweet, he wish'd not to control.

* Brightness, splendour. The word is used by some late writers, as well as by Milton.

'O ye wild groves, O where is now your bloom!
(The Muse interprets thus his tender thought)
'Your flowers, your verdure, and your balmy gloom,
Of late so grateful in the hour of drought!
Why do the birds, that song and rapture brought
To all your bowers, their mansions now forsake?
Ah! why has fickle chance this ruin wrought?
For now the storm howls mournful thro' the brake,
And the dead foliage flies in many a shapeless flake.

'Where now the rill, melodious, pure, and cool,
And meads, with life, and mirth, and beauty crown'd?
Ah! see, th' unsightly slime, and sluggish pool,
Have all the solitary vale embrown'd;
Fled each fair form, and mute each melting sound,
The raven croaks forlorn on naked spray:
And hark! the river, bursting every mound,
Down the vale thunders, and with wasteful sway
Uproots the grove, and rolls the shattered rocks away.

'Yet such the destiny of all on Earth:
So flourishes and fades majestic Man.
Fair is the bud his vernal morn brings forth,
And fostering gales awhile the nursling fan.
O smile, ye Heavens, serene; ye mildews wan,
Ye blighting whirlwinds, spare his balmy prime,
Nor lessen of his life the little span.
Borne on the swift, though silent, wings of Time,
Old age comes on apace to ravage all the clime.

'And be it so. Let those deplore their doom
Whose hope still grovels in this dark sojourn:
But lofty souls, who look beyond the tomb,
Can smile at Fate and wonder how they mourn.
Shall Spring to these sad scenes no more return?
Is yonder wave the Sun's eternal bed?
Soon shall the orient with new lustre burn,

And Spring shall soon her vital influence shed,
Again attune the grove, again adorn the mead.

'Shall I be left forgotten in the dust,
When Fate, relenting, lets the flower revive?
Shall Nature's voice, to man alone unjust,
Bid him, though doom'd to perish, hope to live?
Is it for this fair Virtue oft must strive
With disappointment, penury, and pain?
No: Heaven's immortal spring shall yet arrive,
And man's majestic beauty bloom again,
Bright thro' th' eternal year of Love's triumphant
reign.'

This truth sublime his simple sire had taught.
In sooth, 'twas almost all the shepherd knew.
No subtile nor superfluous lore he sought,
Nor ever wish'd his Edwin to pursue.
'Let man's own sphere,' said he, 'confine his view;
Be man's peculiar work his sole delight.'
And much, and oft, he warn'd him, to eschew
Falsehood and guile, and aye maintain the right,
By pleasure unseduced, unawed by lawless might.

'And, from the prayer of Want, and plaint of Woe,
O never, never turn away thine ear!
Forlorn, in this bleak wilderness below,
Ah! what were man, should Heaven refuse to hear!
To others do (the law is not severe)
What to thyself thou wishest to be done.
Forgive thy foes; and love thy parents dear,
And friends, and native land; nor those alone;
All human weal and woe learn thou to make thine own.'

See, in the rear of the warm sunny shower
The visionary boy from shelter fly;
For now the storm of summer rain is o'er,
And cool, and fresh, and fragrant is the sky.

And, lo! in the dark east, expanded high,
The rainbow brightens to the setting Sun?
Fond fool, that deem'st the streaming glory nigh,
How vain the chase thine ardour has begun!
'Tis fled afar, ere half thy purposed race be run.

Yet couldst thou learn that thus it fares with age,
When pleasure, wealth, or power, the bosom warm,
This baffled hope might tame thy manhood's rage,
And disappointment of her sting disarm.
But why should foresight thy fond heart alarm?
Perish the lore that deadens young desire;
Pursue, poor imp, th' imaginary charm,
Indulge gay hope, and fancy's pleasing fire:
Fancy and hope too soon shall of themselves expire.

When the long-sounding curfew from afar
Loaded with loud lament the lonely gale,
Young Edwin, lighted by the evening star,
Lingering and listening, wander'd down the vale.
There would he dream of graves, and corses pale;
And ghosts that to the charnel-dungeon throng,
And drag a length of clanking chain, and wail,
Till silenced by the owl's terrific song,
Or blast that shrieks by fits the shuddering aisles along.

Or, when the setting Moon, in crimson dyed,
Hung o'er the dark and melancholy deep,
To haunted stream, remote from man, he hied,
Where fays of yore their revels wont to keep;
And there let Fancy rove at large, till sleep
A vision brought to his entranced sight.
And first, a wildly murmuring wind 'gan creep
Shrill to his ringing ear; then tapers bright,
With instantaneous gleam, illumed the vault of night.

Anon in view a portal's blazon'd arch
Arose; the trumpet bids the valves unfold;

And forth an host of little warriors march,
Grasping the diamond lance, and targe of gold.
Their look was gentle, their demeanor bold,
And green their helms, and green their silk attire;
And here and there, right venerably old,
The long-rob'd minstrels wake the warbling wire,
And some with mellow breath the martial pipe inspire.

With merriment, and song, and timbrels clear,
A troop of dames from myrtle bowers advance;
The little warriors doff the targe and spear,
And loud enlivening strains provoke the dance.
They meet, they dart away, they wheel askance:
To right to left they thrid the flying maze;
Now bound aloft with vigorous spring, then glance
Rapid along: with many-colour'd rays
Of tapers, gems, and gold, the echoing forests blaze.

The dream is fled. Proud harbinger of day,
Who scared'st the vision with thy clarion shrill,
Fell chanticleer! who oft hath reft away
My fancied good, and brought substantial ill!
O to thy cursed scream, discordant still,
Let harmony aye shut her gentle ear:
Thy boastful mirth let jealous rivals spill,
Insult thy crest, and glossy pinions tear,
And ever in thy dreams the ruthless fox appear.

Forbear, my Muse. Let Love attune thy line.
Revoke the spell. Thine Edwin frets not so.
For how should he at wicked chance repine,
Who feels from every change amusement flow
Ev'n now his eyes with smiles of rapture glow,
As on he wanders through the scenes of morn,
Where the fresh flowers in living lustre blow,
Where thousand pearls the dewy lawns adorn—
And thousand notes of joy in every breeze are borne.

But who the melodies of morn can tell?
The wild brook babbling down the mountain side;
The lowing herd; the sheepfold's simple bell;
The pipe of early shepherd dim descried;
In the lone valley; echoing far and wide
The clamorous horn along the cliffs above;
The hollow murmur of the ocean tide;
The hum of bees, the linnet's lay of love,
And the full choir that wakes the universal grove.

The cottage-curs at early pilgrim bark;
Crown'd with her pail the tripping milkmaid sings;
The whistling ploughman stalks afield; and, hark!
Down the rough slope the ponderous waggon rings;
Through rustling corn the hare astonish'd springs;
Slow tolls the village-clock the drowsy hour;
The partridge bursts away on whirring wings;
Deep mourns the turtle in sequester'd bower,
And shrill lark carols clear from her aërial tour.

O Nature, how in every charm supreme!
Whose votaries feast on raptures ever new!
O for the voice and fire of seraphim,
To sing thy glories with devotion due!
Blest be the day I 'scaped the wrangling crew,
From Pyrrho's maze, and Epicurus' sty;
And held high converse with the godlike few,
Who to th' enraptured heart, and ear, and eye,
Teach beauty, virtue, truth, and love, and melody.

Hence! ye, who snare and stupify the mind,
Sophists, of beauty, virtue, joy, the bane!
Greedy and fell, though impotent and blind,
Who spread your filthy nets in Truth's fair fane,
And ever ply your venom'd fangs amain,
Hence to dark Error's den, whose rankling slime
First gave you form! Hence! lest the Muse should deign

'Though loth on theme so mean to waste a rhyme),
With vengeance to pursue your sacrilegious crime.

But hail, ye mighty masters of the lay,
Nature's true sons, the friends of man and truth!
Whose songs sublimely sweet, serenely gay,
Amused my childhood, and inform'd my youth.
O let your spirit still my bosom soothe,
Inspire my dreams, and my wild wanderings guide:
Your voice each rugged path of life can smooth,
For well I know, wherever ye reside
There harmony, and peace, and innocence abide.

Ah me! neglected on the lonesome plain,
As yet poor Edwin never knew your lore,
Save when against the winter's drenching rain,
And driving snow, the cottage shut the door.
Then, as instructed by tradition hoar,
Her legend when the beldame 'gan impart,
Or chant the old heroic ditty o'er,
Wonder and joy ran thrilling to his heart;
Much he the tale admired, but more the tuneful art

Various and strange was the long-winded tale;
And halls, and knights, and feats of arms display'd;
Or merry swains, who quaff the nut-brown ale,
And sing enamour'd of the nut-brown maid;
The moonlight revel of the fairy glade;
Or hags, that suckle an infernal brood,
And ply in caves th' unutterable trade,*
'Midst fiends and spectres, quench the Moon in blood,
Yell in the midnight storm, or ride th' infuriate flood.

But when to horror his amazement rose,
A gentler strain the beldame would rehearse,
A tale of rural life, a tale of woes,

* Allusion to Shakspeare.
Macbeth. How now, ye secret, black, and midnight hags.
What is 't ye do?
Witches. A deed without a name.—*Macbeth*, act iv. sc. 1.

The orphan babes, and guardian uncle fierce.
O cruel! will no pang of pity pierce
That heart, by lust of lucre sear'd to stone?
For sure, if aught of virtue last, or verse,
To latest times shall tender souls bemoan
Those hopeless orphan-babes by thy fell arts undone.

Behold, with berries smear'd, with brambles torn,*
The babes now famish'd lay them down to die;
Amidst the howl of darksome woods forlorn,
Folded in one another's arms they lie;
Nor friend, nor stranger, hears their dying cry:
'For from the town the man returns no more.'
But thou, who Heaven's just vengeance darest defy,
This deed with fruitless tears shalt soon deplore,
When Death lays waste thy house, and flames consume
thy store.

A stifled smile of stern vindictive joy
Brighten'd one moment Edwin's starting tear,
'But why should gold man's feeble mind decoy,
And innocence thus die by doom severe?'
O Edwin! while thy heart is yet sincere,
Th' assaults of discontent and doubt repel:
Dark ev'n at noontide is our mortal sphere;
But let us hope; to doubt is to rebel;
Let us exult in hope, that all shall yet be well.

Nor be thy generous indignation check'd,
Nor check'd the tender tear to Misery given·
From Guilt's contagious power shall that protect,
This soften and refine the soul for Heaven.
But dreadful is their doom, whom doubt has driven
To censure Fate, and pious Hope forego:
Like yonder blasted boughs by lightning riven,
Perfection, beauty, life, they never know,
But frown on all that pass, a monument of woe.

* See the fine old ballad called 'The Children in the Wood.

Shall he, whose birth, maturity, and age,
Scarce fill the circle of one summer day,
Shall the poor gnat, with discontent and rage
Exclaim that Nature hastens to decay,
If but a cloud obstruct the solar ray,
If but a momentary shower descend?
Or shall frail man Heaven's dread decree gainsay,
Which bade the series of events extend [end?
Wide through unnumbered worlds, and ages without

One part, one little part, we dimly scan
Through the dark medium of life's feverish dream;
Yet dare arraign the whole stupendous plan,
If but that little part incongruous seem.
Nor is that part perhaps what mortals deem;
Oft from apparent ill our blessings rise.
O then renounce that impious self-esteem,
That aims to trace the secrets of the skies:
For thou art but of dust; be humble, and be wise.

Thus Heaven enlarged his soul in riper years,
For Nature gave him strength, and fire, to soar
On Fancy's wing above this vale of tears;
Where dark cold-hearted sceptics, creeping, pore
Through microscope of metaphysic lore:
And much they grope for Truth, but never hit.
For why? Their powers, inadequate before,
This idle art makes more and more unfit; [wit.
Yet deem they darkness light, and their vain blunders

Nor was this ancient dame a foe to mirth.
Her ballad, jest, and riddle's quaint device
Oft cheer'd the shepherds round their social hearth;
Whom levity or spleen could ne'er entice
To purchase chat, or laughter, at the price
Of decency. Nor let it faith exceed,
That Nature forms a rustic taste so nice.

Ah! had they been of court or city breed,
Such delicacy were right marvellous indeed.

Oft when the winter storm had ceased to rave,
He roam'd the snowy waste at ev'n to view
The cloud stupendous, from th' Atlantic wave
High-tow'ring, sail along th' horizon blue:
Where, 'midst the changeful scenery, ever new,
Fancy a thousand wondrous forms decries,
More wildly great than ever pencil drew,
Rocks, torrents, gulfs, and shapes of giant size,
And glitt'ring cliffs on cliffs, and fiery ramparts rise.

Thence musing onward to the sounding shore,
The lone enthusiast oft would take his way,
Listening, with pleasing dread to the deep roar
Of the wide-weltering waves. In black array
When sulphurous clouds roll'd on th' autumnal day,
Ev'n then he hasten'd from the haunt of man,
Along the trembling wilderness to stray,
What time the lightning's fierce career began, [ran.
And o'er Heaven's rending arch the rattling thunder

Responsive to the sprightly pipe, when all
In sprightly dance the village youth were join'd,
Edwin, of melody aye held in thrall,
From the rude gambol far remote reclined,
Soothed with the soft notes warbling in the wind.
Ah then, all jollity seem'd noise and folly.
To the pure soul by Fancy's fire refin'd,
Ah, what is mirth but turbulence unholy, [choly!
When with the charm compared of heavenly melan-

Is there a heart that music cannot melt?
Alas! how is that rugged heart forlorn;
Is there, who ne'er those mystic transports felt
Of solitude and melancholy born?
He needs not woo the Muse; he is her scorn

The sophist's rope of cobweb he shall twine;
Mope o'er the schoolman's peevish page; or mourn,
And delve for life in Mammon's dirty mine;
Sneak with the scoundrel fox, or grunt with glutton
swine.

For Edwin, Fate a nobler doom had plann'd;
Song was his favourite and first pursuit.
The wild harp rang to his advent'rous hand,
And languish'd to his breath the plaintive flute.
His infant muse, though artless, was not mute·
Of elegance as yet he took no care;
For this of time and culture is the fruit;
And Edwin gain'd at last this fruit so rare:
As in some future verse I purpose to declare.

Meanwhile, whate'er of beautiful, or new,
Sublime, or dreadful, in earth, sea, or sky,
By chance, or search, was offer'd to his view,
He scann'd with curious and romantic eye.
Whate'er of lore tradition could supply
From gothic tale, or song, or fable old,
Roused him, still keen to listen and to pry.
At last, though long by penury controll'd,
And solitude, his soul her graces 'gan unfold.

Thus on the chill Lapponian's dreary land,
For many a long month lost in snow profound,
When Sol from Cancer sends the season bland,
And in their northern cave the storms are bound;
From silent mountains, straight, with startling sound,
Torrents are hurl'd: green hills emerge; and lo,
The trees with foliage, cliffs with flowers are crown'd;
Pure rills through vales of verdure warbling go;
And wonder, love, and joy, the peasant's heart o'erflow.*

* Spring and autumn are hardly known to the Laplanders. About the time the sun enters Cancer, their fields, which a week before were covered with snow, appear on a sudden full of grass and flowers.—*Scheffer's History of Lapland*, p. 16.

Here pause, my gothic lyre, a little while ;
The leisure hour is all that thou canst claim :
But on this verse if Montague should smile,
New strains ere long shall animate thy frame.
And her applause to me is more than fame ;
For still with truth accords her taste refined.
At lucre or renown let others aim,
I only wish to please the gentle mind,
Whom Nature's charms inspire, and love of human-
kind

BOOK II.

Of chance or change O let not man complain,
Else shall he never never cease to wail ;
For, from the imperial dome, to where the swain
Rears the lone cottage in the silent dale,
All feel th' assault of Fortune's fickle gale ;
Art, empire, Earth itself, to change are doom'd ;
Earthquakes have raised to Heaven the humble vale,
And gulfs the mountain's mighty mass entomb'd ;
And where th' Atlantic rolls wide continents have
bloom'd.*

But sure to foreign climes we need not range,
Nor search the ancient records of our race,
To learn the dire effects of time and change,
Which in ourselves, alas! we daily trace.
Yet at the darken'd eye, the wither'd face,
Or hoary hair, I never will repine :
But spare, O Time, whate'er of mental grace,
Of candour, love, or sympathy divine,
Whate'er of fancy's ray or friendship's flame is mine.

* Plato's Timeus.

So I obsequious to Truth's dread command,
Shall here without reluctance change my lay,
And smite the gothic lyre with harsher hand;
Now when I leave that flowery path for aye,
Of childhood, where I sported many a day,
Warbling and sauntering carelessly along;
Where every face was innocent and gay,
Each vale romantic, tuneful every tongue,
Sweet, wild, and artless all, as Edwin's infant song.

'Perish the lore that deadens young desire,'
Is the soft tenor of my song, no more.
Edwin, though lov'd of Heaven, must not aspire
To bliss which mortals never knew before.
On trembling wings let youthful fancy soar,
Nor always haunt the sunny realms of joy:
But now and then the shades of life explore;
Though many a sound and sight of woe annoy,
And many a qualm of care his rising hopes destroy.

Vigour from toil, from trouble patience grows.
The weakly blossom, warm in summer bower,
Some tints of transient beauty may disclose:
But soon it withers in the chilling hour.
Mark yonder oaks! Superior to the power
Of all the warring winds of Heaven they rise,
And from the stormy promontory tower,
And toss their giant arms amid the skies,
While each assailing blast increase of strength supplies.

And now the downy cheek and deepen'd voice
Gave dignity to Edwin's blooming prime;
And walks of wider circuit were his choice,
And vales more mild, and mountains more sublime.
One evening, as he framed the careless rhyme,
It was his chance to wander far abroad,
And o'er a lonely eminence to climb,

Which heretofore his foot had never trode;
A vale appear'd below, a deep retired abode.

Thither he hied, enamour'd of the scene.
For rocks on rocks piled, as by magic spell,
Here scorch'd with lightning, there with ivy green,
Fenced from the north and east this savage dell.
Southward a mountain rose with easy swell,
Whose long long groves eternal murmur made:
And toward the western sun a streamlet fell,
Where, through the cliffs, the eye, remote, survey'd
Blue hills, and glittering waves, and skies in gold
array'd.

Along this narrow valley you might see
The wild deer sporting on the meadow ground,
And, here and there, a solitary tree,
Or mossy stone, or rock with woodbine crown'd.
Oft did the cliffs reverberate the sound
Of parting fragments tumbling from on high;
And from the summit of that craggy mound
The perching eagle oft was heard to cry,
Or on resounding wings to shoot athwart the sky.

One cultivated spot there was, that spread
Its flowery bosom to the noonday beam,
Where many a rose-bud rears its blushing head
And herbs for food with future plenty teem.
Sooth'd by the lulling sound of grove and stream,
Romantic visions swarm on Edwin's soul:
He minded not the Sun's last trembling gleam,
Nor heard from far the twilight curfew toll;
When slowly on his ear these moving accents stole.

'Hail, awful scenes, that calm the troubled breast,
And woo the weary to profound repose!
Can passion's wildest uproar lay to rest,
And whisper comfort to the man of woes?

Here Innocence may wander, safe from foes,
And Contemplation soar on seraph wings.
O solitude! the man who thee foregoes,
When lucre lures him, or ambition stings,
Shall never know the source whence real grandeur
springs.

'Vain man! is grandeur given to gay attire
Then let the butterfly thy pride upbraid:
To friends, attendants, armies, bought with hire
It is thy weakness that requires their aid:
To palaces, with gold and gems inlaid?
They fear the thief, and tremble in the storm;
To hosts, through carnage who to conquest wade?
Behold the victor vanquish'd by the worm!
Behold, what deeds of woe the locust can perform!

'True dignity is his, whose tranquil mind
Virtue has raised above the things below;
Who, every hope and fear to Heaven resign'd,
Shrinks not, though Fortune aim her deadliest blow.'
This strain from 'midst the rocks was heard to flow
In solemn sounds. Now beam'd the evening star;
And from embattled clouds emerging slow
Cynthia came riding on her silver car;
And hoary mountain-cliffs shone faintly from afar.

Soon did the solemn voice its theme renew
(While Edwin, wrapt in wonder, listening stood):
'Ye tools and toys of tyranny, adieu,
Scorn'd by the wise and hated by the good?
Ye only can engage the servile brood
Of Levity and Lust, who all their days,
Ashamed of truth and liberty, have woo'd
And hugg'd the chain, that, glittering on their gaze,
Seems to outshine the pomp of Heaven's empyreal
blaze.

'Like them, abandon'd to Ambition's sway,
I sought for glory in the paths of guile·
And fawn'd and smiled, to plunder and betray,
Myself betray'd and plunder'd all the while;
So gnaw'd the viper the corroding file;
But now, with pangs of keen remorse, I rue
Those years of trouble and debasement vile.
Yet why should I this cruel theme pursue!
Fly, fly, detested thoughts, for ever from my view!

'The gusts of appetite, the clouds of care,
And storms of disappointment, all o'erpast,
Henceforth no earthly hope with Heaven shall share
This heart, where peace serenely shines at last.
And if for me no treasure be amass'd,
And if no future age shall hear my name,
I lurk the more secure from fortune's blast,
And with more leisure feed this pious flame,
Whose rapture far transcends the fairest hopes of fame.

'The end and the reward of toil is rest,
Be all my prayer for virtue and for peace.
Of wealth and fame, of pomp and power possess'd,
Who ever felt his weight of woe decrease?
Ah! what avails the lore of Rome and Greece,
The lay heaven-prompted, and harmonious string,
The dust of Ophir, or the Tyrian fleece,
All that art, fortune, enterprise, can bring,
If envy, scorn, remorse, or pride the bosom wring!

'Let Vanity adorn the marble tomb
With trophies, rhymes, and scutcheons of renown,
In the deep dungeon of some gothic dome,
Where night and desolation ever frown.
Mine to the breezy hill that skirts the down;
Where a green grassy turf is all I crave,
With here and there a violet bestrown,

Fast by a brook, or fountain's murmuring wave,
And many an evening sun shine sweetly on my grave.

'And thither let the village swain repair;
And, light of heart, the village maiden gay,
To deck with flowers her half-dishevell'd hair
And celebrate the merry morn of May.
There let the shepherd's pipe the live-long day
Fill all the grove with love's bewitching woe;
And when mild Evening comes in mantle gray,
Let not the blooming band make haste to go;
No ghost, nor spell, my long and last abode shall know.

'For though I fly to 'scape from Fortune's rage,
And bear the scars of envy, spite, and scorn,
Yet with mankind no horrid war I wage,
Yet with no impious spleen my breast is torn:
For virtue lost, and ruin'd man, I mourn.
O man! creation's pride, Heaven's darling child,
Whom Nature's best, divinest gifts adorn,
Why from thy home are truth and joy exiled,
And all thy favourite haunts with blood and tears
defiled?

'Along yon glittering sky what glory streams!
What majesty attends Night's lovely queen!
Fair laugh our vallies in their vernal beams;
And mountains rise, and oceans roll between,
And all conspire to beautify the scene.
But, in the mental world, what chaos drear;
What forms of mournful, loathsome, furious mien!
O when shall that eternal morn appear,
These dreadful forms to chase, this chaos dark to clear!

'O Thou, at whose creative smile yon heaven,
In all the pomp of beauty, life, and light,
Rose from th' abyss; when dark Confusion driven
Down, down the bottomless profound of night,

I

Fled, where he ever flies, thy piercing sight!
O glance on these sad shades one pitying ray,
To blast the fury of oppressive might,
Melt the hard heart to love and mercy's sway,
And cheer the wandering soul, and light him on the way!'

Silence ensued: and Edwin raised his eyes
In tears, for grief lay heavy at his heart.
'And is it thus in courtly life,' he cries,
'That man to man acts a betrayer's part?
And dares he thus the gifts of Heaven pervert,
Each social instinct, and sublime desire?
Hail Poverty! if honour, wealth, and art,
If what the great pursue, and learn'd admire,
Thus dissipate and quench the soul's ethereal fire!'

He said, and turn'd away; nor did the sage
O'erhear, in silent orisons employ'd.
The youth, his rising sorrow to assuage,
Home as he hied, the evening scene enjoy'd.
For now no cloud obscures the starry void;
The yellow moonlight sleeps on all the hills:*
Nor is the mind with startling sounds annoy'd;
A soothing murmur the lone region fills,
Of groves, and dying gales, and melancholy rills.

But he from day to day more anxious grew,
The voice still seem'd to vibrate on his ear.
Nor durst he hope the hermit's tale untrue;
For man he seem'd to love, and Heaven to fear;
And none speaks false, where there is none to hear.
'Yet, can man's gentle heart become so fell;
No more in vain conjecture let me wear
My hours away, but seek the hermit's cell;
'Tis he my doubt can clear, perhaps my care dispel.'

* How sweet the moonlight sleeps upon this bank.—*Shakspeare.*

At early dawn the youth his journey took,
And many a mountain pass'd and valley wide,
Then reach'd the wild: where, in a flowery nook,
And seated on a mossy stone, he spied
An ancient man: his harp lay him beside.
A stag sprang from the pasture at his call,
And, kneeling, lick'd the wither'd hand that tied
A wreath of woodbine round his antlers tall,
And hung his lofty neck with many a flow'ret small.

And now the hoary sage arose, and saw
The wanderer approaching: innocence
Smiled on his glowing cheek, but modest awe
Depress'd his eye, and fear'd to give offence.
'Who art thou, courteous stranger? and from whence?
Why roam thy steps to this sequester'd dale?'
'A shepherd-boy,' the youth replied; 'far hence
My habitation; hear my artless tale;
Nor levity nor falsehood shall thine ear assail.

'Late as I roam'd, intent on Nature's charms,
I reach'd at eve this wilderness profound;
And, leaning where yon oak expands her arms,
Heard these rude cliffs thine awful voice rebound
(For in thy speech I recognize the sound).
You mourn'd for ruin'd man, and virtue lost,
And seem'd to feel of keen remorse the wound,
Pondering on former days by guilt engross'd,
Or in the giddy storm of dissipation toss'd.

'But say, in courtly life can craft be learn'd,
Where knowledge opens and exalts the soul?
Where Fortune lavishes her gifts unearn'd
Can selfishness the liberal heart control?
Is glory there achieved by arts, as foul
As those that felons, fiends, and furies plan?
Spiders ensnare, snakes poison, tigers prowl:

Love is the godlike attribute of man.
O teach a simple youth this mystery to scan.

'Or else the lamentable strain disclaim,
And give me back the calm, contented mind;
Which, late, exulting, view'd in Nature's frame
Goodness untainted, wisdom unconfined,
Grace, grandeur, and utility combined.
Restore those tranquil days, that saw me still
Well pleased with all, but most with human kind:
When Fancy roam'd through Nature's works at will,
Uncheck'd by cold distrust, and uninform'd of ill.'

'Wouldst thou,' the sage replied, 'in peace return
To the gay dreams of fond romantic youth,
Leave me to hide, in this remote sojourn,
From every gentle ear the dreadful truth:
For if my desultory strain with ruth
And indignation make thine eyes o'erflow,
Alas! what comfort could thy anguish soothe,
Shouldst thou th' extent of human folly know.
Be ignorance thy choice, where knowledge leads to woe.

'But let untender thoughts afar be driven;
Nor venture to arraign the dread decree.
For know, to man, as candidate for heaven,
The voice of the Eternal said, Be free:
And this divine prerogative to thee
Does virtue, happiness, and Heaven convey;
For virtue is the child of liberty,
And happiness of virtue; nor can they
Be free to keep the path, who are not free to stray.

'Yet leave me not. I would allay that grief,
Which else might thy young virtue overpower,
And in thy converse I shall find relief
When the dark shades of melancholy lower;

For solitude has many a dreary hour,
Even when exempt from grief, remorse, and pain:
Come often, then; for, haply, in my bower
Amusement, knowledge, wisdom thou may'st gain:
If I one soul improve, I have not lived in vain.'

And now, at length, to Edwin's ardent gaze
The Muse of History unrols her page.
But few, alas! the scenes her art displays
To charm his fancy, or his heart engage.
Here chiefs their thirst of power in blood assuage,
And straight their flames with tenfold fierceness burn:
Here smiling Virtue prompts the patriot's rage,
But lo, ere long, is left alone to mourn,
And languish in the dust, and clasp th'abandon'd urn!

'Ambition's slippery verge shall mortals tread,
Where ruin's gulf unfathom'd yawns beneath!
Shall life, shall liberty be lost,' he said,
'For the vain toys that pomp and power bequeath!
The car of victory, the plume, the wreath,
Defend not from the bolt of fate the brave:
No note the clarion of renown can breathe,
T' alarm the long night of the lonely grave,
Or check the headlong haste of time's o'erwhelming
wave.

'Ah, what avails it to have traced the springs,
That whirl of empire the stupendous wheel!
Ah, what have I to do with conquering kings,
Hands drench'd in blood, and breasts begirt with steel:
To those, whom Nature taught to think and feel,
Heroes, alas! a e things of small concern;
Could History man's secret heart reveal,
And what imports a heaven-born mind to learn,
Her transcripts to explore what bosom would not
yearn!

This praise, O Cheronean sage,* is thine!
(Why should this praise to thee alone belong?)
All else from Nature's moral path decline,
Lured by the toys that captivate the throng;
To herd in cabinets and camps, among
Spoil, carnage, and the cruel pomp of pride;
Or chant of heraldry the drowsy song,
How tyrant blood, o'er many a region wide,
Rolls to a thousand thrones its execrable tide.

'O who of man the story will unfold,
Ere victory and empire wrought annoy,
In that elysian age (misnamed of gold),
The age of love, and innocence, and joy,
When all were great and free! man's sole employ
To deck the bosom of his parent earth;
Or toward his bower the murmuring stream decoy;
To aid the flow'ret's long-expected birth,
And lull the bed of peace, and crown the board of
mirth.

'Sweet were your shades, O ye primeval groves!
Whose boughs to man his food and shelter lent,
Pure in his pleasures, happy in his loves,
His eye still smiling, and his heart content.
Then, hand in hand, health, sport, and labour went.
Nature supplied the wish she taught to crave.
None prowl'd for prey, none watch'd to circumvent.
To all an equal lot Heaven's bounty gave:
No vassal fear'd his lord, no tyrant fear'd his slave.

'But ah! the historic Muse has never dared
To pierce those hallow'd bowers: 'tis Fancy's beam
Pour'd on the vision of th' enraptured bard,
That paints the charms of that delicious theme.

* Plutarch.

Then hail, sweet Fancy's ray! and hail the dream
That weans the weary soul from guilt and woe!
Careless what others of my choice may deem,
I long, where Love and Fancy lead, to go
And meditate on Heaven, enough of Earth I know.'

'I cannot blame thy choice,' the sage replied,
'For soft and smooth are Fancy's flowery ways.
And yet, ev'n there, if left without a guide,
The young adventurer unsafely plays.
Eyes dazzled long by fiction's gaudy rays
In modest truth no light nor beauty find.
And who, my child, would trust the meteor-blaze,
That soon must fail, and leave the wanderer blind,
More dark and helpless far than if it ne'er had
shined?

'Fancy enervates, while it soothes, the heart,
And, while it dazzles, wounds the mental sight:
To joy each heightening charm it can impart,
But wraps the hour of woe in tenfold night.
And often, where no real ills affright,
Its visionary fiends, an endless train,
Assail with equal or superior might,
And through the throbbing heart, and dizzy brain,
And shivering nerves, shoot stings of more than mor-
tal pain.

'And yet, alas! the real ills of life
Claim the full vigour of a mind prepared,
Prepared for patient, long, laborious strife,
Its guide experience, and truth its guard.
We fare on earth as other men have fared.
Were they successful? Let us not despair.
Was disappointment oft their sole reward?
Yet shall their tale instruct, if it declare [bear.
How they have borne the load ourselves are doom'd to

'What charms th' historic Muse adorn, from spoils,
And blood, and tyrants, when she wings her flight,
To hail the patriot prince, whose pious toils
Sacred to science, liberty, and right,
And peace, through every age divinely bright
Shall shine the boast and wonder of mankind!
Sees yonder Sun, from his meridian height,
A lovelier scene, than virtue thus enshrined
In power, and man with man for mutual aid combined?

'Hail sacred Polity, by Freedom rear'd!
Hail sacred Freedom, when by law restrain'd!
Without you what were man? A groveling herd,
In darkness, wretchedness, and want enchain'd.
Sublimed by you, the Greek and Roman reign'd
In arts unrivall'd: O, to latest days
In Albion may your influence unprofaned
To godlike worth the generous bosom raise,
And prompt the sage's lore, and fire the poet's lays!

'But now let other themes our care engage.
For lo, with modest yet majestic grace,
To curb Imagination's lawless rage,
And from within the cherish'd heart to brace
Philosophy appears! The gloomy race
By Indolence and moping Fancy bred,
Fear, Discontent, Solicitude, give place,
And Hope and Courage brighten in their stead,
While on the kindling soul her vital beams are shed

'Then waken from long lethargy to life*
The seeds of happiness, and powers of thought;
Then jarring appetites forego their strife,
A strife by ignorance to madness wrought.
Pleasure by savage man is dearly bought

* The influence of the philosophic spirit in humanizing the mind, and preparing it for intellectual exertion and delicate pleasure;—in exploring, by the help of geometry, the system of the universe;—in banishing superstition;—in promoting navigation, agriculture, medicine, and moral and political science.

With fell revenge, lust that defies control,
With gluttony and death. The mind untaught
Is a dark waste, where fiends and tempests howl:
As Phœbus to the world, is science to the soul.

'And reason now through number, time, and space,
Darts the keen lustre of her serious eye,
And learns, from facts compared, the laws to trace,
Whose long progression leads to Deity.
Can mortal strength presume to soar so high!
Can mortal sight, so oft bedimm'd with tears,
Such glory bear!—for lo, the shadows fly
From Nature's face; confusion disappears,
And order charms the eye, and harmony the ears!

'In the deep windings of the grove, no more
The hag obscene and grisly phantom dwell;
Nor in the fall of mountain stream, or roar
Of winds, is heard the angry spirit's yell;
No wizard mutters the tremendous spell,
Nor sinks convulsive in prophetic swoon;
Nor bids the noise of drums and trumpets swell,
To ease of fancied pangs the labouring Moon,
Or chase the shade that blots the blazing orb of noon.

'Many a long-lingering year, in lonely isle,
Stunn'd with th' eternal turbulence of waves,
Lo, with dim eyes, that never learn'd to smile,
And trembling hands, the famish'd native craves
Of Heaven his wretched fare; shivering in caves,
Or scorch'd on rocks, he pines from day to day;
But science gives the word; and lo, he braves
The surge and tempest, lighted by her ray,
And to a happier land wafts merrily away!

'And ev'n where Nature loads the teeming plain
With the full pomp of vegetable store,
Her bounty, unimproved is deadly bane:
Dark woods and rankling wilds, from shore to shore

Stretch their enormous gloom; which to explore
Ev'n Fancy trembles, in her sprightliest mood;
For there, each eye-ball gleams with lust of gore,
Nestles each murderous and each monstrous brood,
Plague lurks in every shade, and steams from every
flood.

'Twas from Philosophy man learn'd to tame
The soil, by plenty to intemperance fed.
Lo, from the echoing axe, and thunder flame,
Poison and plague and yelling rage are fled!
The waters, bursting from their slimy bed,
Bring health and melody to every vale:
And, from the breezy main, and mountain's head,
Ceres and Flora, to the sunny dale,
To fan their glowing charms, invite the fluttering gale.

'What dire necessities on every hand
Our art, our strength, our fortitude require!
Of foes intestine what a numerous band
Against this little throb of life conspire!
Yet Science can elude their fatal ire
Awhile, and turn aside Death's level'd dart,
Soothe the sharp pang, allay the fever's fire,
And brace the nerves once more, and cheer the heart,
And yet a few soft nights and balmy days impart.

'Nor less to regulate man's moral frame
Science exerts her all-composing sway.
Flutters thy breast with fear, or pants for fame,
Or pines, to indolence and spleen a prey,
Or avarice, a fiend more fierce than they?
Flee to the shade of Academus' grove;
Where cares molest not, discord melts away
In harmony, and the pure passions prove
How sweet the words of Truth, breathed from the lips
of Love

'What cannot Art and Industry perform,
When Science plans the progress of their toil!
They smile at penury, disease, and storm;
And oceans from their mighty mounds recoil.
When tyrants scourge, or demagogues embroil
A land, or when the rabble's headlong rage
Order transforms to anarchy and spoil,
Deep-versed in man the philosophic sage
Prepares with lenient hand their frenzy to assuage.

''Tis he alone, whose comprehensive mind,
From situation, temper, soil, and clime
Explored, a nation's various powers can bind,
And various orders, in one form sublime
Of policy, that midst the wrecks of time,
Secure shall lift its head on high, nor fear
Th'assault of foreign or domestic crime,
While public faith, and public love sincere,
And industry and law maintain their sway severe.'

Enraptured by the hermit's strain, the youth
Proceeds the path of Science to explore.
And now, expanded to the beam of truth,
New energies and charms unknown before
His mind discloses: Fancy now no more
Wantons on fickle pinion through the skies;
But, fix'd in aim, and conscious of her power,
Aloft from cause to cause exults to rise,
Creation's blended stores arranging as she flies.

Nor love of novelty alone inspires
Their laws and nice dependencies to scan;
For, mindful of the aids that life requires,
And of the services man owes to man,
He meditates new arts on Nature's plan;
The cold desponding breast of sloth to warm,
The flame of industry and genius fan,

And emulation's noble rage alarm,
And the long hours of toil and solitude to charm.

But she, who set on fire his infant heart,
And all his dreams, and all his wanderings shared
And blessed, the Muse, and her celestial art,
Still claim th' enthusiast's fond and first regard.
From Nature's beauties variously compared
And variously combined, he learns to frame
Those forms of bright perfection,* which the bard,
While boundless hopes and boundless views inflame,
Enamour'd consecrates to never-dying fame.

Of late, with cumbersome, though pompous show,
Edwin would oft his flowery rhyme deface,
Through ardour to adorn; but Nature now
To his experienced eye a modest grace
Presents, where ornament the second place
Holds, to intrinsic worth and just design
Subservient still. Simplicity apace
Tempers his rage: he owns her charms divine,
And clears th' ambiguous phrase, and lops the unwieldy line.

Fain would I sing (much yet unsung remains)
What sweet delirium o'er his bosom stole,
When the great shepherd of the Mantuan plains†
His deep majestic melody 'gan roll:
Fain would I sing what transport storm'd his soul,
How the red current throbb'd his veins along,
When, like Pelides, bold beyond control,
Without art graceful, without effort strong,
Homer raised high to Heaven the loud, th' impetuous song

And how his lyre, though rude her first essays,
Now skill'd to soothe, to triumph, to complain,
Warbling at will through each harmonious maze,
Was taught to modulate the artful strain,

* See Aristotle's Poetics, and the Discourses of Sir Joshua Reynolds
† Virgil.

I fain would sing: but ah! I strive in vain.
Sighs from a breaking heart my voice confound
With trembling step, to join yon weeping train
I haste, where gleams funereal glare around,
And mix'd with shrieks of woe, the knells of death
resound.

Adieu, ye lays, that Fancy's flowers adorn,
The soft amusement of the vacant mind!
He sleeps in dust, and all the Muses mourn,
He, whom each virtue fired, each grace refined,
Friend, teacher, pattern, darling of mankind!
He sleeps in dust.* Ah, how shall I pursue
My theme! To heart-consuming grief resign'd,
Here on his recent grave I fix my view,
And pour my bitter tears. Ye flowery lays, adieu!

Art thou, my *Gregory*, for ever fled!
And am I left to unavailing woe!
When fortune's storms assail this weary head,
Where cares long since have shed untimely snow!
Ah, now for comfort whither shall I go!
No more thy soothing voice my anguish cheers:
Thy placid eyes with smiles no longer glow,
My hopes to cherish and allay my fears.
'Tis meet that I should mourn: flow forth afresh,
my tears.

* This excellent person died suddenly on the 10th of February 1773. The conclusion of the poem was written a few days after.

POEMS.

TO

MRS. MONTAGU,

THESE

LITTLE POEMS,

NOW REVISED AND CORRECTED FOR THE LAST TIME,

ARE,

WITH EVERY SENTIMENT OF ESTEEM AND GRATITUDE,

MOST RESPECTFULLY INSCRIBED,

BY THE AUTHOR.

ADVERTISEMENT.

January, 1777.

HAVING lately seen in print some poems ascribed to me which I never wrote, and some of my own inaccurately copied, I thought it would not be improper to publish, in this little volume, all the verses of which I am willing to be considered as the author. Many others I did indeed write in the early part of my life; but they were in general so incorrect, that I would not rescue them from oblivion, even if a wish could do it.

Some of the few now offered to the public would perhaps have been suppressed, if in making this collection I had implicitly followed my own judgment. But in so small a matter, who would refuse to submit his opinion to that of a friend?

It is of no consequence to the reader to know the date of any of these little poems. But some private reasons determined the author to add, that most of them were written many years ago, and that the greater part of the *Minstrel* which is his latest attempt in this way, was composed in the year 1768.

ODE TO PEACE.

I. 1.

PEACE, heaven-descended maid! whose powerful voice
From ancient darkness call'd the morn,
Of jarring elements composed the noise:
When Chaos, from his old dominion torn,
With all his bellowing throng,
Far, far was hurl'd the void abyss along;
And all the bright angelic choir
To loftiest raptures tuned the heavenly lyre,
Pour'd in loud symphony th' impetuous strain;
And every fiery orb and planet sung,
And wide through night's dark desolate domain
Rebounding long and deep the lays triumphant rung.

I. 2.

Oh whither art thou fled, Saturnian reign?
Roll round again, majestic years!
To break fell Tyranny's corroding chain,
From Woe's wan cheek to wipe the bitter tears,
Ye years, again roll round!
Hark from afar what loud tumultuous sound,
While echoes sweep the winding vales,
Swells full along the plains, and loads the gales!
Murder deep-roused, with the wild whirlwind's haste
And roar of tempest, from her cavern springs,
Her tangled serpents girds around her waist,
Smiles ghastly-stern, and shakes her gore-distilling
wings.

I. 3.

Fierce up the yielding skies
The shouts redoubling rise:
Earth shudders at the dreadful sound,
And all is listening trembling round

Torrents, that from yon promontory's head
Dash'd furious down in desperate cascade,
Heard from afar amid the lonely night
That oft have led the wanderer right,
Are silent at the noise.
The mighty ocean's more majestic voice
Drown'd in superior din is heard no more;
The surge in silence sweeps along the foamy shore.

II. 1.

The bloody banner streaming in the air
Seen on yon sky-mix'd mountain's brow,
The mingling multitudes, the madding car
Pouring impetuous on the plain below,
War's dreadful lord proclaim.
Bursts out by frequent fits th' expansive flame.
Whirl'd in tempestuous eddies flies
The surging smoke o'er all the darken'd skies.
The cheerful face of heaven no more is seen,
Fades the morn's vivid blush to deadly pale,
The bat flits transient o'er the dusky green
Night's shrieking birds along the sullen twilight sail.

II. 2.

Involv'd in fire-streak'd gloom the car comes on;
The mangled steeds grim Terror guides.
His forehead writhed to a relentless frown,
Aloft the angry power of battles rides:
Grasp'd in his mighty hand
A mace tremendous desolates the land;
Thunders the turret down the steep,
The mountain shrinks before its wasteful sweep;
Chill horror the dissolving limbs invades;
Smit by the blasting lightning of his eyes,
A bloated paleness beauty's bloom o'erspreads,
Fades every flowery field, and every verdure dies.

II. 3.

How startled Phrenzy stares,
Bristling her ragged hairs!
Revenge the gory fragment gnaws;
See, with her griping vulture-claws
Imprinted deep, she rends the opening wound!
Hatred her torch blue streaming tosses round;
The shrieks of agony and clang of arms
Re-echo to the fierce alarms
Her trump terrific blows.
Disparting from behind, the clouds disclose
Of kingly gesture a gigantic form,
That with his scourge sublime directs the whirling
storm.

III. 1.

Ambition, outside fair! within more foul
Than fellest fiend from Tartarus sprung,
In caverns hatch'd, where the fierce torrents roll
Of Phlegethon, the burning banks along,
Yon naked waste survey;
Where late was heard the flute's mellifluous lay;
Where late the rosy-bosom'd Hours
In loose array danced lightly o'er the flowers;
Where late the shepherd told his tender tale;
And, waked by the soft-murmuring breeze of morn,
The voice of cheerful labour fill'd the dale;
And dove eyed Plenty smiled, and wav'd her liberal
horn.

III. 2.

Yon ruins sable from the wasting flame
But mark the once resplendent dome;
The frequent corse obstructs the sullen stream,
And ghosts glare horrid from the sylvan gloom.
How sadly silent all!
Save where out-stretch'd beneath yon hanging wall

Pale Famine moans with feeble breath,
And torture yells, and grinds her bloody teeth—
Though vain the Muse, and every melting lay
To touch thy heart, unconscious of remorse!
Know, monster, know, thy hour is on the way,
I see, I see the years begin their mighty course.

III. 3.

What scenes of glory rise
Before my dazzled eyes!
Young Zephyrs wave their wanton wings,
And melody celestial rings:
Along the lilied lawn the nymphs advance,
Flush'd with love's bloom, and range the sprightly dance:
The gladsome shepherds on the mountain-side
Array'd in all their rural pride
Exalt the festive note,
Inviting Echo from her inmost grot—
But ah! the landscape glows with fainter light,
It darkens, swims, and flies for ever from my sight.

IV. 1.

Illusions vain! Can sacred Peace reside
Where sordid gold the breast alarms,
Where cruelty inflames the eye of Pride,
And Grandeur wantons in soft Pleasure's arms?
Ambition! these are thine:
These from the soul erase the form divine;
These quench the animating fire,
That warms the bosom with sublime desire.
Thence the relentless heart forgets to feel,
Hate rides tremendous on th' o'erwhelming brow,
And midnight Rancour grasps the cruel steel,
Blaze the funereal flames, and sound the shrieks of Woe.

IV. 2.

From Albion fled, thy once-beloved retreat,
What region brightens in thy smile,
Creative Peace, and underneath thy feet
Sees sudden flowers adorn the rugged soil?
In bleak Siberia blows,
Waked by thy genial breath, the balmy rose?
Waved o'er by thy magic wand
Does life inform fell Lybia's burning sand?
Or does some isle thy parting flight detain,
Where roves the Indian through primeval shades:
Haunts the pure pleasures of the woodland reign,
And, led by reason's ray, the path of Nature treads?

IV. 3.

On Cuba's utmost steep*
Far leaning o'er the deep
The goddess' pensive form was seen.
Her robe of Nature's varied green
Waved on the gale: grief dimm'd her radiant eyes,
Her swelling bosom heaved with boding sighs:
She eyed the main; where, gaining on the view,
Emerging from th' ethereal blue,
'Midst the dread pomp of war
Gleam'd the Iberian streamer from afar.
She saw; and on refulgent pinions borne
Slow wing'd her way sublime, and mingled with the
morn.

* Alluding to the discovery of America by the Spaniards under Columbus. These ravagers are supposed to have made their first descent on the islands in the gulf of Florida, of which Cuba is one.

THE

TRIUMPH OF MELANCHOLY.

MEMORY, be still! why throng upon the thought
These scenes deep-stain'd with Sorrow's sable dye?
Hast thou in store no joy-illumined draught,
To cheer bewilder'd Fancy's tearful eye?

Yes—from afar a landscape seems to rise,
Deckt gorgeous by the lavish hand of Spring;
Thin gilded clouds float light along the skies,
And laughing Loves disport on fluttering wing.

How blest the youth in yonder valley laid!
Soft smiles in every conscious feature play,
While to the gale low-murmuring through the glade
He tempers sweet his sprightly warbling lay.

Hail Innocence! whose bosom all serene,
Feels not fierce passion's raving tempest roll!
Oh ne'er may Care distract that placid mien!
Oh ne'er may Doubt's dark shades o'erwhelm thy soul

Vain wish! for lo, in gay attire conceal'd
Yonder she comes! the heart-inflaming fiend!
(Will no kind power the helpless stripling shield?)
Swift to her destined prey see Passion bend!

O smile accurst to hide the worst designs!
Now with blithe eye she wooes him to be blest,
While round her arm unseen a serpent twines—
And lo, she hurls it hissing at his breast!

And, instant, lo, his dizzy eye ball swims
Ghastly, and, reddening, darts a threatful glare:
Pain with strong grasp distorts his writhing limbs,
And Fear's cold hand erects his bristling hair!

Is this, O life, is this thy boasted prime?
And does thy spring no happier prospect yield?
Why gilds the vernal sun thy gaudy clime,
When nipping mildews waste the flowery field

How memory pains! Let some gay theme beguile
The musing mind, and soothe to soft delight.
Ye images of woe, no more recoil;
Be life's past scenes wrapt in oblivious night.

Now when fierce Winter, arm'd with wasteful power,
Heaves the wild deep that thunders from afar,
How sweet to sit in this sequester'd bower,
To hear, and but to hear, the mingling war!

Ambition here displays no gilded toy
That tempts on desperate wing the soul to rise,
Nor Pleasure's flower-embroider'd paths decoy,
Nor Anguish lurks in Grandeur's gay disguise.

Oft has Contentment cheer'd this lone abode
With the mild languish of her smiling eye;
Here Health has oft in blushing beauty glow'd,
While loose-robed Quiet stood enamour'd by.

E'en the storm lulls to more profound repose:
The storm these humble walls assails in vain;
Screen'd is the lily when the whirlwind blows,
While the oak's stately ruin strews the plain.

Blow on, ye winds! Thine, Winter, be the skies,
Roll the old ocean, and the vales lay waste:
Nature thy momentary rage defies;
To her relief the gentler seasons haste.

Throned in her emerald-car see Spring appear!
(As Fancy wills the landscape starts to view)
Her emerald-car the youthful Zephyrs bear,
Fanning her bosom with their pinions blue.

Around the jocund Hours are fluttering seen;
And lo, her rod the rose lip'd power extends!
And lo, the lawns are deckt in living green,
And Beauty's bright-eyed train from heaven descends!

Haste, happy days, and make all nature glad—
But will all nature joy at your return?
Say, can ye cheer pale Sickness' gloomy bed,
Or dry the tears that bathe th' untimely urn?

Will ye one transient ray of gladness dart
'Cross the dark cell where hopeless slavery lies?
To ease tired Disappointment's bleeding heart,
Will all your stores of softening balm suffice?

When fell Oppression in his harpy-fangs
From Want's weak grasp the last sad morsel bears,
Can ye allay the heart wrung parent's pangs,
Whose famish'd child craves help with fruitless tears?

For ah! thy reign, Oppression, is not past.
Who from the shivering limbs the vestment rends
Who lays the once-rejoicing village waste,
Bursting the ties of lovers and of friends?

O ye, to Pleasure who resign the day,
As loose in Luxury's clasping arms you lie,
O yet let pity in your breast bear sway,
And learn to melt at Misery's moving cry.

But hop'st thou, Muse, vain glorious as thou art,
With the weak impulse of thy humble strain,
Hop'st thou to soften Pride's obdurate heart,
When Errol's bright example shines in vain?

Then cease the theme. Turn, Fancy, turn thine eye,
Thy weeping eye, nor farther urge thy flight;
Thy haunts, alas! no gleams of joy supply,
Or transient gleams, that flash, and sink in night.

Yet fain the mind its anguish would forego—
Spread then, historic Muse, thy pictured scroll;
Bid thy great scenes in all their splendour glow,
And swell to thought sublime th' exalted soul.

What mingling pomps rush boundless on the gaze!
What gallant navies ride the heaving deep!
What glittering towns their cloud-wrapt turrets raise!
What bulwarks frown horrific o'er the steep!

Bristling with spears, and bright with burnish'd
shields,
Th' embattled legions stretch their long array;
Discord's red torch, as fierce she scours the fields,
With bloody tincture stains the face of day.

And now the hosts in silence wait the sign.
How keen their looks whom Liberty inspires!
Quick as the goddess darts along the line,
Each breast impatient burns with noble fires.

Her form how graceful! In her lofty mien
The smiles of Love stern Wisdom's frown control;
Her fearless eye, determined though serene,
Speaks the great purpose, and th' unconquered soul.

Mark, where Ambition leads the adverse band,
Each feature fierce and haggard, as with pain!
With menace loud he cries, while from his hand
He vainly strives to wipe the crimson stain.

Lo, at his call, impetuous as the storms,
Headlong to deeds of death the hosts are driven;
Hatred to madness wrought each face deforms,
Mounts the black whirlwind, and involves the heaven

Now, Virtue, now thy powerful succour lend,
Shield them for Liberty who dare to die—
Ah Liberty! will none thy cause befriend?
Are these thy sons, thy generous sons, that fly?

Not Virtue's self, when Heaven its aid denies,
Can brace the loosen'd nerves, or warm the heart;
Not Virtue's self can still the burst of sighs,
When festers in the soul Misfortune's dart.

See, where by heaven-bred terror all dismay'd
The scattering legions pour along the plain.
Ambition's car with bloody spoils array'd
Hews its broad way, as Vengeance guides the rein.

But who is he, that by yon lonely brook
With woods o'erhung and precipices rude,*
Abandon'd lies, and with undaunted look
Sees streaming from his breast the purple flood?

Ah, Brutus! ever thine be Virtue's tear!
Lo, his dim eyes to Liberty he turns,
As scarce supported on her broken spear
O'er her expiring son the goddess mourns.

Loose to the wind her azure mantle flies,
From her dishevell'd locks she rends the plume;
No lustre lightens in her weeping eyes,
And on her tear-stain'd cheek no roses bloom.

Meanwhile the world, Ambition, owns thy sway,
Fame's loudest trumpet labours in thy praise;
For thee the Muse awakes her sweetest lay,
And flattery bids for thee her altars blaze.

Nor in life's lofty bustling sphere alone,
The sphere where monarchs and where heroes toil,
Sink Virtue's sons beneath Misfortune's frown,
While Guilt's thrill'd bosom leaps at Pleasure's smile;

Full oft, where Solitude and Silence dwell
Far, far remote amid the lowly plain,
Resounds the voice of Woe from Virtue's cell.
Such is man's doom, and Pity weeps in vain.

* Such, according to Plutarch, was the scene of Brutus's death.

Still grief recoils—How vainly have I strove
Thy power, O Melancholy, to withstand!
Tired I submit; but yet, O yet remove,
Or ease the pressure of thy heavy hand.

Yet for awhile let the bewilder'd soul
Find in society relief from woe;
O yield awhile to Friendship's soft control;
Some respite, Friendship, wilt thou not bestow?

Come, then, Philander! for thy lofty mind
Looks down from far on all that charms the great:
For thou canst bear, unshaken and resign'd,
The brightest smiles, the blackest frowns of Fate:

Come thou, whose love unlimited, sincere,
Nor faction cools, nor injury destroys;
Who lend'st to Misery's moans a pitying ear,
And feel'st with ecstasy another's joys:

Who know'st man's frailty; with a favouring eye,
And melting heart, behold'st a brother's fall;
Who, unenslaved by custom's narrow tie,
With manly freedom follow'st reason's call.

And bring thy Delia, softly smiling fair,
Whose spotless soul no sordid thoughts deform;
Her accents mild would still each throbbing care,
And harmonize the thunder of the storm:

Though blest with wisdom and with wit refined;
She courts not homage, nor desires to shine;
In her each sentiment sublime is join'd
To female sweetness, and a form divine.

Come, and dispel the deep-surrounding shade:
Let chasten'd mirth the social hours employ;
O catch the swift-wing'd hour before 'tis fled,
On swiftest pinion flies the hour of joy.

Even while the careless disencumber'd soul
Dissolving sinks to joy's oblivious dream,
Even then to time's tremendous verge we roll
With haste impetuous down life's surgy stream.

Can gaiety the vanish'd years restore,
Or on the withering limbs fresh beauty shed,
Or soothe the sad inevitable hour,
Or cheer the dark dark mansions of the dead?

Still sound the solemn knell in fancy's ear,
That call'd Cleora to the silent tomb;
To her how jocund roll'd the sprightly year!
How shone the nymph in beauty's brightest bloom!

Ah! Beauty's bloom avails not in the grave,
Youth's lofty mien, nor age's awful grace;
Moulder unknown the monarch and the slave,
Whelm'd in th' enormous wreck of human race.

The thought-fix'd portraiture, the breathing bust,
The arch with proud memorials array'd,
The long-lived pyramid shall sink in dust,
To dumb oblivion's ever-desert shade.

Fancy from comfort wanders still astray.
Ah, Melancholy! how I feel thy power!
Long have I labour'd to elude thy sway!
But 'tis enough, for I resist no more.

The traveller thus, that o'er the midnight waste
Through many a lonesome path is doom'd to roam,
'Wilder'd and weary sits him down at last;
For long the night, and distant far his home.

EPITAPH

ON ***** *******.†

ESCAPED the gloom of mortal life, a soul
Here leaves its mouldering tenement of clay,
Safe, where no cares their whelming billows roll,
No doubts bewilder, and no hopes betray.

Like thee, I once have stemm'd the sea of life;
Like thee, have languish'd after empty joys;
Like thee, have labour'd in the stormy strife;
Been grieved for trifles, and amused with toys.

Yet for awhile 'gainst Passion's threatful blast
Let steady Reason urge the struggling oar;
Shot through the dreary gloom the morn at last
Gives to thy longing eye the blissful shore.

Forget my frailties, thou art also frail;
Forgive my lapses, for thyself may'st fall;
Nor read unmoved my artless tender tale,
I was a friend, O man, to thee, to all

† James Beattie: intended for himself.

EPITAPH.*

Nov. 1, 175*.

To this grave is committed
All that the grave can claim
Of two brothers * * * * * and * * * * * * * *†
Who on the vii of October, MDCCLVII,
Both unfortunately perished in the * * * water:
The one in his xxii, the other in his xviii year.
Their disconsolate father * * * * * * * * * * *
Erects this monument to the memory of
These amiable youths:
Whose early virtues promised
Uncommon comfort to his declining years
And singular emolument to society.

O thou! whose steps in sacred rev'rence tread
These lone dominions of the silent dead,
On this sad stone a pious look bestow,
Nor uninstructed read this tale of woe;
And while the sigh of sorrow heaves thy breast,
Let each rebellious murmur be suppress;
Heaven's hidden ways to trace, for us how vain!
Heaven's wise decrees how impious to arraign!
Pure from the stains of a polluted age,
In early bloom of life, they left the stage:
Not doom'd in lingering woe to waste their breath,
One moment snatch'd them from the power of Death:
They lived united, and united died;
Happy the friends, whom death cannot divide!

* Engraved on a tomb-stone in the church-yard of Lethnet, in the shire of Angus.

† Named Leitch, who were drowned in crossing the river Southesk.

ELEGY.

TIRED with the busy crowds, that all the day
Impatient throng where Folly's altars flame,
My languid powers dissolve with quick decay,
Till genial Sleep repair the sinking frame.

Hail, kind reviver! that canst lull the cares,
And every weary sense compose to rest,
Lighten th' oppressive load which languish bears,
And warm with hope the cold desponding breast.

Touch'd by thy rod, from Power's majestic brow
Drops the gay plume; he pines a lowly clown;
And on the cold earth stretch'd the son of Woe
Quaffs Pleasure's draught, and wears a fancied crown.

When roused by thee, on boundless pinions borne
Fancy to fairy scenes exults to rove,
Now scales the cliff gay gleaming on the morn,
Now sad and silent treads the deepening grove;

Or skims the main, and listens to the storms,
Marks the long waves roll far remote away;
Or mingling with ten thousand glittering forms,
Floats on the gale, and basks in purest day.

Haply, ere long, pierced by the howling blast,
Through dark and pathless deserts I shall roam,
Plunge down th' unfathom'd deep, or shrink aghast
Where bursts the shrieking spectre from the tomb:

Perhaps loose Luxury's enchanting smile
Shall lure my steps to some romantic dale,
Where Mirth's light freaks th' unheeded hours beguile
And airs of rapture warble in the gale.

Instructive emblem of this mortal state!
Where scenes as various every hour arise
In swift succession, which the hand of Fate
Presents, then snatches from our wondering eyes.

Be taught, vain man, how fleeting all thy joys,
Thy boasted grandeur, and thy glittering store;
Death comes and all thy fancied bliss destroys,
Quick as a dream it fades, and is no more.

And, sons of Sorrow! though the threatening storm
Of angry Fortune overhang awhile,
Let not her frowns your inward peace deform;
Soon happier days in happier climes shall smile.

Through Earth's throng'd visions while we toss forlorn,
'Tis tumult all, and rage, and restless strife;
But these shall vanish like the dreams of morn,
When Death awakes us to immortal life.

SONG,

IN IMITATION OF

Shakspeare's 'Blow, blow, thou winter wind.

Blow, blow, thou vernal gale!
Thy balm will not avail
To ease my aching breast;
Though thou the billows smooth,
Thy murmurs cannot soothe
My weary soul to rest.

Flow, flow, thou tuneful stream;
Infuse the easy dream
Into the peaceful soul;
But thou canst not compose
The tumult of my woes,
Though soft thy waters roll.

Blush, blush, ye fairest flowers!
Beauties surpassing yours
My Rosalind adorn;
Nor is the Winter's blast
That lays your glories waste,
So killing as her scorn.

Breathe, breathe, ye tender lays,
That linger down the maze
Of yonder winding grove;
O let your soft control
Bend her relenting soul
To pity and to love.

Fade, fade, ye flowrets fair!
Gales, fan no more the air!
Ye streams forget to glide!
Be hush'd, each vernal strain;
Since nought can soothe my pain,
Nor mitigate her pride.

RETIREMENT.

1758.

WHEN in the crimson cloud of even
The lingering light decays,
And Hesper on the front of Heaven
His glittering gem displays;
Deep in the silent vale, unseen,
Beside a lulling stream,
A pensive youth, of placid mien,
Indulged this tender theme.

'Ye cliffs, in hoary grandeur piled
High o'er the glimmering dale;
Ye woods, along whose windings wild
Murmurs the solemn gale:

Where Melancholy strays forlorn,
And Woe retires to weep,
What time the wan Moon's yellow horn
Gleams on the western deep:

'To you, ye wastes, whose artless charms
Ne'er drew ambition's eye,
'Scaped a tumultuous world's alarms,
To your retreats I fly.
Deep in your most sequester'd bower
Let me at last recline,
Where Solitude, mild, modest power,
Leans on her ivy'd shrine.

'How shall I woo thee, matchless fair!
Thy heavenly smile how win?
Thy smile that smooths the brow of Care,
And stills the storm within.
O wilt thou to thy favourite grove
Thine ardent votary bring,
And bless his hours, and bid them move
Serene, on silent wing?

'Oft let Remembrance soothe his mind
With dreams of former days,
When in the lap of Peace reclined
He framed his infant lays;
When Fancy roved at large, nor Care
Nor cold Distrust alarm'd,
Nor Envy with malignant glare
His simple youth had harm'd.

''Twas then, O Solitude! to thee
His early vows were paid,
From heart sincere, and warm, and free,
Devoted to the shade.

Ah why did Fate his steps decoy
In stormy paths to roam.
Remote from all congenial joy !--
O take the wanderer home.

'Thy shades, thy silence now be mine,
Thy charms my only theme;
My haunt the hollow cliff, whose pine
Waves o'er the gloomy stream.
Whence the scared owl on pinions gray
Breaks from the rustling boughs,
And down the lone vale sails away
To more profound repose.

'O, while to thee the woodland pours
Its wildly warbling song,
And balmy from the bank of flowers
The Zephyr breathes along;
Let no rude sound invade from far,
No vagrant foot be nigh,
No ray fom Grandeur's gilded car
Flash on the startled eye.

'But if some pilgrim through the glade
Thy hallow'd bowers explore,
O guard from harm his hoary head,
And listen to his lore;
For he of joys divine shall tell,
That wean from earthly woe,
And triumph o'er the mighty spell
That chains his heart below.

'For me, no more the path invites
Ambition loves to tread;
No more I climb those toilsome heights,
By guileful Hope misled;

Leaps my fond fluttering heart no more
To Mirth's enlivening strain;
For present pleasure soon is o'er,
And all the past is vain.'

ELEGY,

Written in the Year 1758.

STILL shall unthinking man substantial deem
The forms that fleet through life's deceitful dream?
Till at some stroke of Fate the vision flies,
And sad realities in prospect rise;
And, from elysian slumbers rudely torn,
The startled soul awakes, to think and mourn.
O ye, whose hours in jocund train advance,
Whose spirits to the song of gladness dance,
Who flowery plains in endless pomp survey,
Glittering in beams of visionary day;
O, yet while Fate delays th' impending woe,
Be roused to thought, anticipate the blow;
Lest, like the lightning's glance, the sudden ill
Flash to confound, and penetrate to kill;
Lest, thus encompass'd with funereal gloom,
Like me, ye bend o'er some untimely tomb,
Pour your wild ravings in Night's frighted ear,
And half pronounce Heaven's sacred doom severe.
Wise, beauteous, good! O every grace combined,
That charms the eye, or captivates the mind!
Fresh as the floweret opening on the morn,
Whose leaves bright drops of liquid pearl adorn!
Sweet as the downy-pinion'd gale, that roves
To gather fragrance in Arabian groves!
Mild as the melodies at close of day,
That heard remote along the vale decay!

Yet, why with these compared? What tints so fine,
What sweetness, mildness, can be match'd with thine?
Why roam abroad, since recollection true
Restores the lovely form to Fancy's view;
Still let me gaze, and every care beguile,
Gaze on that cheek, where all the Graces smile;
That soul-expressing eye, benignly bright,
Where Meekness beams ineffable delight;
That brow, where Wisdom sits enthroned serene,
Each feature forms, and dignifies the mien:
Still let me listen, while her words impart
The sweet effusions of the blameless heart,
Till all my soul, each tumult charm'd away,
Yields, gently led, to Virtue's easy sway.
By thee inspired, O Virtue, age is young,
And music warbles from the faltering tongue·
Thy ray creative cheers the clouded brow,
And decks the faded cheek with rosy glow;
Brightens the joyless aspect, and supplies
Pure heavenly lustre to the languid eyes:
But when youth's living bloom reflects thy beams
Resistless on the view the glory streams,
Love, wonder, joy, alternately alarm,
And beauty dazzles with angelic charm.
Ah, whither fled! ye dear illusions, stay!
Lo, pale and silent lies the lovely clay.
How are the roses on that cheek decay'd,
Which late the purple light of youth display'd!
Health on her form each sprightly grace bestow'd:
With life and thought each speaking feature glow'd.
Fair was the blossom, soft the vernal sky;
Elate with hope we deem'd no tempest nigh:
When lo, a whirlwind's instantaneous gust
Left all its beauties withering in the dust.
Cold the soft hand, that sooth'd Woe's weary head!
And quench'd the eye, the pitying tear that shed!

And mute the voice, whose pleasing accents stole,
Infusing balm, into the rankled soul!
O Death, why arm with cruelty thy power,
And spare the idle weed, yet lop the flower?
Why fly thy shafts in lawless error driven?
Is Virtue then no more the care of Heaven?
But peace, bold thought! be still, my bursting heart.
We, not Eliza, felt the fatal dart.
Escaped the dungeon, does the slave complain,
Nor bless the friendly hand that broke the chain?
Say, pines not Virtue for the lingering morn,
On this dark wild condemn'd to roam forlorn!
Where Reason's meteor-rays, with sickly glow,
O'er the dun gloom a dreadful glimmering throw;
Disclosing dubious to th' affrighted eye
O'erwhelming mountains tottering from on high,
Black billowy deeps in storms perpetual toss'd,
And weary ways in wildering labyrinths lost.
O happy stroke, that burst the bonds of clay,
Darts through the rending gloom the blaze of day,
And wings the soul with boundless flight to soar,
Where dangers threat and fears alarm no more.
Transporting thought! here let me wipe away
The tear of Grief, and wake a bolder lay.
But ah! the swimming eye o'erflows anew;
Nor check the sacred drops to Pity due;
Lo, where in speechless, hopeless anguish, bend
O'er her loved dust, the parent, brother, friend!
How vain the hope of man! but cease thy strain,
Nor sorrow's dread solemnity profane;
Mix'd with yon drooping mourners, on her bier
In silence shed the sympathetic tear.

ODE TO HOPE.

I. 1.

O THOU, who gladd'st the pensive soul,
More than Aurora's smile the swain forlorn,
Left all night long to mourn
Where desolation frowns, and tempests howl;
And shrieks of woe, as intermits the storm,
Far o'er the monstrous wilderness resound,
And 'cross the gloom darts many a shapeless form,
And many a fire-eyed visage glares around.
O come, and be once more my guest:
Come, for thou oft thy suppliant's vow hast heard,
And oft with smiles indulgent cheer'd
And sooth'd him into rest.

I. 2.

Smit by thy rapture-beaming eye
Deep flashing through the midnight of their mind,
The sable bands combined,
Where Fear's black banner bloats the troubled sky
Appall'd retire. Suspicion hides her head,
Nor dares th' obliquely gleaming eye-ball raise;
Despair, with gorgon-figured veil o'erspread,
Speeds to dark Phlegethon's detested maze.
Lo, startled at the heavenly ray,
With speed unwonted Indolence upsprings,
And, heaving, lifts her leaden wings,
And sullen glides away:

I. 3.

Ten thousand forms, by pining Fancy view'd,
Dissolve.—Above the sparkling flood
When Phœbus rears his awful brow,
From lengthening lawn and valley low

The troops of fe - orn mists retire.
Along the plain
The joyous swain
Eyes the gay villages again,
And gold-illumined spire;
While on the billowy ether borne
Floats the loose lay's jovial measure;
And light along the fairy Pleasure,
Her green robes glittering to the morn,
Wantons on silken wing. And goblins all
To the damp dungeon shrink, or hoary hall;
Or westward, with impetuous flight,
Shoot to the desert realms of their congenial night.

II. 1.

When first on childhood's eager gaze
Life's varied landscape, stretch'd immense around,
Starts out of night profound,
Thy voice incites to tempt th' untrodden maze.
Fond he surveys thy mild maternal face,
His bashful eye still kindling as he views,
And, while thy lenient arm supports his pace,
With beating heart the upland path pursues:
The path that leads, where, hung sublime,
And seen afar, youth's gallant trophies, bright
In Fancy's rainbow ray, invite
His wingy nerves to climb.

II. 2.

Pursue thy pleasurable way,
Safe in the guidance of thy heavenly guard,
While melting airs are heard,
And soft-eyed cherub-forms around thee play:
Simplicity, in careless flowers array'd,
Prattling amusive in his accent meek;
And Modesty, half turning as afraid,
The smile just dimpling on his glowing cheek!

Content and Leisure, hand in hand
With Innocence and Peace, advance, and sing;
And Mirth, in many a mazy ring,
Frisks o'er the flowery land.

II. 3.

Frail man, how various is thy lot below!
To-day though gales propitious blow,
And Peace soft gliding down the sky
Lead Love along, and Harmony,
To-morrow the gay scene deforms;
Then all around
The thunder's sound
Rolls rattling on through Heaven's profound,
And down rush all the storms.
Ye days, that balmy influence shed,
When sweet childhood, ever sprightly,
In paths of pleasure sported lightly,
Whither, ah whither are ye fled?
Ye cherub train, that brought him on his way,
O leave him not 'midst tumult and dismay;
For now youth's eminence he gains:
But what a weary length of lingering toil remains!

III. 1.

They shrink, they vanish into air,
Now Slander taints with pestilence the gale;
And mingling cries assail,
The wail of Woe, and groan of grim Despair.
Lo, wizard Envy from his serpent eye
Darts quick destruction in each baleful glance
Pride smiling stern, and yellow Jealousy,
Frowning Disdain, and haggard Hate advance;
Behold, amidst the dire array,
Pale wither'd Care his giant-stature rears,
And lo, his iron hand prepares
To grasp its feeble prey.

III. 2.

Who now will guard bewilder'd youth
Safe from the fierce assault of hostile rage?
Such war can Virtue wage,
Virtue, that bears the sacred shield of Truth?
Alas! full oft on Guilt's victorious car
The spoils of Virtue are in triumph borne;
While the fair captive, mark'd with many a scar,
In long obscurity, oppress'd, forlorn,
Resigns to tears her angel form.
Ill-fated youth, then whither wilt thou fly?
No friend, no shelter now is nigh,
And onward rolls the storm.

III. 3.

But whence the sudden beam that shoots along?
Why shrink aghast the hostile throng?
Lo, from amidst affliction's night
Hope bursts all radiant on the sight:
Her words the troubled bosom soothe.
'Why thus dismay'd?
Though foes invade,
Hope ne'er is wanting to their aid,
Who read the path of truth.
'Tis I, who smooth the rugged way,
I, who close the eyes of Sorrow,
And with glad visions of to-morrow
Repair the weary soul's decay.
When Death's cold touch thrills to the freezing heart,
Dreams of Heaven's opening glories I impart,
Till the freed spirit springs on high
In rapture too severe for weak mortality.'

PYGMÆO-GERANO-MACHIA:

THE

BATTLE OF THE PYGMIES AND CRANES.

FROM THE LATIN OF ADDISON.

1762.

THE pygmy-people, and the feather'd train,
Mingling in mortal combat on the plain,
I sing. Ye Muses, favour my designs,
Lead on my squadrons, and arrange the lines:
The flashing swords and fluttering wings display,
And long bills nibbling in the bloody fray;
Cranes darting with disdain on tiny foes,
Conflicting birds and men, and war's unnumber'd woe
  The wars and woes of heroes six feet long
Have oft resounded in Pierian song.
Who has not heard of Colchos' golden fleece,
And Argo mann'd with all the flower of Greece?
Of Thebes' fell brethren, Theseus stern of face,
And Peleus' son unrivall'd in the race,
Eneas, founder of the Roman line,
And William, glorious on the banks of Boyne?
Who has not learn'd to weep at Pompey's woes;
And over Blackmore's epic page to doze?
'Tis I, who dare attempt unusual strains
Of hosts unsung, and unfrequented plains;
The small shrill trump, and chiefs of little size,
And armies rushing down the darken'd skies.
  Where India reddens to the early dawn,
Winds a deep vale from vulgar eye withdrawn:
Bosom'd in groves the lowly region lies,
And rocky mountains round the border rise.

Here, till the doom of fate its fall decreed,
The empire flourish'd of the pygmy breed;
Here Industry perform'd, and Genius plann'd,
And busy multitudes o'erspread the land.
But now to these long bounds if pilgrim stray,
Tempting through craggy cliffs the desperate way,
He finds the puny mansion fallen to earth,
Its godlings mouldering on th' abandon'd hearth;
And starts, where small white bones are spread around,
'Or little footsteps lightly print the ground;'
While the proud crane her nest securely builds,
Chattering amid the desolated fields.
  But different fates befel her hostile rage,
While reign'd, invincible through many an age,
The dreaded pygmy: roused by war's alarms,
Forth rush'd the madding mannikin to arms.
Fierce to the field of death the hero flies;
The faint crane fluttering flaps the ground, and dies;
And by the victor borne (o'erwhelming load!)
With bloody bill loose-dangling marks the road.
And oft the wily dwarf in ambush lay,
And often made the callow young his prey;
With slaughter'd victims heap'd his board, and smil'd,
T' avenge the parent's trespass on the child.
Oft, where his feather'd foe had rear'd her nest,
And laid her eggs and household gods to rest,
Burning for blood, in terrible array,
The eighteen-inch militia burst their way;
All went to wreck: the infant foeman fell,
Whence scarce his chirping bill had broke the shell.
  Loud uproar hence, and rage of arms arose,
And the fell rancour of encountering foes;
Hence dwarfs and cranes one general havoc whelms,
And Death's grim visage scares the pygmy-realms.
Not half so furious blazed the warlike fire
Of mice, high theme of the Meonian lyre;

When bold to battle march'd th' accoutred frogs,
And the deep tumult thunder'd through the bogs,
Pierced by the javelin bulrush on the shore
Here agonizing roll'd the mouse in gore;
And there the frog (a scene full sad to see!)
Shorn of one leg, slow sprawl'd along on three:
He vaults no more with vigorous hops on high,
But mourns in hoarsest croaks his destiny.
  And now the day of woe drew on apace,
A day of woe to all the pygmy-race,
When dwarfs were doom'd (but penitence was vain)
To rue each broken egg, and chicken slain.
For, roused to vengeance by repeated wrong,
From distant climes the long-bill'd legions throng:
From Strymon's lake, Caÿster's plashy meads,
And fens of Scythia, green with rustling reeds,
From where the Danube winds through many a land,
And Mareotis laves th' Egyptian strand,
To rendezvous they waft on eager wing,
And wait assembled the returning spring.
Meanwhile they trim their plumes for length of flight,
Whet their keen beaks, and twisting claws, for fight;
Each crane the pygmy power in thought o'erturns,
And every bosom for the battle burns.
  When genial gales the frozen air unbind,
The screaming legions wheel, and mount the wind;
Far in the sky they form their long array,
And land and ocean stretch'd immense survey
Deep deep beneath; and, triumphing in pride,
With clouds and winds commix'd, innumerous ride:
'Tis wild obstreperous clangour all, and heaven
Whirls, in tempestuous undulation driven.
  Nor less th' alarm that shook the world below,
Where march'd in pomp of war th' embattled foe:
Where manuikins with haughty step advance,
And grasp the shield, and couch the quivering lance:

To right and left the lengthening lines they form,
And rank'd in deep array await the storm.
High in the midst the chieftain-dwarf was seen,
Of giant stature, and imperial mien:
Full twenty inches tall, he strode along,
And view'd with lofty eye the wondering throng:
And while with many a scar his visage frown'd,
Bared his broad bosom, rough with many a wound
Of beaks and claws, disclosing to their sight
The glorious meed of high heroic might.
For with insatiate vengeance he pursued,
And never-ending hate, the feathery brood.
Unhappy they, confiding in the length
Of horny beak, or talon's crooked strength,
Who durst abide his rage; the blade descends,
And from the panting trunk the pinion rends:
Laid low in dust the pinion waves no more,
The trunk disfigured stiffens in its gore.
What hosts of heroes fell beneath his force!
What heaps of chicken carnage mark'd his course!
How oft, O Strymon, thy lone banks along,
Did wailing Echo waft the funeral song!
And now from far the mingling clamours rise,
Loud and more loud rebounding through the skies.
From skirt to skirt of Heaven, with stormy sway,
A cloud rolls on, and darkens all the day.
Near and more near descends the dreadful shade,
And now in battailous array display'd,
On sounding wings, and screaming in their ire,
The cranes rush onward, and the fight require.
The pygmy warriors eye with fearless glare
The host thick swarming o'er the burthen'd air;
Thick swarming now, but to their native land
Doom'd to return a scanty straggling band.—
When sudden, darting down the depth of Heaven,
Fierce on th' expecting foe the cranes are driven,

The kindling frenzy every bosom warms,
The region echoes to the crash of arms:
Loose feathers from th' encountering armies fly,
And in careering whirlwinds mount the sky.
To breathe from toil upsprings the panting crane,
Then with fresh vigour downward darts again.
Success in equal balance hovering hangs.
Here, on the sharp spear, mad with mortal pangs,
The bird transfix'd in bloody vortex whirls,
Yet fierce in death the threatening talon curls;
There, while the life-blood bubbles from his wound,
With little feet the pygmy beats the ground;
Deep from his breast the short short sob he draws,
And, dying, curses the keen-pointed claws.
Trembles the thundering field, thick cover'd o'er
With falchions, mangled wings, and streaming gore,
And pygmy arms, and beaks of ample size,
And here a claw, and there a finger lies.
  Encompass'd round with heaps of slaughter'd foes,
All grim in blood the pigmy champion glows,
And on th' assailing host impetuous springs,
Careless of nibbling bills, and flapping wings;
And 'midst the tumult, wheresoe'er he turns,
The battle with redoubled fury burns;
From ev'ry side th' avenging cranes amain
Throng, to o'erwhelm this terror of the plain.
When suddenly (for such the will of Jove)
A fowl enormous, sousing from above,
The gallant chieftain clutch'd, and soaring high,
(Sad chance of battle!) bore him up the sky.
The cranes pursue, and clustering in a ring,
Chatter triumphant round the captive king.
But ah! what pangs each pygmy bosom wrung,
When, now to cranes a prey, on talons hung,
High in the clouds they saw their helpless lord,
His wriggling form still lessening as he soar'd.

Lo! yet again, with unabated rage,
In mortal strife the mingling hosts engage.
The crane with darted bill assaults the foe,
Hovering; then wheels aloft to 'scape the blow:
The dwarf in anguish aims the vengeful wound:
But whirls in empty air the falchion round.
Such was the scene, when 'midst the loud alarms
Sublime th' eternal Thunderer rose in arms.
When Briareus, by mad ambition driven,
Heaved Pelion huge, and hurl'd it high at Heaven,
Jove roll'd redoubling thunders from on high,
Mountains and bolts encounter'd in the sky;
Till one stupendous ruin whelm'd the crew,
Their vast limbs weltering wide in brimstone blue.
But now at length the pygmy legions yield,
And wing'd with terror fly the fatal field.
They raise a weak and melancholy wail,
All in distraction scattering o'er the vale.
Prone on their routed rear the cranes descend;
Their bills bite furious, and their talons rend:
With unrelenting ire they urge the chase,
Sworn to exterminate the hated race.
'Twas thus the pygmy name, once great in war,
For spoils of conquer'd cranes renown'd afar,
Perish'd. For, by the dread decree of Heaven,
Short is the date to earthly grandeur given,
And vain are all attempts to roam beyond
Where fate has fix'd the everlasting bound.
Fallen are the trophies of Assyrian power,
And Persia's proud dominion is no more;
Yea, though to both superior far in fame,
Thine empire, Latium, is an empty name.
And now with lofty chiefs of ancient time,
The pygmy heroes roam th' elysian clime.
Or, if belief to matron tales be due,
Full oft, in the belated shepherd's view,

Their frisking forms, in gentle green array'd,
Gambol secure amid the moonlight glade.
Secure, for no alarming cranes molest,
And all their woes in long oblivion rest:
Down the deep vale, and narrow winding way,
They foot it featly, ranged in ringlets gay:
'Tis joy and frolic all, where'er they rove,
And Fairy-people is the name they love.

THE HARES.

A FABLE.

Yes, yes, I grant the sons of Earth
Are doom'd to trouble from their birth.
We all of sorrow have our share;
But say, is yours without compare?
Look round the world; perhaps you'll find
Each individual of our kind
Press'd with an equal load of ill,
Equal at least. Look further still,
And own your lamentable case
Is little short of happiness.
In yonder hut that stands alone
Attend to Famine's feeble moan;
Or view the couch where Sickness lies,
Mark his pale cheek, and languid eyes,
His frame by strong convulsion torn,
His struggling sighs, and looks forlorn.
Or see, transfix'd with keener pangs,
Where o'er his hoard the miser hangs;
Whistles the wind; he starts, he stares,
Nor Slumber's balmy blessing shares;
Despair, Remorse, and Terror roll
Their tempests on his harass'd soul.

But here perhaps it may avail
T' enforce our reasoning with a tale.
Mild was the morn, the sky serene,
The jolly hunting band convene,
The beagle's breast with ardour burns,
The bounding steed the champaign spurns,
And Fancy oft the game descries
Through the hound's nose, and huntsman's eyes.
Just then, a council of the hares
Had met, on national affairs.
The chiefs were set; while o'er their head
The furze its frizzled covering spread.
Long lists of grievances were heard,
And general discontent appear'd.
'Our harmless race shall every savage
Both quadruped and biped ravage?
Shall horses, hounds, and hunters still
Unite their wits to work us ill?
The youth, his parent's sole delight,
Whose tooth the dewy lawns invite,
Whose pulse in every vein beats strong,
Whose limbs leap light the vales along,
May yet ere noontide meet his death,
And lie dismember'd on the heath.
For youth, alas, nor cautious age,
Nor strength, nor speed, eludes their rage.
In every field we meet the foe,
Each gale comes fraught with sounds of woe;
The morning but awakes our fears,
The evening sees us bathed in tears.
But must we ever idly grieve,
Nor strive our fortunes to relieve?
Small is each individual's force:
To stratagem be our recourse;
And then, from all our tribes combined,
The murderer to his cost may find

No foes are weak, whom Justice arms,
Whom Concord leads, and Hatred warms.
Be roused : or liberty acquire,
Or in the great attempt expire.'
He said no more, for in his breast
Conflicting thoughts the voice suppress'd :
The fire of vengeance seem'd to stream
From his swoln eyeball's yellow gleam.
And now the tumults of the war,
Mingling confusedly from afar,
Swell in the wind. Now louder cries
Distinct of hounds and men arise.
Forth from the brake, with beating heart,
Th' assembled hares tumultuous start,
And, every straining nerve on wing,
Away precipitately spring.
The hunting band, a signal given,
Thick thundering o'er the plain are driven ;
O'er cliff abrupt, and shrubby mound,
And river broad, impetuous bound :
Now plunge amid the forest shades,
Glance through the openings of the glades ;
Now o'er the level valley sweep,
Now with short steps strain up the steep ;
While backward from the hunter's eyes
The landscape like a torrent flies.
At last an ancient wood they gain'd,
By pruner's axe yet unprofaned.
High o'er the rest, by Nature rear'd,
The oak's majestic boughs appear'd :
Beneath, a copse of various hue
In barbarous luxuriance grew.
No knife had curb'd the rambling sprays,
No hand had wove th' implicit maze.
The flowering thorn, self-taught to wind,
The hazel's stubborn stem intwined,

And bramble twigs were wreath'd around,
And rough furze crept along the ground.
Here sheltering from the sons of murther,
The hares drag their tired limbs no further.
But lo, the western wind ere long
Was loud, and roar'd the woods among;
From rustling leaves and crashing boughs
The sound of woe and war arose.
The hares distracted scour the grove,
As terror and amazement drove;
But danger, wheresoe'er they fled,
Still seem'd impending o'er their head.
Now crowded in a grotto's gloom,
All hope extinct, they wait their doom.
Dire was the silence, till, at length,
Even from despair deriving strength,
With bloody eye and furious look,
A daring youth arose and spoke.
'O wretched race, the scorn of Fate,
Whom ills of every sort await!
O, cursed with keenest sense to feel
The sharpest sting of every ill!
Say ye, who fraught with mighty scheme,
Of liberty and vengeance dream,
What now remains? To what recess
Shall we our weary steps address,
Since Fate is evermore pursuing
All ways, and means to work our ruin?
Are we alone, of all beneath,
Condemn'd to misery worse than death?
Must we, with fruitless labour, strive
In misery worse than death to live?
No. Be the smaller ill our choice:
So dictates Nature's powerful voice.
Death's pang will in a moment cease;
And then, All hail, eternal peace!'

Thus while he spoke, his words impart
The dire resolve to every heart.
  A distant lake in prospect lay,
That, glittering in the solar ray,
Gleam'd through the dusky trees, and shot
A trembling light along the grot.
Thither with one consent they bend,
Their sorrows with their lives to end;
While each, in thought, already hears
The water hissing in his ears.
Fast by the margin of the lake,
Conceal'd within a thorny brake,
A linnet sate, whose careless lay
Amused the solitary day.
Careless he sung, for on his breast
Sorrow no lasting trace impress'd;
When suddenly he heard a sound
Of swift feet traversing the ground.
Quick to the neighbouring tree he flies,
Thence trembling casts around his eyes;
No foe appear'd, his fears were vain;
Pleased he renews the sprightly strain.
  The hares, whose noise had caused his fright,
Saw with surprise the linnet's flight.
'Is there on earth a wretch,' they said,
'Whom our approach can strike with dread?'
An instantaneous change of thought
To tumult every bosom wrought.
So fares the system-building sage,
Who, plodding on from youth to age,
At last on some foundation-dream
Has rear'd aloft his goodly scheme,
And proved his predecessors fools,
And bound all nature by his rules;
So fares he in that dreadful hour,
When injured Truth exerts her power,

Some new phenomenon to raise,
Which, bursting on his frighted gaze,
From its proud summit to the ground
Proves the whole edifice unsound.
'Children,' thus spoke a hare sedate,
Who oft had known th' extremes of fate,
'In slight events the docile mind
May hints of good instruction find.
That our condition is the worst,
And we with such misfortunes curst
As all comparison defy,
Was late the universal cry;
When lo, an accident so slight
As yonder little linnet's flight,
Has made your stubborn heart confess
(So your amazement bids me guess)
That all our load of woes and fears
Is but a part of what he bears.
Where can he rest secure from harms,
Whom even a helpless hare alarms?
Yet he repines not at his lot,
When past, the danger is forgot:
On yonder bough he trims his wings,
And with unusual rapture sings:
While we, less wretched, sink beneath
Our lighter ills, and rush to death.
No more of this unmeaning rage,
But hear, my friends, the words of age.
'When by the winds of autumn driven
The scatter'd clouds fly 'cross the Heaven,
Oft have we, from some mountain's head,
Beheld th' alternate light and shade
Sweep the long vale. Here hovering lowers
The shadowy cloud; there downwards pours,
Streaming direct, a flood of day,
Which from the view flies swift away;

It flies, while other shades advance,
And other streaks of sunshine glance.
Thus chequer'd is the life below
With gleams of joy and clouds of woe.
Then hope not, while we journey on,
Still to be basking in the sun:
Nor fear, though now in shades ye mourn
That sunshine will no more return.
If, by your terrors overcome,
Ye fly before th' approaching gloom,
The rapid clouds your flight pursue,
And darkness still o'ercasts your view.
Who longs to reach the radiant plain
Must onward urge his course amain;
For doubly swift the shadow flies,
When 'gainst the gale the pilgrim plies.
At least be firm, and undismay'd
Maintain your ground! the fleeting shade
Ere long spontaneous glides away,
And gives you back th' enlivening ray.
Lo, while I speak, our danger past!
No more the shrill horn's angry blast
Howls in our ear; the savage roar
Of war and murder is no more.
Then snatch the moment fate allows,
Nor think of past or future woes.'
He spoke; and hope revives; the lake
That instant one and all forsake,
In sweet amusement to employ
The present sprightly hour of joy.
Now from the western mountain's brow,
Compass'd with clouds of various glow,
The Sun a broader orb displays,
And shoots aslope his ruddy rays.
The lawn assumes a fresher green,
And dew-drops spangle all the scene.

The balmy zephyr breathes along,
The shepherd sings his tender song;
With all their lays the groves resound,
And falling waters murmur round,
Discord and care were put to flight,
And all was peace, and calm delight.

EPITAPH:

Being Part of an Inscription for a Monument to be erected by a Gentleman to the Memory of his Lady.

FAREWELL, my best beloved! whose heavenly mind
Genius with virtue, strength with softness join'd;
Devotion, undebased by pride or art,
With meek simplicity, and joy of heart;
Though sprightly, gentle; though polite, sincere;
And only of thyself a judge severe;
Unblamed, unequall'd in each sphere of life,
The tenderest daughter, sister, parent, wife.
In thee their patroness th' afflicted lost;
Thy friends, their pattern, ornament, and boast;
And I—but ah, can words my loss declare,
Or paint th' extremes of transport and despair!
O thou, beyond what verse or speech can tell,
My guide, my friend, my best-beloved, farewell!

ODE ON LORD H**'s BIRTH-DAY.

A MUSE, unskill'd in venal praise,
Unstain'd with flatt'ry's art;
Who loves simplicity of lays
Breathed ardent from the heart;
While gratitude and joy inspire,
Resumes the long-unpractised lyre,

To hail, O, H**, thy natal morn:
No gaudy wreath of flowers she weaves,
But twines with oak the laurel leaves,
Thy cradle to adorn.

For not on beds of gaudy flowers
Thine ancestors reclined,
Where sloth dissolves, and spleen devours
All energy of mind.
To hurl the dart, to ride the car,
To stem the deluges of war,
And snatch from fate a sinking land;
Trample th' invader's lofty crest,
And from his grasp the dagger wrest,
And desolating brand:

'Twas this that raised th' illustrious line
To match the first in fame!
A thousand years have seen it shine
With unabated flame:
Have seen thy mighty sires appear
Foremost in glory's high career,
The pride and pattern of the brave.
Yet, pure from lust of blood their fire,
And from ambition's wild desire,
They triumph'd but to save.

The Muse with joy attends their way
The vale of peace along:
There to its lord the village gay
Renews the grateful song.
Yon castle's glittering towers contain
No pit of woe, nor clanking chain,
Nor to the suppliant's wail resound;
The open doors the needy bless,
Th' unfriended hail their calm recess,
And gladness smiles around.

There to the sympathetic heart
Life's best delights belong,
To mitigate the mourner's smart,
To guard the weak from wrong.
Ye sons of luxury, be wise:
Know, happiness for ever flies
The cold and solitary breast;
Then let the social instinct glow,
And learn to feel another's woe,
And in his joy be blest.

O yet, ere Pleasure plant her snare
For unsuspecting youth;
Ere Flattery her song prepare
To check the voice of Truth;
O may his country's guardian power
Attend the slumbering infant's bower,
And bright, inspiring dreams impart,
To rouse th' hereditary fire,
To kindle each sublime desire,
Exalt, and warm the heart.

Swift to reward a parent's fears,
A parent's hopes to crown,
Roll on in peace, ye blooming years,
That rear him to renown;
When in his finish'd form and face
Admiring multitudes shall trace
Each patrimonial charm combined,
The courteous yet majestic mien,
The liberal smile, the look serene,
The great and gentle mind.

Yet, though thou draw a nation's eyes,
And win a nation's love,
Let not thy towering mind despise
The village and the grove.

No slander there shall wound thy fame,
No ruffian take his deadly aim,
No rival weave the secret snare:
For Innocence with angel smile,
Simplicity that knows no guile,
And Love and Peace are there.

When winds the mountain oak assail,
And lay its glories waste,
Content may slumber in the vale,
Unconscious of the blast.
Through scenes of tumult while we roam,
The heart, alas! is ne'er at home,
It hopes in time to roam no more;
The mariner, not vainly brave,
Combats the storm, and rides the wave,
To rest at last on shore.

Ye proud, ye selfish, ye severe,
How vain your mask of state!
The good alone have joy sincere,
The good alone are great:
Great, when, amid the vale of peace,
They bid the plaint of sorrow cease,
And hear the voice of artless praise;
As when along the trophy'd plain
Sublime they lead the victor train,
While shouting nations gaze.

TO THE RIGHT HON.

LADY CHARLOTTE GORDON,

Dressed in a Tartan Scotch Bonnet, with Plumes, &c.

WHY, lady, wilt thou bind thy lovely brow
With the dread semblance of that warlike helm,
That nodding plume, and wreath of various glow,
That graced the chiefs of Scotia's ancient realm?

Thou knowest that Virtue is of power the source,
And all her magic to thy eyes is given;
We own their empire, while we feel their force,
Beaming with the benignity of heaven.

The plumy helmet, and the martial mien,
Might dignify Minerva's awful charms;
But more resistless far th' Idalian queen—
Smiles, graces, gentleness, her only arms.

THE HERMIT.

At the close of the day, when the hamlet is still,
And mortals the sweets of forgetfulness prove,
When nought but the torrent is heard on the hill,
And nought but the nightingale's song in the grove:
'Twas thus, by the cave of the mountain afar,
While his harp rung symphonious, a hermit began:
No more with himself or with nature at war,
He thought as a sage, though he felt as a man.

'Ah! why, all abandon'd to darkness and woe,
Why, lone Philomela, that languishing fall?
For spring shall return, and a lover bestow,
And sorrow no longer thy bosom inthral:
But, if pity inspire thee, renew the sad lay,
Mourn, sweetest complainer, man calls thee to mourn;
O soothe him, whose pleasures like thine pass away:
Full quickly they pass—but they never return.

'Now gliding remote, on the verge of the sky,
The Moon, half extinguish'd, her crescent displays:
But lately I mark'd, when majestic on high
She shone, and the planets were lost in her blaze.
Roll on, thou fair orb, and with gladness pursue
The path that conducts thee to splendour again.
But man's faded glory what change shall renew?
Ah fool! to exult in a glory so vain!

''Tis night, and the landscape is lovely no more;
I mourn, but, ye woodlands, I mourn not for you;
For morn is approaching, your charms to restore,
Perfumed with fresh fragrance, and glittering with dew:
Nor yet for the ravage of winter I mourn;
Kind Nature the embryo blossom will save.
But when shall spring visit the mouldering urn!
O when shall it dawn on the night of the grave!

''Twas thus, by the glare of false science betray'd,
That leads, to bewilder; and dazzles, to blind;
My thoughts wont to roam, from shade onward to
shade,
Destruction before me, and sorrow behind.
O pity, great Father of Light,' then I cried,
'Thy creature, who fain would not wander from thee;
Lo, humbled in dust, I relinquish my pride:
From doubt and from darkness thou only canst free!

—'And darkness and doubt are now flying away,
No longer I roam in conjecture forlorn.
So breaks on the traveller, faint, and astray,
The bright and the balmy effulgence of morn.
See Truth, Love, and Mercy, in triumph descending,
And nature all glowing in Eden's first bloom!
On the cold cheek of Death smiles and roses are
blending,
And Beauty immortal awakes from the tomb.'

ON THE REPORT OF A MONUMENT TO BE ERECTED IN WESTMINSTER ABBEY, TO THE MEMORY OF A LATE AUTHOR, (CHURCHILL.)

(Written in 1765.)

[Part of a letter to a person of quality.]

——LEST your lordship, who are so well acquainted with every thing that relates to true honour, should think hardly of me for attacking the memory of the dead, I beg leave to offer a few words in my own vindication.

If I had composed the following verses with a view to gratify private resentment, to promote the interest of any faction, or to recommend myself to the patronage of any person whatsoever, I should have been altogether inexcusable. To attack the memory of the dead from selfish considerations, or from mere wantonness or malice, is an enormity which none can hold in greater detestation than I. But I composed them from very different motives; as every intelligent reader, who peruses them with attention, and who is willing to believe me upon my own testimony, will undoubtedly perceive. My motives proceeded from a sincere desire to do some small service to my country, and to the cause of truth and virtue. The promoters of faction I ever did, and ever will consider as the enemies of mankind: to the memory of such I owe no veneration: to the writings of such I owe no indulgence.

Your lordship knows that (Churchill) owed the greatest share of his renown to the most incompetent of all judges, the mob: actuated by the most unworthy of all principles, a spirit of insolence, and inflamed by the vilest of all human passions, hatred to their fellow-citizens. Those who joined the cry in his favour seemed to me to be swayed rather by fashion than by real sentiment; he therefore might have lived and died unmolested by me, confident as I am, that posterity, when the present unhappy dissensions are forgotten, will do ample justice to his real character. But when I saw the extravagant honours that were paid to his memory, and heard that a monument in Westminster Abbey was intended for one whom even his admirers acknowledge to have been an incendiary, and a debauchee, I could not help wishing that my countrymen would reflect a little on what they were doing, before they consecrated, by what posterity would think the public voice, a character, which no friend to virtue or true taste can approve. It was this sentiment, enforced by the earnest request of a friend, which produced the following little poem; in which I have said nothing of (Churchill's) manners that is not warranted by the best authority; nor of his writings, that is not perfectly agreeable to the opinion of many of the most competent judges in Britain.

(Aberdeen,) January, 1765.

BUFO, begone! with thee may faction's fire,
That hatch'd thy salamander-fame, expire.
Fame, dirty idol of the brainless crowd,
What half-made moon-calf can mistake for good!
Since shared by knaves of high and low degree—
Cromwell and Catiline; Guido Faux, and thee.
By nature uninspired, untaught by art,
With not one thought that breathes the feeling heart,
With not one offering vow'd to Virtue's shrine,
With not one pure unprostituted line;
Alike debauch'd in body, soul, and lays;—
For pension'd censure, and for pension'd praise,

For ribaldry, for libels, lewdness, lies,
For blasphemy of all the good and wise:
Coarse violence in coarser doggrel writ,
Which bawling blackguards spell'd, and took for wit:
For conscience, honour, slighted, spurn'd, o'erthrown:
Lo, Bufo shines the minion of renown.
Is this the land that boasts a Milton's fire,
And magic Spenser's wildly warbling lyre!
The land that owns th' omnipotence of song,
When Shakspeare whirls the throbbing heart along?
The land, where Pope, with energy divine,
In one strong blaze bade wit and fancy shine:
Whose verse, by truth in virtue's triumph borne,
Gave knaves to infamy, and fools to scorn;
Yet pure in manners, and in thought refined,
Whose life and lays adorn'd and bless'd mankind?
Is this the land, where Gray's unlabour'd art
Soothes, melts, alarms, and ravishes the heart:
While the lone wanderer's sweet complainings flow
In simple majesty of manly woe:
Or while, sublime, on eagle-pinion driven, [Heaven?
He soars Pindaric heights, and sails the waste of
Is this the land, o'er Shenstone's recent urn
Where all the Loves and gentler Graces mourn?
And where, to crown the hoary bard of night*
The Muses and the Virtues all unite?
Is this the land, where Akenside displays
The bold yet temperate flame of ancient days?
Like the rapt sage,† in genius as in theme,
Whose hallow'd strain renown'd Ilyssus' stream:
Or him, the indignant bard,‡ whose patriot ire,
Sublime in vengeance, smote the dreadful lyre:
For truth, for liberty, for virtue warm,
Whose mighty song unnerved a tyrant's arm,

* Dr. Young. † Plato.
‡ Alceus. See Akenside's Ode on Lyric Poetry.

Hush'd the rude roar of discord, rage, and lust,
And spurn'd licentious demagogues to dust.
Is this the queen of realms! the glorious isle,
Britannia, blest in Heaven's indulgent smile!
Guardian of truth, and patroness of art,
Nurse of th' undaunted soul, and generous heart
Where, from a base unthankful world exiled,
Freedom exults to roam the careless wild:
Where taste to science every charm supplies,
And genius soars unbounded to the skies!
And shall a Bufo's most polluted name
Stain her bright tablet of untainted fame?
Shall his disgraceful name with theirs be join'd,
Who wish'd and wrought the welfare of their kind?
His name accurst, who leagued with ****** and Hell,
Labour'd to rouse, with rude and murderous yell,
Discord the fiend, to toss rebellion's brand,
To whelm in rage and woe a guiltless land:
To frustrate wisdom's, virtue's noblest plan,
And triumph in the miseries of man.
Drivelling and dull, when crawls the reptile Muse,
Swoln from the sty, and rankling from the stews,
With envy, spleen, and pestilence replete,
And gorged with dust she lick'd from Treason's feet:
Who once, like Satan, raised to Heaven her sight,
But turn'd abhorrent from the hated light:—
O'er such a Muse shall wreaths of glory bloom?
No—shame and execration be her doom.
Hard-fated Bufo! could not dulness save
Thy soul from sin, from infamy thy grave?
Blackmore and Quarles, those blockheads of renown,
Lavish'd their ink, but never harm'd the town.
Though this, thy brother in discordant song,
Harass'd the ear, and cramp'd the labouring tongue:
And that, like thee, taught staggering prose to stand,
And limp on stilts of rhyme around the land.

Harmless they dozed a scribbling life away,
And yawning nations own'd th' innoxious lay:
But from thy graceless, rude, and beastly brain
What fury breathed th' incendiary strain?
Did hate to vice exasperate thy style?
No—Bufo match'd the vilest of the vile.
Yet blazon'd was his verse with Virtue's name—
Thus prudes look down to hide their want of shame:
Thus hypocrites to truth, and fools to sense,
And fops to taste, have sometimes made pretence:
Thus thieves and gamesters swear by honour's laws:
Thus pension-hunters bawl 'their country's cause:'
Thus furious Teague for moderation raved,
And own'd his soul to liberty enslaved.
Nor yet, though thousand cits admire thy rage,
Though less of fool than felon marks thy page:
Nor yet, though here and there one lonely spark
Of wit half brightens through th' involving dark,
To shew the gloom more hideous for the foil,
But not repay the drudging reader's toil;
(For who for one poor pearl of clouded ray
Through Alpine dunghills delves his desperate way?)
Did genius to thy verse such bane impart?
No. 'Twas the demon of thy venom'd heart
(Thy heart with rancour's quintessence endued),
And the blind zeal of a misjudging crowd.
Thus from rank soil a poison'd mushroom sprung,
Nursling obscene of mildew and of dung:
By Heaven design'd on its own native spot
Harmless t' enlarge its bloated bulk, and rot.
But Gluttony th' abortive nuisance saw;
It roused his ravenous undiscerning maw:
Gulp'd down the tasteless throat, the mess abhorr'd
Shot fiery influence round the maddening board.
O had thy verse been impotent as dull,
Nor spoke the rancorous heart, but lumpish skull;

Had mobs distinguish'd, they who howl'd thy fame,
The icicle from the pure diamond's flame,
From fancy's soul thy gross imbruted sense,
From dauntless truth thy shameless insolence,
From elegance confusion's monstrous mass,
And from the lion's spoils the sculking ass,
From rapture's strain the drawling doggrel line,
From warbling seraphim the grunting swine;
With gluttons, dunces, rakes, thy name had slept,
Nor o'er her sullied fame Britannia wept;
Nor had the Muse, with honest zeal possess'd,
T' avenge her country, by thy name disgraced,
Raised this bold strain for virtue, truth, mankind,
And thy fell shade to infamy resign'd.
When frailty leads astray the soul sincere,
Let mercy shed the soft and manly tear.
When to the grave descends the sensual sot,
Unnamed, unnoticed, let his carrion rot.
When paltry rogues, by stealth, deceit, or force,
Hazard their necks, ambitious of your purse:
For such the hangman wreaths his trusty gin,
And let the gallows expiate their sin.
But when a ruffian, whose portentous crimes
Like plagues and earthquakes terrify the times,
Triumphs through life, from legal judgment free,
For Hell may hatch what law could ne'er foresee;
Sacred from vengeance shall his memory rest?—
Judas though dead, though damn'd, we still detest.

THE JUDGMENT OF PARIS.

(Published in 1765.)

FAR in the depth of Ida's inmost grove,
A scene for love and solitude design'd;
Where flowery woodbines wild by Nature wove
Form'd the lone bower, the royal swain reclined.

All up the craggy cliffs, that tower'd to Heaven,
  Green waved the murmuring pines on every side,
Save where, fair opening to the beam of even,
  A dale sloped gradual to the valley wide.

Echo'd the vale with many a cheerful note;
  The lowing of the herds resounded long,
The shrilling pipe, and mellow horn remote
  And social clamours of the festive throng.

For now, low hovering o'er the western main,
  Where amber clouds begirt his dazzling throne,
The Sun with ruddier verdure deckt the plain;
  And lakes and streams, and spires triumphal shone.

And many a band of ardent youths were seen;
  Some into rapture fired by glory's charms,
Or hurl'd the thundering car along the green,
  Or march'd embattled on in glittering arms.

Others more mild, in happy leisure gay,
  The darkening forest's lonely gloom explore,
Or by Scamander's flowery margin stray,
  Or the blue Hellespont's resounding shore.

But chief the eye to Ilion's glories turn'd,
  That gleam'd along th' extended champaign far,
And bulwarks in terrific pomp adorn'd,
  Where Peace sat smiling at the frowns of War.

Rich in the spoils of many a subject-clime,
  In pride luxurious blaz'd th' imperial dome;
Tower'd 'mid th' encircling grove the fane sublime;
  And dread memorials mark'd the hero's tomb.

Who from the black and bloody cavern led
  The savage stern, and sooth'd his boisterous breast;
Who spoke, and Science rear'd her radiant head,
  And brighten'd o'er the long benighted waste;

Or, greatly daring in his country's cause,
  Whose heaven-taught soul the awful plan design'd,
Whence Power stood trembling at the voice of Laws;
  Whence soar'd on Freedom's wing th' ethereal mind.

But not the pomp that royalty displays,
  Nor all the imperial pride of lofty Troy,
Nor Virtue's triumph of immortal praise
  Could rouse the languor of the lingering boy.

Abandon'd all to soft Enone's charms,
  He to oblivion doom'd the listless day;
Inglorious lull'd in Love's dissolving arms,
  While flutes lascivious breathed th' enfeebling lay.

To trim the ringlets of his scented hair;
  To aim, insidious, Love's bewitching glance;
Or cull fresh garlands for the gaudy fair,
  Or wanton loose in the voluptuous dance:

These were his arts; these won Enone's love,
  Nor sought his fettered soul a nobler aim.
Ah why should Beauty's smile those arts approve,
  Which taint with infamy the lover's flame!

Now laid at large beside a murmuring spring,
  Melting he listen'd to the vernal song,
And Echo, listening, waved her airy wing,
  While the deep winding dales the lays prolong.

When slowly floating down the azure skies
  A crimson cloud flash'd on his startled sight;
Whose skirts gay sparkling with unnumber'd dies
  Launched the long billowy trails of flickery light.

That instant hush'd was all the vocal grove,
  Hush'd was the gale, and every ruder sound,
And strains aërial, warbling far above,
  Rung in the ear a magic peal profound.

Near, and more near, the swimming radiance roll'd;
  Along the mountains stream the lingering fires,
Sublime the groves of Ida blaze with gold,
  And all the Heaven resounds with louder lyres.

The trumpet breathed a note: and all in air,
  The glories vanish'd from the dazzled eye;
And three ethereal forms, divinely fair,
  Down the steep glade were seen advancing nigh.

The flowering glade fell level where they moved;
  O'er-arching high the clustering roses hung,
And gales from Heaven on balmy pinion roved,
  And hill and dale with gratulation rung.

The *first* with slow and stately step drew near,
  Fix'd was her lofty eye, erect her mien:
Sublime in grace, in majesty severe,
  She look'd and moved a goddess and a queen.

Her robe along the gale profusely stream'd,
  Light lean'd the sceptre on her bending arm;
And round her brow a starry circlet gleam'd,
  Heightening the pride of each commanding charm.

Milder the *next* came on with artless grace,
  And on a javelin's quivering length reclined:
T' exalt her mien she bade no splendour blaze,
  Nor pomp of vesture fluctuate on the wind.

Serene, though awful, on her brow the light
  Of heavenly wisdom shone: nor roved her eyes,
Save to the shadowy cliff's majestic height,
  Or the blue concave of th' involving skies.

Keen were her eyes to search the inmost soul:
  Yet Virtue triumph'd in their beams benign,
And impious Pride oft felt their dread control,
  When in fierce lightning flash'd the wrath divine.*

* This is agreeable to the theology of Homer, who often represents Pallas as the executioner of divine vengeance.

With awe and wonder gazed th' adoring swain;
His kindling cheeks great Virtue's power confess'd,
But soon 'twas o'er, for Virtue prompts in vain,
When Pleasure's influence numbs the nerveless breast.

And now advanced the *queen of melting joy*,
Smiling supreme in unresisted charms:
Ah, then, what transports fired the trembling boy!
How throbb'd his sickening frame with fierce alarms!

Her eyes in liquid light luxurious swim,
And languish with unutterable love. [limb,
Heaven's warm bloom glows along each bright'ning
Where fluttering bland the veil's thin mantlings rove.

Quick, blushing as abash'd, she half withdrew:
One hand a bough of flowering myrtle waved,
One graceful spread, where, scarce conceal'd from view,
Soft through the parting robe her bosom heaved,

'Offspring of Jove supreme! beloved of Heav'n!
Attend.' Thus spoke the empress of the skies.
'For know, to thee, high-fated prince, 'tis given
Through the bright realms of Fame sublime to rise,

'Beyond man's boldest hope; if nor the wiles
Of Pallas triumph o'er th' ennobling thought;
Nor Pleasure lure with artificial smiles
To quaff the poison of her luscious draught.

'When Juno's charms the prize of beauty claim,
Shall aught on Earth, shall aught in Heav'n contend?
Whom Juno calls to high triumphant fame,
Shall he to meaner sway inglorious bend?

'Yet lingering comfortless in lonesome wild,
Where Echo sleeps 'mid cavern'd vales profound,
The pride of Troy, Dominion's darling child,
Pines while the slow hour stalks its sullen round.

'Hear thou, of Heav'n unconscious! From the blaze
Of glory, stream'd from Jove's eternal throne,
Thy soul, O mortal, caught th' inspiring rays
That to a god exalt Earth's raptured son.

'Hence the bold wish, on boundless pinion borne,
That fires, alarms, impels the maddening soul;
The hero's eye, hence, kindling into scorn,
Blasts the proud menace, and defies control.

'But, unimproved, Heav'n's noblest boons are vain,
No sun with plenty crowns th' uncultured vale:
Where green lakes languish on the silent plain,
Death rides the billows of the western gale.

'Deep in yon mountain's womb, where the dark cave
Howls to the torrent's everlasting roar,
Does the rich gem its flashy radiance wave?
Or flames with steady ray th' imperial ore?

'Toil deck'd with glittering domes yon champaign wide,
And wakes yon grove-embosom'd lawns to joy,
And rends the rough ore from the mountain's side,
Spangling with starry pomp the thrones of Troy.

'Fly these soft scenes. Even now with playful art,
Love wreathes the flowery ways with fatal snare.
And nurse th' ethereal fire that warms thy heart,
That fire ethereal lives but by thy care.

'Lo, hovering near on dark and dampy wing,
Sloth with stern patience waits the hour assign'd,
From her chill plume the deadly dews to fling,
That quench Heav'n's beam, and freeze the cheer-
less mind.

'Vain, then, th' enlivening sound of Fame's alarms,
For Hope's exulting impulse prompts no more:
Vain even the joys that lure to Pleasure's arms,
The throb of transport is for ever o'er

'O who shall then to Fancy's darkening eyes
Recal th' Elysian dreams of joy and light!
Dim through the gloom the formless visions rise,
Snatch'd instantaneous down the gulf of night.

'Thou, who securely lull'd in youth's warm ray
Mark'st not the desolations wrought by Time,
Be roused or perish. Ardent for its prey
Speeds the fell hour that ravages thy prime.

'And, 'midst the horrors shrined of midnight storm,
The fiend Oblivion eyes thee from afar,
Black with intolerable frowns her form,
Beckoning th' embattled whirlwinds into war.

'Fanes, bulwarks, mountains, worlds, their tempest whelms:
Yet glory braves unmoved th' impetuous sweep.
Fly then, ere, hurl'd from life's delightful realms,
Thou sink t' Oblivion's dark and boundless deep.

'Fly, then, where Glory points the path sublime,
See her crown dazzling with eternal light!
'Tis Juno prompts thy daring steps to climb,
And girds thy bounding heart with matchless might.

'Warm in the raptures of divine desire,
Burst the soft chain that curbs th' aspiring mind:
And fly, where Victory, borne on wings of fire,
Waves her red banner to the rattling wind.

'Ascend the car. Indulge the pride of arms,
Where clarions roll their kindling strains on high
Where the eye maddens to the dread alarms,
And the long shout tumultuous rends the sky.

'Plunged in the uproar of the thundering field
I see thy lofty arm the tempest guide:
Fate scatters lightning from thy meteor shield,
And Ruin spreads around the sanguine tide

'Go, urge the terrors of thy headlong car
  On prostrate Pride, and Grandeur's spoils o'erthrown,
While all amazed even heroes shrink afar,
  And hosts embattled vanish at thy frown.

'When glory crowns thy godlike toils, and all
  The triumph's lengthening pomp exalts thy soul,
When lowly at thy feet the mighty fall,
  And tyrants tremble at thy stern control:

'When conquering millions hail thy sovereign might,
  And tribes unknown dread acclamation join;
How wilt thou spurn the forms of low delight!
  For all the ecstasies of Heav'n are thine:

'For thine the joys, that fear no length of days,
  Whose wide effulgence scorns all mortal bound:
Fame's trump in thunder shall announce thy praise,
  Nor bursting worlds her clarion's blast confound.'

The goddess ceased, not dubious of the prize:
  Elate she mark'd his wild and rolling eye,
Mark'd his lip quiver, and his bosom rise,
  And his warm cheek suffused with crimson die.

But Pallas now drew near. Sublime, serene,
  In conscious dignity, she view'd the swain:
Then, love and pity softening all her mien,
  Thus breathed with accents mild the solemn strain.

'Let those, whose arts to fatal paths betray,
  The soul with passion's gloom tempestuous blind,
And snatch from Reason's ken th' auspicious ray
  Truth darts from Heaven to guide th' exploring mind.

'But Wisdom loves the calm and serious hour,
  When Heaven's pure emanation beams confess'd:
Rage, ecstasy, alike disclaim her power,
  She wooes each gentler impulse of the breast.

'Sincere th' unalter'd bliss her charms impart,
 Sedate th' enlivening ardours they inspire:
She bids no transient rapture thrill the heart,
 She wakes no feverish gust of fierce desire.

'Unwise, who, tossing on the watery way,
 All to the storm th' unfetter'd sail devolve:
Man more unwise resigns the mental sway,
 Borne headlong on by passion's keen resolve.

'While storms remote but murmur on thine ear,
 Nor waves in ruinous uproar round thee roll,
Yet, yet a moment check thy prone career,
 And curb the keen resolve that prompts thy soul.

'Explore thy heart, that, roused by glory's name,
 Pants all enraptured with the mighty charm—
And, does Ambition quench each milder flame?
 And is it Conquest that alone can warm?

'To indulge fell Rapine's desolating lust,
 To drench the balmy lawn in streaming gore,
To spurn the hero's cold and silent dust—
 Are these thy joys? Nor throbs thy heart for more?

'Pleased canst thou listen to the patriot's groan,
 And the wild wail of innocence forlorn?
And hear th' abandon'd maid's last frantic moan,
 Her love for ever from her bosom torn?

'Nor wilt thou shrink, when Virtue's fainting breath
 Pours the dread curse of vengeance on thy head?
Nor when the pale ghost bursts the cave of death,
 To glare destruction on thy midnight bed?

'Was it for this, though born to regal power,
 Kind Heav'n to thee did nobler gifts consign,
Bade Fancy's influence gild thy natal hour,
 And bade Philanthropy's applause be thine?

Theirs be the dreadful glory to destroy,
And theirs the pride of pomp and praise suborn'd,
Whose eye ne'er lighten'd at the smile of Joy,
Whose cheek the tear of Pity ne'er adorn'd:

'Whose soul, each finer sense instinctive quell'd,
The lyre's mellifluous ravishment defies:
Nor marks where Beauty roves the flowery field,
Or Grandeur's pinion sweeps th' unbounded skies.

'Hail to sweet Fancy's unexpressive charm!
Hail to the pure delights of social love!
Hail, pleasures mild, that fire not while ye warm,
Nor rack th' exulting frame, but gently move!

'But Fancy soothes no more, if stern Remorse
With iron grasp the tortured bosom wring.
Ah then, even Fancy speeds the venom's course,
Even Fancy points with rage the maddening sting.

'Her wrath a thousand gnashing fiends attend,
And roll the snakes, and toss the brands of Hell:
The beam of Beauty blasts: dark Heavens impend
Tottering: and Music thrills with startling yell.

'What then avails, that with exhaustless store
Obsequious Luxury loads thy glittering shrine?
What then avails, that prostrate slaves adore,
And Fame proclaims thee matchless and divine?

'What though bland Flattery all her arts apply—
Will these avail to calm th' infuriate brain?
Or will the roaring surge, when heaved on high,
Headlong hang, hush'd, to hear the piping swain?

'In health how fair, how ghastly in decay
Man's lofty form! how heavenly fair the mind
Sublimed by Virtue's sweet enlivening sway!
But ah, to Guilt's outrageous rule resign'd,

'How hideous and forlorn! when ruthless Care
With cankering tooth corrodes the seeds of life,
And deaf with passion's storms when pines Despair,
And howling furies rouse th' eternal strife.

'O, by thy hopes of joy that restless glow,
Pledges of Heaven! be taught by Wisdom's lore:
With anxious haste each doubtful path forego,
And life's wild ways with cautious fear explore.

'Straight be thy course: nor tempt the maze that leads
Where fell Remorse his shapeless strength conceals,
And oft Ambition's dizzy cliff he treads,
And slumbers oft in Pleasure's flowery vales.

'Nor linger unresolved: Heaven prompts the choice,
Save when Presumption shuts the ear of Pride:
With grateful awe attend to Nature's voice,
The voice of Nature Heaven ordain'd thy guide.

'Warn'd by her voice, the arduous path pursue,
That leads to Virtue's fane a hardy band:
What, though no gaudy scenes decoy their view,
Nor clouds of fragrance roll along the land?

'What, though rude mountains heave the flinty way?
Yet there the soul drinks light and life divine,
And pure aërial gales of gladness play,
Brace every nerve, and every sense refine.

'Go, prince, be virtuous, and be blest. The throne
Rears not its state to swell the couch of Lust:
Nor dignify Corruption's daring son,
T' o'erwhelm his humbler brethren of the dust.

'But yield an ampler scene to Bounty's eye,
An ampler range to Mercy's ear expand:
And, 'midst admiring nations, set on high
Virtue's fair model, framed by Wisdom's hand.

'Go, then: the moan of Woe demands thine aid:
  Pride's licensed outrage claims thy slumbering ire.
Pale Genius roams the bleak neglected shade,
  And battening Avarice mocks his tuneless lyre.

'Even Nature pines by vilest chains oppress'd:
  Th' astonish'd kingdoms crouch to Fashion's nod.
O ye pure inmates of the gentle breast,
  Truth, Freedom, Love, O where is your abode?

'O yet once more shall Peace from Heaven return,
  And young Simplicity with mortals dwell!
Nor Innocence th' august pavilion scorn,
  Nor meek Contentment fly the humble cell!

'Wilt thou, my prince, th' beauteous train implore,
  'Midst Earth's forsaken scenes once more to bide?
Then shall the shepherd sing in every bower,
  And Love with garlands wreath the domes of Pride.

'The bright tear starting in th' impassion'd eyes
  Of silent gratitude; the smiling gaze
Of gratulation, faltering while he tries
  With voice of transport to proclaim thy praise;

'Th' ethereal glow that stimulates thy frame,
  When all th' according powers harmonious move,
And wake to energy each social aim,
  Attuned spontaneous to the will of Jove;

'Be these, O man, the triumphs of thy soul;
  And all the conqueror's dazzling glories slight,
That, meteor like, o'er trembling nations roll,
  To sink at once in deep and dreadful night.

'Like thine, yon orb's stupendous glories burn
  With genial beam; nor, at th' approach of even,
In shades of horror leave the world to mourn,
  But gild with lingering light th' impurpled Heaven.

Thus while she spoke, her eye, sedately meek,
  Look'd the pure fervour of maternal love.
No rival zeal intemperate flush'd her cheek—
  Can Beauty's boast the soul of Wisdom move?

Worth's noble pride can Envy's leer appal,
  Or staring Folly's vain applauses soothe?
Can jealous Fear Truth's dauntless heart inthral?
  Suspicion lurks not in the heart of Truth.

And now the shepherd raised his pensive head:
  Yet unresolved and fearful roved his eyes,
Scared at the glances of the awful maid;
  For young unpractised Guilt distrusts the guise

Of shameless Arrogance—His wav'ring breast,
  Though warm'd by Wisdom, own'd no constant fire.
While lawless Fancy roam'd afar, unblest,
  Save in the oblivious lap of soft Desire.

When thus the queen of soul-dissolving smiles:
  'Let gentler fate my darling prince attend;
Joyless and cruel are the warrior's spoils,
  Dreary the path stern Virtue's sons ascend.

'Of human joy full short is the career,
  And the dread verge still gains upon your sight:
While idly gazing, far beyond your sphere,
  Ye scan the dream of unapproach'd delight:

'Till every sprightly hour, and blooming scene,
  Of life's gay morn unheeded glides away,
And clouds of tempests mount the blue serene,
  And storms and ruin close the troublous day.

'Then still exult to hail the present joy;
  Thine be the boon that comes unearn'd by toil;
No froward vain desire thy bliss annoy,
  No flattering hope thy longing hours beguile.

'Ah! why should man pursue the charms of Fame,
  For ever luring, yet for ever coy?
Light as the gaudy rainbow's pillar'd gleam,
  That melts illusive from the wondering boy!

'What though her throne irradiate many a clime,
  If hung loose-tottering o'er th' unfathom'd tomb?
What though her mighty clarion, rear'd sublime,
  Display the imperial wreath, and glittering plume?

'Can glittering plume, or can th' imperial wreath
  Redeem from unrelenting fate the brave?
What note of triumph can her clarion breathe,
  T' alarm th' eternal midnight of the grave?

'That night draws on: nor will the vacant hour
  Of expectation linger as it flies:
Nor Fate one moment unenjoy'd restore:
  Each moment's flight how precious to the wise!

'O shun th' annoyance of the bustling throng,
  That haunt with zealous turbulence the great;
There coward Office boasts th' unpunished wrong,
  And sneaks secure in insolence of state.

'O'er fancied injury Suspicion pines,
  And in grim silence gnaws the festering wound;
Deceit the rage-embitter'd smile refines,
  And Censure spreads the viperous hiss around.

'Hope not, fond prince, though Wisdom guard thy throne,
  Though Truth and Bounty prompt each generous aim,
Though thine the palm of peace, the victor's crown,
  The Muse's rapture, and the patriot's flame:

'Hope not, though all that captivates the wise,
  All that endears the good exalt thy praise:
Hope not to taste repose: for Envy's eyes
  At fairest worth still point their deadly rays.

'Envy, stern tyrant of the flinty heart,
Can aught of Virtue, Truth, or Beauty charm?
Can soft Compassion thrill with pleasing smart,
Repentance melt, or Gratitude disarm?

'Ah no. Where Winter Scythia's waste enchains,
And monstrous shapes roar to the ruthless storm,
Not Phœbus' smile can cheer the dreadful plains,
Or soil accursed with balmy life inform.

'Then, Envy, then is thy triumphant hour,
When mourns Benevolence his baffled scheme:
When Insult mocks the clemency of Power,
And loud Dissension's livid firebrands gleam:

'When squint-eyed Slander plies th' unhallow'd tongue,
From poison'd maw when Treason weaves his line,
And muse apostate (infamy to song!)
Grovels, low-muttering, at Sedition's shrine.

'Let not my prince forego the peaceful shade,
The whispering grove, the fountain and the plain:
Power, with th' oppressive weight of pomp array'd,
Pants for simplicity and ease in vain.

'The yell of frantic Mirth may stun his ear,
But frantic Mirth soon leaves the heart forlorn:
And Pleasure flies that high tempestuous sphere,
Far different scenes her lucid paths adorn.

'She loves to wander on th' untrodden lawn,
Or the green bosom of reclining hill,
Soothed by the careless warbler of the dawn,
Or the lone plaint of ever-murmuring rill.

'Or from the mountain-glade's aërial brow,
While to her song a thousand echoes call,
Marks the wild woodland wave remote below,
Where shepherds pipe unseen, and waters fall.

'Her influence oft the festive hamlet proves,
  Where the high carol cheers th' exulting ring:
And oft she roams the maze of wildering groves,
  Listening th' unnumber'd melodies of Spring.

'Or to the long and lonely shore retires;
  What time, loose-glimmering to the lunar beam,
Faint heaves the slumberous wave, and starry fires
  Gild the blue deep with many a lengthening gleam.

'Then to the balmy bower of Rapture borne,
  While strings self-warbling breathe elysian rest,
Melts in delicious vision, till the morn
  Spangle with twinkling dew the flowery waste.

'The frolic Moments, purple-pinion'd, dance
  Around, and scatter roses as they play:
And the blithe Graces, hand in hand, advance,
  Where, with her loved compeers, she deigns to stray.

'Mild Solitude, in veil of rustic die,
  Her sylvan spear with moss-grown ivy bound:
And Indolence, with sweetly-languid eye,
  And zoneless robe that trails along the ground.

'But chiefly Love—O thou, whose gentle mind
  Each soft indulgence Nature framed to share,
Pomp, wealth, renown, dominion, all resign'd,
  O haste to Pleasure's bower, for Love is there.

'Love, the desire of gods! the feast of Heaven!
  Yet to Earth's favour'd offspring not denied!
Ah, let not thankless man the blessing given
  Enslave to Fame, or sacrifice to Pride.

'Nor I from Virtue's call decoy thine ear;
  Friendly to Pleasure are her sacred laws:
Let Temperance' smile the cup of gladness cheer;
  That cup is death, if he withhold applause.

'Far from thy haunt be Envy's baneful sway,
And Hate, that works the harass'd soul to storm:
But woo Content to breathe her soothing lay,
And charm from Fancy's view each angry form

'No savage joy th' harmonious hours profane!
Whom Love refines, can barbarous tumults please?
Shall rage of blood pollute the sylvan reign?
Shall Leisure wanton in the spoils of Peace?

'Free let the feathery race indulge the song,
Inhale the liberal beam, and melt in love:
Free let the fleet hind bound her hills along,
And in pure streams the watery nations rove

'To joy in Nature's universal smile
Well suits, O man, thy pleasurable sphere;
But why should Virtue doom thy years to toil?
Ah, why should Virtue's law be deem'd severe?

'What meed, Beneficence, thy care repays?
What, Sympathy, thy still returning pang?
And why his generous arm should Justice raise,
To dare the vengeance of a tyrant's fang?

'From thankless spite no bounty can secure;
Or froward wish of discontent fulfil,
That knows not to regret thy bounded power,
But blames with keen reproach thy partial will

'To check th' impetuous all involving tide
Of human woes, how impotent thy strife!
High o'er thy mounds devouring surges ride,
Nor reek thy baffled toils, or lavish'd life.

The bower of bliss, the smile of love be thine,
Unlabour'd ease, and leisure's careless dream:
Such be their joys, who bend at *Venus'* shrine,
And own her charms beyond compare supreme.

. S

Warm'd as she spoke, all panting with delight,
  Her kindling beauties breathed triumphant bloom:
And Cupids flutter'd round in circlets bright,
  And Flora pour'd from all her stores perfume.

'Thine be the prize,' exclaim'd th' enraptured youth,
  'Queen of unrivall'd charms, and matchless joy.'—
O blind to fate, felicity, and truth!—
  But such are they, whom Pleasure's snares decoy.

The sun was sunk; the vision was no more;
  Night downward rush'd tempestuous, at the frown
Of Jove's awaken'd wrath: deep thunders roar,
  And forests howl afar and mountains groan.

And sanguine meteors glare athwart the plain;
  With horror's scream the Ilian towers resound,
Raves the hoarse storm along the bellowing main,
  And the strong earthquake rends the shuddering ground.

THE WOLF AND SHEPHERDS.

A FABLE.

(Written in 1757, and first published in 1766.)

LAWS, as we read in ancient sages,
Have been like cobwebs in all ages.
Cobwebs for little flies are spread,
And laws for little folks are made;
But if an insect of renown,
Hornet or beetle, wasp or drone,
Be caught in quest of sport or plunder,
The flimsy fetter flies in sunder.
  Your simile perhaps may please one
With whom wit holds the place of reason:

But can you prove that this in fact is
Agreeable to life and practice?
Then hear what in his simple way
Old Æsop told me t' other day.
In days of yore, but (which is very odd)
Our author mentions not the period,
We mortal men, less given to speeches,
Allow'd the beasts sometimes to teach us.
But now we all are prattlers grown,
And suffer no voice but our own;
With us no beast has leave to speak,
Although his honest heart should break
'Tis true, your asses and your apes,
And other brutes in human shapes,
And that thing made of sound and show
Which mortals have misnamed a beau,
(But in the language of the sky
Is call'd a two legg'd butterfly)
Will make your very heartstrings ache
With loud and everlasting clack,
And beat your auditory drum,
Till you grow deaf, and they grow dumb.
But to our story we return:
'Twas early on a summer morn
A wolf forsook the mountain-den,
And issued hungry on the plain.
Full many a stream and lawn he pass'd,
And reach'd a winding vale at last;
Where from a hollow rock he spied
The shepherds drest in flowery pride.
Garlands were strew'd, and all was gay,
To celebrate an holiday,
The merry tabor's gamesome sound
Provoked the sprightly dance around.
Hard by a rural board was rear'd,
On which in fair array appear'd

The peach, the apple, and the raisin,
And all the fruitage of the season.
But, more distinguished than the rest,
Was seen a wether ready drest,
That smoking, recent from the flame,
Diffused a stomach-rousing steam.
Our wolf could not endure the sight,
Courageous grew his appetite :
His entrails groan'd with tenfold pain,
He lick'd his lips, and lick'd again ;
At last, with lightning in his eyes,
He bounces forth, and fiercely cries,
'Shepherds, I am not given to scolding,
But now my spleen I cannot hold in.
By Jove! such scandalous oppression
Would put an elephant in passion.
You, who your flocks (as you pretend)
By wholesome laws from harm defend,
Which make it death for any beast,
How much soe'er by hunger press'd,
To seize a sheep by force or stealth,
For sheep have right to life and health ;
Can you commit, uncheck'd by shame,
What in a beast so much you blame?
What is a law, if those who make it
Become the forwardest to break it?
The case is plain : you would reserve
All to yourselves, while others starve.
Such laws from base self-interest spring,
Not from the reason of the thing—'
He was proceeding, when a swain
Burst out:—' And dares a wolf arraign
His betters, and condemn their measures,
And contradict their wills and pleasures?
We have establish'd laws, 'tis true,
But laws are made for such as you.

Know, sirrah, in its very nature
A law can't reach the legislature.
For laws, without a sanction join'd,
As all men know, can never bind:
But sanctions reach not us the makers,
For who dares punish us, though breakers?
'Tis therefore plain beyond denial,
That laws were ne'er design'd to tie all,
But those, whom sanctions reach alone;
We stand accountable to none.
Besides, 'tis evident, that seeing
Laws from the great derive their being,
They as in duty bound should love
The great, in whom they live and move,
And humbly yield to their desires:
'Tis just, what gratitude requires.
What suckling dandled on the lap
Would tear away its mother's pap?
But hold—Why deign I to dispute
With such a scoundrel of a brute?
Logic is lost upon a knave,
Let action prove the law our slave.'
  An angry nod his will declared,
To his gruff yeomen of the guard;
The full-fed mongrels, train'd to ravage,
Fly to devour the shaggy savage.
  The beast had now no time to lose
In chopping logic with his foes;
'This argument,' quoth he, 'has force,
And swiftness is my sole resource.'
  He said, and left the swains their prey,
And to the mountains scower'd away.

TRANSLATIONS.

ANACREON. ODE XXII.

Παρὰ τὴν σκίην, βάθυλλε,
Κάθισον·——

BATHYLLUS, in yonder lone grove
All carelessly let us recline:
To shade us the branches above
Their leaf waving tendrils combine;
While a streamlet, inviting repose,
Soft-murmuring, wanders away,
And gales warble wild through the boughs:
Who there would not pass the sweet day?

THE BEGINNING OF THE

FIRST BOOK OF LUCRETIUS.

Æneadum Genetrix——v. 1—45.

MOTHER of mighty Rome's imperial line,
Delight of man, and of the powers divine,
Venus, all bounteous queen! whose genial power
Diffuses beauty in unbounded store
Through seas, and fertile plains, and all that lies
Beneath the starr'd expansion of the skies.
Prepared by thee, the embryo springs to day,
And opes its eyelids on the golden ray.
At thy approach, the clouds tumultuous fly,
And the hush'd storms in gentle breezes die;
Flowers instantaneous spring; the billows sleep;
A wavy radiance smiles along the deep:

At thy approach, th' untroubled sky refines,
And all serene Heaven's lofty concave shines.
Soon as her blooming form the Spring reveals,
And Zephyr breathes his warm prolific gales,
The feather'd tribes first catch the genial flame,
And to the groves thy glad return proclaim.
Thence to the beasts the soft infection spreads;
The raging cattle spurn the grassy meads,
Burst o'er the plains, and frantic in their course
Cleave the wild torrents with resistless force.
Won by thy charms, thy dictates all obey,
And eager follow where thou lead'st the way.
Whatever haunts the mountains, or the main,
The rapid river, or the verdant plain,
Or forms its leafy mansion in the shades,
All, all thy universal power pervades,
Each panting bosom melts to soft desires,
And with the love of propagation fires.
And since thy sovereign influence guides the reins
Of nature, and the universe sustains;
Since nought without thee bursts the bonds of night,
To hail the happy realms of heavenly light;
Since love, and joy, and harmony are thine,
Guide me, O goddess, by thy power divine,
And to my rising lays thy succour bring,
While I the universe attempt to sing.
O may my verse deserved applause obtain
Of him, for whom I try the daring strain,
My Memmius, him, whom thou profusely kind
Adorn'st with every excellence refined.
And that immortal charms my song may grace,
Let war, with all its cruel labours, cease;
O hush the dismal din of arms once more,
And calm the jarring world from shore to shore.
By thee alone the race of man foregoes
The rage of blood, and sinks in soft repose:

For mighty Mars, the dreadful god of arms,
Who wakes or stills the battle's dire alarms,
In love's strong fetters by thy charms is bound,
And languishes with an eternal wound.
Oft from his bloody toil the god retires
To quench in thy embrace his fierce desires.
Soft on thy heaving bosom he reclines,
And round thy yielding neck transported twines;
There fix'd in ecstacy intense surveys
Thy kindling beauties with insatiate gaze,
Grows to thy balmy mouth, and ardent sips
Celestial sweets from thy ambrosial lips.
O while the god with fiercest raptures blest
Lies all dissolving on thy sacred breast,
O breathe thy melting whispers to his ear,
And bid him still the loud alarms of war.
In these tumultuous days the Muse in vain,
Her steady tenour lost, pursues the strain,
And Memmius's generous soul disdains to taste
The calm delights of philosophic rest;
Paternal fires his beating breast inflame,
To rescue Rome, and vindicate her name

HORACE, BOOK II. ODE X.

Rectius vives, Licini ——

Wouldst thou through life securely glide,
Nor boundless o'er the ocean ride;
Nor ply too near th' insidious shore,
Scared at the tempest's threat'ning roar.
The man who follows Wisdom's voice,
And makes the golden mean his choice,
Nor plunged in antique gloomy cells
'Midst hoary desolation dwells;

Nor to allure the envious eye
Rears his proud palace to the sky.
The pine, that all the grove transcends,
With every blast the tempest rends;
Totters the tower with thund'rous sound,
And spreads a mighty ruin round;
Jove's bolt with desolating blow
Strikes the ethereal mountain's brow.
The man, whose steadfast soul can bear
Fortune indulgent or severe,
Hopes when she frowns, and when she smiles
With cautious fear eludes her wiles.
Jove with rude winter wastes the plain,
Jove decks the rosy spring again.
Life's former ills are overpast,
Nor will the present always last.
Now Phœbus wings his shafts, and now
He lays aside th' unbended bow,
Strikes into life the trembling string,
And wakes the silent Muse to sing.
With unabating courage, brave
Adversity's tumultuous wave;
When too propitious breezes rise,
And the light vessel swiftly flies,
With timid caution catch the gale,
And shorten the distended sail.

HORACE, BOOK III. ODE XIII.

O Fons Blandusiæ ——

BLANDUSIA! more than crystal clear!
Whose soothing murmurs charm the ear!
Whose margin soft with flowrets crown'd
Invites the festive band around,

Their careless limbs diffused supine,
To quaff the soul-enlivening wine.
  To thee a tender kid I vow,
That aims for fight his budding brow;
In thought, the wrathful combat prove
Or wantons with his little loves:
But vain are all his purposed schemes,
Delusive all his flattering dreams;
To-morrow shall his fervent blood
Stain the pure silver of thy flood.
  When fiery Sirius blasts the plain,
Untouch'd thy gelid streams remain.
To thee, the fainting flocks repair,
To taste thy cool reviving air;
To thee, the ox with toil opprest,
And lays his languid limbs to rest.
  As springs of old renown'd, thy name,
Blest fountain! I devote to fame;
Thus while I sing in deathless lays,
The verdant holm, whose waving sprays,
Thy sweet retirement to defend,
High o'er the moss-grown rock impend,
Whence prattling in loquacious play
Thy sprightly waters leap away.

THE PASTORALS OF VIRGIL.

Non ita certandi cupidus, quam propter amorem
Quod te imitari aveo — *Lucret.* lib. iii.

PASTORAL I.*

MELIBŒUS, TITYRUS.

Melibœus.

Where the broad beech an ample shade displays,
Your slender reed resounds the sylvan lays,
O happy Tityrus! while we, forlorn,
Driven from our lands, to distant climes are borne,
Stretch'd careless in the peaceful shade you sing,
And all the groves with Amaryllis ring.

* It has been observed by some critics, who have treated of pastoral poetry, that, in every poem of this kind, it is proper that the scene or landscape, connected with the little plot or fable on which the poem is founded, be delineated with at least as much accuracy as is sufficient to render the description particular and picturesque. How far Virgil has thought fit to attend to such a rule may appear from the remarks which the translator has subjoined to every pastoral.

The scene of the first pastoral is pictured out with great accuracy. The shepherds Melibœus and Tityrus are represented as conversing together beneath a spreading beech-tree. Flocks and herds are feeding hard by. At a little distance we behold, on the one hand a great rock, and on the other a fence of flowering willows. The prospect as it widens is diversified with groves, and streams, and some tall trees, particularly elms. Beyond all these appear marshy grounds, and rocky hills. The ragged and drooping flock of the unfortunate shepherd particularly the she-goat which he leads along, are no inconsiderable figures in this picture.—The time is the evening of a summer-day, a little before sunset. See of the original, v. 1. 5. 9. 52. 54. 57. 59. 81, &c.

This pastoral is said to have been written on the following occasion. Augustus, in order to reward the services of his veterans, by means of whom he had established himself in the Roman empire, distributed among them the lands that lay contiguous to Mantua and Cremona. To make way for these intruders, the rightful owners, of whom Virgil was one, were turned out. But our poet, by the intercession of Mecænus, was reinstated in his possessions. Melibœus here personates one of the unhappy exiles, and Virgil is represented under the character of Tityrus.

Tityrus.

This peace to a propitious god I owe;
None else, my friend, such blessings could bestow.
Him will I celebrate with rights divine,
And frequent lambs shall stain his sacred shrine.
By him, these feeding herds in safety stray;
By him, in peace I pipe the rural lay.

Melibœus.

I envy not, but wonder at your fate,
That no alarms invade this blest retreat;
While neighbouring fields the voice of woe resound,
And desolation rages all around.
Worn with fatigue I slowly onward bend,
And scarce my feeble fainting goats attend.
My hand this sickly dam can hardly bear,
Whose young new-yean'd (ah once an hopeful pair!)
Amid the tangling hazels as they lay,
On the sharp flint were left to pine away.
These ills I had foreseen, but that my mind
To all portents and prodigies was blind.
Oft have the blasted oaks foretold my woe:
And often has the inauspicious crow,
Perch'd on the wither'd holm, with fateful cries
Scream'd in my ear her dismal prophecies.
But say, O Tityrus, what god bestows
This blissful life of undisturb'd repose?

Tityrus.

Imperial Rome, while yet to me unknown,
I vainly liken'd to our country-town,
Our little Mantua, at which is sold
The yearly offspring of our fruitful fold:
As in the whelp the father's shape appears,
And as the kid its mother's semblance bears,
Thus greater things my inexperienced mind
Rated by others of inferior kind.

But she, 'midst other cities, rears her head
High, as the cypress overtops the reed.

Melibœus.

And why to visit Rome was you inclin'd?

Tityrus.

'Twas there I hoped my liberty to find.
And there my liberty I found at last,
Though long with listless indolence opprest;
Yet not till Time had silver'd o'er my hairs,
And I had told a tedious length of years;
Nor till the gentle Amaryllis charm'd,*
And Galatea's love no longer warm'd.
For (to my friend I will confess the whole)
While Galatea captive held my soul,
Languid and lifeless all I dragg'd the chain,
Neglected liberty, neglected gain,
Though from my fold the frequent victim bled,
Though my fat cheese th' ungrateful city fed,
For this I ne'er perceived my wealth increase;
I lavish'd all her haughty heart to please.

Melibœus.

Why Amaryllis pined, and pass'd away
In lonely shades the melancholy day;
Why to the gods she breathed incessant vows;
For whom her mellow apples press'd the boughs
So late, I wonder'd—Tityrus was gone,
And she (ah luckless maid!) was left alone.
Your absence every warbling fountain mourn'd,
And woods and wilds the wailing strains return'd.

Tityrus.

What could I do? to break th' enslaving chain
All other efforts had (alas!) been vain;

* The refinements of Taubmannus, De La Cerda, and others, who will have Amaryllis to signify Rome, and Galatea to signify Mantua, have perplexed this passage not a little: if the literal meaning be admitted, the whole becomes obvious and natural.

Nor durst my hopes presume, but there, to find
The gods so condescending and so kind.
'Twas there these eyes the Heaven born youth*
beheld,
To whom our altars monthly incense yield:
My suit he even prevented, while he spoke,
'Manure your ancient farm, and feed your former
flock.'

Melibœus.

Happy old man! then shall your lands remain,
Extent sufficient for th' industrious swain!
Though bleak and bare yon ridgy rocks arise,
And lost in lakes the neighbouring pasture lies.
Your herds on wonted grounds shall safely range,
And never feel the dire effects of change.
No foreign flock shall spread infecting bane
To hurt your pregnant dams, thrice happy swain!
You by known streams and sacred fountains laid
Shall taste the coolness of the fragrant shade,
Beneath yon fence, where willow-boughs unite,
And to their flowers the swarming bees invite,
Oft shall the lulling hum persuade to rest,
And balmy slumbers steal into your breast;
While warbled from this rock the pruner's lay
In deep repose dissolves your soul away;
High on yon elm the turtle wails alone,
And your loved ring doves breathe a hoarser moan.

Tityrus.

The nimble harts shall graze in empty air,
And seas retreating leave their fishes bare,
The German dwell where rapid Tigris flows,
The Parthian, banish'd by invading foes,
Shall drink the Gallic Arar, from my breast
Ere his majestic image be effaced.

* Augustus Cæsar.

Melibœus.

But we must travel o'er a .ength of lands,
O'er Scythian snows, or Afric's burning sands;
Some wander where remote Oäxes laves
The Cretan meadows with his rapid waves;
In Britain some, from every comfort torn,
From all the world removed, are doom'd to mourn.
When long long years have tedious roll'd away,
Ah! shall I yet at last, at last, survey
My dear paternal lands, and dear abode,
Where once I reign'd in walls of humble sod!
These lands, these harvests must the soldier share!
For rude barbarians lavish we our care!
How are our fields become the spoil of wars!
How are we ruin'd by intestine jars!
Now, Melibœus, now ingraff the pear,
Now teach the vine its tender sprays to rear!—
Go then, my goats!—go, once a happy store—
Once happy!—happy now (alas!) no more!
No more shall I, beneath the bowery shade
In rural quiet indolently laid,
Behold you from afar the cliffs ascend,
And from the shrubby precipice depend;
No more to music wake my melting flute,
While on the thyme you feed, and willow's whole-
some shoot.

Tityrus.

This night at least with me you may repose
On the green foliage, and forget our woes.
Apples and nuts mature our boughs afford,
And curdled milk in plenty crowns my board,
Now from yon hamlets clouds of smoke arise,
And slowly roll along the evening skies;
And see, projected from the mountain's brow,
A lengthen'd shade obscures the plain below.

N

II.*

ALEXIS.

YOUNG Corydon for fair Alexis pined,
But hope ne'er gladden'd his desponding mind;
Nor vows nor tears the scornful boy could move,
Distinguish'd by his wealthier master's love.
Oft to the beech's deep-embow'ring shade
Pensive and sad this hapless shepherd stray'd;
There told in artless verse his tender pain
To echoing hills and groves, but all in vain.
In vain the flute's complaining lays I try!
And am I doom'd, unpitying boy, to die;
Now to faint flocks the grove a shade supplies,
And in the thorny brake the lizard lies;
Now Thestylis with herbs of savory taste
Prepares the weary harvest-man's repast:
And all is still, save where the buzzing sound
Of chirping grasshoppers is heard around:
While I, exposed to all the rage of heat,
Wander the wilds in search of thy retreat.
Was it not easier to support the pain
I felt from Amaryllis' fierce disdain?

* The chief excellency of this poem consists in its delicacy and simplicity. Corydon addresses his favourite in such a purity of sentiment as one would think might effectually discountenance the prepossessions which generally prevail against the subject of this eclogue. The nature of his affection may easily be ascertained from his ideas of the happiness which he hopes to enjoy in the company of his beloved Alexis.

O tantum libeat——
O deign at last amid these lonely fields, &c.

It appears to have been no other than that friendship, which was encouraged by the wisest legislators of ancient Greece, as a noble incentive to virtue, and recommended by the example even of Agesilaus, Pericles, and Socrates: an affection wholly distinct from the infamous attachments that prevailed among the licentious. The reader will find a full and satisfying account of this generous passion in Dr. Potter's Antiquities of Greece, Book iv. chap. 9. Mons Bayle in his Dictionary, at the article Virgile, has at great length vindicated our poet from the charge of immorality which the critics have grounded upon this pastoral.

The scene of this pastoral is a grove interspersed with beech-trees; the season, harvest.

Easier Menalcas' cold neglect to bear,
Black though he was, though thou art blooming fair?
Yet be relenting, nor too much presume,
O beauteous boy, on thy celestial bloom;
The sable violet* yields a precious die,
While useless on the field the withering lilies lie.
Ah, cruel boy! my love is all in vain,
No thoughts of thine regard thy wretched swain.
How rich my flock thou carest not to know,
Nor how my pails with generous milk o'erflow.
With bleat of thousand lambs my hills resound,
And all the year my milky stores abound.
Not Amphion's lays were sweeter than my song,
Those lays that led the listening herds along;
And if the face be true I lately view'd,
Where calm and clear th' uncurling ocean stood,
I lack not beauty, nor could'st thou deny,
That even with Daphnis I might dare to vie.
O deign at last, amid these lonely fields,
To taste the pleasures which the country yields,
With me to dwell in cottages resign'd,
To roam the woods, to shoot the bounding hind;
With me the weanling kids from home to guide
To the green mallows on the mountain side;
With me in echoing groves the song to raise,
And emulate ev'n Pan's celestial lays.
Pan taught the jointed reed its tuneful strain,
Pan guards the tender flock, and shepherd swain.
Nor grudge, Alexis, that the rural pipe
So oft hath stain'd the roses of thy lip:
How did Amyntas strive thy skill to gain!
How grieve at last to find his labour vain!
Of seven unequal reeds a pipe I have,
The precious gift which good Damœtas gave;

* Vaccinium (here translated violet) yielded a purple colour used in dying the garments of slaves, according to Plin. l. xvi. c. 28.

'Take this,' the dying shepherd said, 'for none
Inherits all my skill but thou alone.'
He said; Amyntas murmurs at my praise,
And with an envious eye the gift surveys.
Besides, as presents for my soul's delight
Two beauteous kids I keep, bestreak'd with white,
Nourish'd with care, nor purchased without pain;
An ewe's full udder twice a day they drain,
These to obtain oft Thestylis hath tried
Each winning art, while I her suit denied:
But I at last shall yield what she requests,
Since thy relentless pride my gifts detests.
Come, beauteous boy, and bless my rural bowers,
For thee the nymphs collect the choicest flowers:
Fair Naïs culls amid the blooming dale
The drooping poppy, and the violet pale,
To marygolds the hyacinth applies,
Shading the glossy with the tawny dies:
Narcissus' flower with daffodil entwined,
And Cassia's breathing sweets to these are join'd,
With every bloom that paints the vernal grove,
And all to form a garland for my love.
Myself with sweetest fruits will crown thy feast;
The luscious peach shall gratify thy taste.
And chesnut brown (once high in my regard,
For Amaryllis this to all preferr'd;
But if the blushing plum thy choice thou make,
The plum shall more be valued for thy sake).
The myrtle wreath'd with laurel shall exhale
A blended fragrance to delight thy smell.
Ah, Corydon! thou rustic, simple swain!
Thyself, thy prayers, thy offers all are vain.
How few, compared with rich Iolas' store,
Thy boasted gifts, and all thy wealth how poor,
Wretch that I am! while thus I pine forlorn,
And all the live-long day inactive mourn,

The boars have laid my silver fountains waste,
My flowers are fading in the southern blast,—
Fly'st thou, ah foolish boy, the lonesome grove?
Yet gods for this have left the realm above.
Paris with scorn the pomp of Troy survey'd,
And sought th' Idæan bowers and peaceful shade.
In her proud palaces let Pallas shine;
The lowly woods and rural life be mine.
The lioness all dreadful in her course
Pursues the wolf, and he with headlong force
Flies at the wanton goat, that loves to climb
The cliff's steep side, and crop the flowering thyme,
Thee Corydon pursues, O beauteous boy:
Thus each is drawn along by some peculiar joy.
  Now evening soft comes on; and homeward now
From field the weary oxen bear the plough.
The setting sun now beams more mildly bright,
The shadows lengthening with the level light,
While with love's flame my restless bosom glows,
For love no interval of ease allows.
Ah, Corydon! to weak complaints a prey!
What madness thus to waste the fleeting day!
Be roused at length; thy half-pruned vines demand
The needful culture of thy curbing hand.
Haste, lingering swain, the flexile willows weave,
And with thy wonted care thy wants relieve.
Forget Alexis' unrelenting scorn,
Another love thy passion will return.

III.

MENALCAS, DAMŒTAS, PALÆMON.*

Menalcas.

To whom belongs this flock, Damœtas, pray:
To Meliboeus?

Damœtas.

No: the other day
The shepherd Ægon gave it me to keep.

Menalcas.

Ah still neglected, still unhappy sheep!†
He plies Neæra with assiduous love,
And fears lest she my happier flame approve;
Meanwhile this hireling wretch (disgrace to swains!)
Defrauds his master, and purloins his gains,
Milks twice an hour, and drains the famish'd dams,
Whose empty dugs in vain attract the lambs.

Damœtas.

Forbear, on men such language to bestow.
Thee, stain of manhood! thee, full well I know.
I know, with whom—and where—‡ (their grove defiled
The nymphs revenged not, but indulgent smiled)
And how the goats beheld, then browsing near,
The shameful sight with a lascivious leer.

* The contending shepherds, Menalcas and Damœtas, together with their umpire Palæmon, are seated on the grass, not far from a row of beech-trees. Flocks are seen feeding hard by. The time of the day seems to be noon, the season between spring and summer.

† Throughout the whole of this altercation, notwithstanding the untoward subject, the reader will find in the original such a happy union of simplicity and force of expression, and harmony of verse, as it is vain to look for in an English translation.

‡ The abruptness and obscurity of the original is here imitated.

Menalcas.

No doubt, when Mycon's tender trees I broke,
And gash'd his young vines with a blunted hook.

Damœtas.

Or when, conceal'd behind this ancient row
Of beech, you broke young Daphnis' shafts and bow,
With sharpest pangs of rancorous anguish stung
To see the gift conferr'd on one so young:
And had you not thus wreak'd your sordid spite,
Of very envy you had died outright.

Menalcas.

Gods! what may masters dare, when such a pitch
Of impudence their thievish hirelings reach:
Did I not, wretch (deny it if you dare),
Did I not see you Damon's goat ensnare?
Lycisca bark'd; then I the felon spied,
And 'Whither slinks yon sneaking thief?' I cried.
The thief discover'd straight his prey forsook,
And sculk'd amid the sedges of the brook.

Damœtas.

That goat my pipe from Damon fairly gain'd,
A match was set, and I the prize obtain'd.
He own'd it due to my superior skill,
And yet refused his bargain to fulfil.

Menalcas.

By your superior skill the goat was won!
Have you a jointed pipe, indecent clown!
Whose whizzing straws with hars' est discord jarr'd,
As in the streets your wretched rhymes you marr'd.

Damœtas.

Boasts are but vain. I'm ready, when you will,
To make a solemn trial of our skill.

I stake this heifer, no ignoble prize;
Two calves from her full udder she supplies,
And twice a day her milk the pail o'erflows;
What pledge of equal worth will you expose?

Menalcas.

Aught from the flock I dare not risk: I fear
A cruel step dame, and a sire severe,
Who of their store so strict a reckoning keep,
That twice a day they count the kids and sheep.
But since you purpose to be mad to day,
Two beechen cups I scruple not to lay
(Whose far superior worth yourself will own),
The labour'd work of famed Alcimedon.
Raised round the brims by the engraver's care
The flaunting vine unfolds its foliage fair;
Entwined the ivy's tendrils seem to grow,
Half-hid in leaves its mimic berries glow;
Two figures rise below, of curious frame,
Conon, and—what's that other sage's name,
Who with his rod described the world's vast round,
Taught when to reap, and when to till the ground?
At home I have reserved them unprofaned,
No lip has e'er their glossy polish stain'd.

Damœtas.

Two cups for me that skilful artist made;
Their handles with acanthus are array'd;
Orpheus is in the midst, whose magic song
Leads in tumultuous dance the lofty groves along.
At home I have reserved them unprofaned,
No lip has e'er their glossy polish stain'd.
But my pledged heifer if aright you prize,
The cups so much extoll'd you will despise.

Menalcas.

These arts, proud boaster, all are lost on me;
To any terms I readily agree.

You shall not boast your victory to-day,
Let him be judge who passes first this way:
And see the good Palæmon! trust me, swain,
You'll be more cautious how you brag again.

Damœtas.

Delays I brook not; if you dare, proceed;
At singing no antagonist I dread.
Palæmon, listen to th' important songs,
To such debates attention strict belongs.

Palæmon.

Sing then. A couch the flowery herbage yields:
Now blossom all the trees, and all the fields;
And all the woods their pomp of foliage wear,
And Nature's fairest robe adorns the blooming year.
Damœtas first th' alternate lay shall raise:
Th' inspiring Muses love alternate lays.

Damœtas.

Jove first I sing; ye Muses, aid my lay;
All Nature owns his energy and sway;
The Earth and Heavens his sovereign bounty share,
And to my verses he vouchsafes his care.

Menalcas.

With great Apollo I begin the strain,
For I am great Apollo's favourite swain;
For him the purple hyacinth I wear,
And sacred bay to Phœbus ever dear.

Damœtas.

The sprightly Galatea at my head
An apple flung, and to the willows fled;
But as along the level lawn she flew,
The wanton wish'd not to escape my view.

Menalcas.

I languish'd long for fair Amyntas' charms,
But now he comes unbidden to my arms,

And with my dogs is so familiar grown,
That my own Delia is no better known.

Damœtas.

I lately mark'd where, 'midst the verdant shade,
Two parent-doves had built their leafy bed;
I from the nest the young will shortly take,
And to my love a handsome present make.

Menalcas.

Ten ruddy wildings, from a lofty bough,
That through the green leaves beam'd with yellow glow,
I brought away, and to Amyntas bore;
To-morrow I shall send as many more.

Damœtas.

Ah the keen raptures! when my yielding fair
Breathed her kind whispers to my ravish'd ear!
Waft, gentle gales, her accents to the skies,
That gods themselves may hear with sweet surprise

Menalcas.

What, though I am not wretched by your scorn.
Say, beauteous boy, say can I cease to mourn,
If, while I hold the nets, the boar you face,
And rashly brave the dangers of the chase?

Damœtas.

Send Phyllis home, Iolas, for to-day
I celebrate my birth, and all is gay;
When for my crop the victim I prepare,
Iolas in our festival may share.

Menalcas.

Phyllis I love; she more than all can charm,
And mutual fires her gentle bosom warm:
Tears, when I leave her, bathe her beauteous eyes;
'A long, a long adieu, my love" she cries.

Damœtas.

The wolf is dreadful to the woolly train,
Fatal to harvests is the crushing rain,
To the green woods the winds destructive prove,
To me the rage of mine offended love.

Menalcas.

The willow's grateful to the pregnant ewes,
Showers to the corn, to kids the mountain-brows;
More grateful far to me my lovely boy,—
In sweet Amyntas centres all my joy.

Damœtas.

Even Pollio deigns to hear my rural lays;
And cheers the bashful Muse with generous praise:
Ye sacred Nine, for your great patron feed
A beauteous heifer of the noblest breed.

Menalcas.

Pollio the art of heavenly song adorns;
Then let a bull be bred with butting horns,
And ample front, that bellowing, spurns the ground,
Tears up the turf, and throws the sands around.

Damœtas.

Him whom my Pollio loves may naught annoy;
May he like Pollio every wish enjoy;
O may his happy lands with honey flow,
And on his thorns Assyrian roses blow!

Menalcas.

Who hates not foolish Bavius, let him love
Thee, Mævius, and thy tasteless rhymes approve!
Nor needs it thy admirer's reason shock
To milk the he goats, and the foxes yoke.

Damœtas.

Ye boys, on garlands who employ your care,
And pull the creeping strawberries, beware.

Fly for your lives, and leave that fatal place,
A deadly snake lies lurking in the grass.

Menalcas.

Forbear, my flocks, and warily proceed,
Nor on that faithless bank securely tread;
The heedless ram late plunged amid the pool,
And in the sun now dries his reeking wool.

Damœtas.

Ho, Tityrus! lead back the browsing flock,
And let them feed at distance from the brook;
At bathing time I to the shade will bring
My goats, and wash them in the cooling spring.

Menalcas.

Haste, from the sultry lawn the flocks remove
To the cool shelter of the shady grove:
When burning noon the curdling udder dries,
Th' ungrateful teats in vain the shepherd plies.

Damœtas.

How lean my bull in yonder mead appears,
Though the fat soil the richest pasture bears!
Ah Love! thou reign'st supreme in every heart,
Both flocks and shepherds languish with thy dart.

Menalcas.

Love has not injured my consumptive flocks,
Yet bare their bones, and faded are their looks:
What envious eye hath squinted on my dams,
And sent its poison to my tender lambs?

Damœtas.

Say in what distant land the eye descries
But three short ells of all th' expanded skies?
Tell this, and great Apollo be your name?
Your skill is equal, equal be your fame.

Menalcas.

Say in what soil a wondrous flower is born,
Whose leaves the sacred name of kings adorn?
Tell this, and take my Phyllis to your arms,
And reign th' unrivall'd sovereign of her charms.

Palæmon.

'Tis not for me these high disputes to end;
Each to the heifer justly may pretend.
Such be their fortune, who so well can sing
From love what painful joys, what pleasing torments spring.
Now, boys, obstruct the course of yonder rill;
The meadows have already drunk their fill.

PASTORAL IV.*

Pollio.

SICILIAN Muse, sublimer strains inspire,
And warm my bosom with diviner fire!
All take not pleasure in the rural scene,
In lowly tamarisks, and forests green.
If sylvan themes we sing, then let our lays
Deserve a consul's ear, a consul's praise.

* In this fourth pastoral no particular landscape is delineated. The whole is a prophetic song of triumph. But as almost all the images and allusions are of the rural kind, it is no less a true bucolic than the others; if we admit the definition of a pastoral, given us by an author of the first rank,† who calls it 'A poem in which any action or passion is represented by its effects upon country life.'

It is of little importance to inquire on what occasion this poem was written. The spirit of prophetic enthusiasm that breathes through it, and the resemblance it bears in many places to the oriental manner, makes it not improbable that our poet composed it partly from some pieces of ancient prophecy that might have fallen into his hands, and that he afterwards inscribed it to his friend and patron Pollio, on occasion of the birth of his son Salonnius.

† The author of the Rambler.

The age comes on, that future age of gold
In Cuma's mystic prophecies foretold.
The years begin their mighty course again,
The Virgin now returns, and the Saturnian reign.
Now from the lofty mansions of the sky
To Earth descends an heaven-born progeny.
Thy Phœbus reigns, Lucina, lend thine aid,
Nor be his birth, his glorious birth, delay'd!
An iron race shall then no longer rage,
But all the world regain the golden age.
This child, the joy of nations, shall be born,
Thy consulship, O Pollio, to adorn:
Thy consulship these happy times shall prove,
And see the mighty months begin to move;
Then all our former guilt shall be forgiven,
And man shall dread no more th' avenging doom of Heav'n.
The son with heroes and with gods shall shine,
And lead, enroll'd with them, the life divine.
He o'er the peaceful nations shall preside,
And his sire's virtues shall his sceptre guide.
To thee, auspicious babe, th' unbidden earth
Shall bring the earliest of her flowery birth:
Acanthus soft in smiling beauty gay,
The blossom'd bean, and ivy's flaunting spray.
Th' untended goats shall to their homes repair,
And to the milker's hand the loaded udder bear.
The mighty lion shall no more be fear'd,
But graze innoxious with the friendly herd.
Sprung from thy cradle fragrant flowers shall spr
And, fanning bland, shall wave around thy head.
Then shall the serpent die, with all his race:
No deadly herb the happy soil disgrace:
Assyrian balm on every bush shall bloom,
And breathe in every gale its rich perfume.
But when thy father's deeds thy youth shall fire,
And to great actions all thy soul inspire,

When thou shalt read of heroes and of kings,
And mark the glory that from virtue springs;
Then boundless o'er the far-extended plain
Shall wave luxuriant crops of golden grain,
With purple grapes the loaded thorn shall bend,
And streaming honey from the oak descend.
Nor yet old fraud shall wholly be effaced;
Navies for wealth shall roam the watery waste;
Proud cities fenced with towery walls appear,
And cruel shares shall earth's soft bosom tear:
Another Typhys o'er the swelling tide
With steady skill the bounding ship shall guide;
Another Argo with the flower of Greece
From Colchos' shore shall waft the golden fleece;
Again the world shall hear war's loud alarms,
And great Achilles shine again in arms.
When riper years thy strengthen'd nerves shall brace,
And o'er thy limbs diffuse a manly grace,
The mariner no more shall plough the deep,
Nor load with foreign wares the trading ship;
Each country shall abound in every store,
Nor need the products of another shore.
Henceforth no plough shall cleave the fertile ground,
No pruning-hook the tender vine shall wound;
The husbandman, with toil no longer broke,
Shall loose his ox for ever from the yoke.
No more the wool a foreign die shall feign,
But purple flocks shall graze the flowery plain;
Glittering in native gold the ram shall tread,
And scarlet lambs shall wanton on the mead.
In concord join'd with fate's unalter'd law
The Destinies these happy times foresaw,
They bade the sacred spindle swiftly run,
And hasten the auspicious ages on.
O dear to all thy kindred gods above!
O thou, the offspring of eternal Jove!

Receive thy dignities, begin thy reign,
And o'er the world extend thy wide domain.
See nature's mighty frame exulting round,
Ocean, and earth, and heaven's immense profound!
See nations yet unborn with joy behold
Thy glad approach, and hail the age of gold!
O would th' immortals lend a length of days,
And give a soul sublime to sound thy praise;
Would Heaven this breast, this labouring breast inflame
With ardour equal to the mighty theme;
Not Orpheus with diviner transports glow'd,
When all her fire his mother-muse bestow'd;
Nor loftier numbers flow'd from Linus' tongue,
Although his sire Apollo gave the song;
Even Pan, in presence of Arcadian swains,
Would vainly strive to emulate my strains.
Repay a parent's care, O beauteous boy,
And greet thy mother with a smile of joy;
For thee, to loathing languors all resign'd,
Ten slow-revolving months thy mother pined,
If cruel fate thy parent's bliss denies,*
If no fond joy sits smiling in thine eyes,
No nymph of heavenly birth shall crown thy love,
Nor shalt thou share the immortal feast above.

* This passage has perplexed all the critics. Out of a number of significations that have been offered, the translator has pitched upon one, which he thinks the most agreeable to the scope of the poem and most consistent with the language of the original. The reader who wants more particulars on this head, may consult Servius, De La Cerda, or Ruæus.

V.*

MENALCAS, MOPSUS.

Menalcas.

SINCE you with skill can touch the tuneful reed,
Since few my verses or my voice exceed;
In this refreshing shade shall we recline,
Where hazels with the lofty elms combine?

Mopsus.

Your riper age a due respect requires,
'Tis mine to yield to what my friend desires;
Whether you choose the zephyr's fanning breeze,
That shakes the wavering shadows of the trees;
Or the deep-shaded grotto's cool retreat:—
And see yon cave screen'd from the scorching heat,
Where the wild vine its curling tendrils weaves,
Whose grapes glow ruddy through the quivering leaves.

Menalcas.

Of all the swains that to our hills belong,
Amyntas only vies with you in song.

Mopsus.

What, though with me that haughty shepherd vie,
Who proudly dares Apollo's self defy?

Menalcas.

Begin; let Alcon's praise inspire your strains,†
Or Codrus' death, or Phyllis' amorous pains;
Begin whatever theme your Muse prefer.
To feed the kids be, Tityrus, thy care.

* Here we discover Menalcas and Mopsus seated in an arbour formed by the interwoven twigs of a wild vine. A grove of hazels and elms surrounds this arbour. The season seems to be summer. The time of the day is not specified.

† From this passage it is evident that Virgil thought pastoral poetry capable of a much greater variety in its subjects than some modern critics will allow.

Mopsus.

I rather will repeat that mournful song,
Which late I carved the verdant beech along;
(I carved and trill'd by turns the labour'd lay)
And let Amyntas match me if he may.

Menalcas.

As slender willows where the olive grows,
Or sordid shrubs when near the scarlet rose,
Such (if the judgment I have form'd be true)
Such is Amyntas when compared with you.

Mopsus.

No more, Menalcas; we delay too long,
The grot's dim shade invites my promised song.
When Daphnis fell by fate's remorseless blow*
The weeping nymphs pour'd wild the plaint of woe;
Witness, O hazel-grove, and winding stream,
For all your echoes caught the mournful theme.
In agony of grief his mother prest
The clay-cold carcase to her throbbing breast,
Frantic with anguish wail'd his hapless fate,
Raved at the stars, and Heaven's relentless hate.
'Twas then the swains in deep despair forsook
Their pining flocks, nor led them to the brook;
The pining flocks for him their pastures slight,
Nor grassy plains nor cooling streams invite.
The doleful tidings reach'd the Libyan shores,
And lions mourn'd in deep repeated roars.
His cruel doom the woodlands wild bewail,
And plaintive hills repeat the melancholy tale.

* It is the most general and most probable conjecture, that Julius Cæsar is the Daphnis whose death and deification are here celebrated. Some however are of opinion, that by Daphnis is meant a real shepherd of Sicily of that name, who is said to have invented bucolic poetry, and in honour of whom the Sicilians performed yearly sacrifices.

'Twas he, who first Armenia's tigers broke,
And tamed their stubborn natures to the yoke;
He first with ivy wrapt the thyrsus round,
And made the hills with Bacchus' rites resound.*
As vines adorn the trees which they entwine,
As purple clusters beautify the vine,
As bulls the herd, as corns the fertile plains,
The godlike Daphnis dignified the swains.
When Daphnis from our eager hopes was torn,
Phœbus and Pales left the plains to mourn.
Now weeds and wretched tares the crops subdue,
Where store of generous wheat but lately grew.
Narcissus' lovely flower no more is seen,
No more the velvet violet decks the green;
Thistles for these the blasted meadow yields,
And thorns and frizzled burs deform the fields.
Swains, shade the springs, and let the ground be drest
With verdant leaves; 'twas Daphnis' last request.
Erect a tomb in honour to his name,
Mark'd with this verse to celebrate his fame:
'The swains with Daphnis' name this tomb adorn,
Whose high renown above the skies is borne;
Fair was his flock, he fairest on the plain,
The pride, the glory of the sylvan reign.'

Menalcas.

Sweeter, O bard divine, thy numbers seem
Than to the scorched swain the cooling stream,
Or soft on fragrant flow'rets to recline,
And the tired limbs to balmy sleep resign.
Blest youth! whose voice and pipe demand the praise
Due but to thine, and to thy master's lays.
I in return the darling theme will choose,
And Daphnis' praises shall inspire my Muse:

* This can be applied only to Julius Cæsar; for it was he who introduced at Rome the celebration of the Bacchanalian revels.—*Servius.*

He in my song shall high as Heaven ascend,
High as the Heavens, for Daphnis was my friend.

Mopsus.

His virtues sure our noblest numbers claim;
Nought can delight me more than such a theme,
Which in your song new dignity obtains;
Oft has our Stimichon extoll'd the strains.

Menalcas.

Now Daphnis shines, among the gods a god,
Struck with the splendours of his new abode.
Beneath his footstool far remote appear
The clouds slow sailing, and the starry sphere.
Hence lawns and groves with gladsome raptures ring,
The swains, the nymphs, and Pan in concert sing.
The wolves to murder are no more inclined,
No guileful nets ensnare the wandering hind,
Deceit and violence and rapine cease,
Fo Daphnis loves the gentle arts of peace.
From savage mountains shouts of transport rise
Borne in triumphant echoes to the skies;
The rocks and shrubs emit melodious sounds,
Through nature's vast extent the god, the god rebounds.
Be gracious still, still present to our prayer;
Four altars, lo! we build with pious care,
Two for the inspiring god of song divine,
And two, propitious Daphnis, shall be thine.
Two bowls white-foaming with their milky store,
Of generous oil two brimming goblets more,
Each year we shall present before thy shrine,
And cheer the feast with liberal draughts of wine;
Before the fire when winter-storms invade,
In summer's heat beneath the breezy shade:
The hallow'd bowls with wines of Chios crown'd,
Shall pour their sparkling nectar to the ground.

Damœtas shall with Lyctian* Ægon play,
And celebrate with festive strains the day.
Alphesibœus to the sprightly song
Shall like the dancing Satyrs trip along.
These rites shall still be paid, so justly due,
Both when the nymphs receive our annual vow,
And when with solemn songs, and victims crown'd,
Our lands in long procession we surround,
While fishes love the streams and briny deep,
And savage boars the mountain's rocky steep,
While grasshoppers their dewy food delights,
While balmy thyme the busy bee invites;
So long shall last thine honours and thy fame,
So long the shepherds shall resound thy name.
Such rites to thee shall husbandmen ordain,
As Ceres and the god of wine obtain.
Thou to our prayers propitiously inclined
Thy grateful suppliants to their vows shalt bind.

Mopsus.

What boon, dear shepherd, can your song requite?
For nought in nature yields so sweet delight.
Not the soft sighing of the southern gale,
That faintly breathes along the flowery vale;
Nor, when light breezes curl the liquid plain,
To tread the margin of the murmuring main;
Nor melody of streams, that roll away
Through rocky dales, delights me as your lay.

Menalcas.

No mean reward, my friend, your verses claim;
Take then this flute that breathed the plaintive theme
Of Corydon;† when proud Damœtas‡ tried
To match my skill, it dash'd his hasty pride.

* Lyctium was a city of Crete.
† See Pastoral second. ‡ See Pastoral third.

Mopsus.

And let this sheep-crook by my friend be worn,
Which brazen studs in beamy rows adorn;
This fair Antigenes oft begg'd to gain,
But all his beauty, all his prayers were vain.

PASTORAL VI.*

Silenus.

My sportive Muse first sung Sicilian strains,
Nor blush'd to dwell in woods and lowly plains.
To sing of kings and wars when I aspire,
Apollo checks my vainly-rising fire.
'To swains the flock and sylvan pipe belong,
Then choose some humbler theme, nor dare heroic song.'
The voice divine, O Varus, I obey,
And to my reed shall chant a rural lay;
Since others long thy praises to rehearse,
And sing thy battles in immortal verse.
Yet if these songs, which Phœbus bids me write,
Hereafter to the swains shall yield delight,
Of thee the trees and humble shrubs shall sing,
And all the vocal grove with Varus ring.
The song inscribed to Varus' sacred name
To Phœbus' favour has the justest claim.
Come then, my Muse, a sylvan song repeat.
'Twas in his shady arbour's cool retreat
Two youthful swains the god Silenus found,
In drunkenness and sleep his senses bound,
His turgid veins the late debauch betray;
His garland on the ground neglected lay,

* The cave of Silenus, which is the scene of this eclogue, is delineated with sufficient accuracy. The time seems to be the evening; at least the song does not cease till the flocks are folded, and the evening star appears.

Fallen from his head: and by the well-worn ear
His cup of ample size depended near.
Sudden the swains the sleeping god surprise,
And with his garland bind him as he lies
(No better chain at hand), incensed so long
To be defrauded of their promised song.
To aid their project, and remove their fears,
Ægle, a beauteous fountain nymph appears;
Who, while he hardly opes his heavy eyes,
His stupid brow with bloody berries dies.
Then smiling at the fraud Silenus said,
'And dare you thus a sleeping god invade?
To see me was enough; but haste, unloose
My bonds; the song no longer I refuse;
Unloose me, youths: my song shall pay your pains;
For this fair nymph another boon remains.'
  He sung; responsive to the heavenly sound
The stubborn oaks and forests dance around,
Tripping the Satyrs and the Fauns advance,
Wild beasts forget their rage, and join the general dance.
Not so Parnassus' listening rocks rejoice,
When Phœbus raises his celestial voice;
Nor Thracia's echoing mountains so admire,
When Orpheus strikes the loud-lamenting lyre.
  For first he sung of Nature's wond'rous birth;
How seeds of water, air, and flame, and earth,
Down the vast void with casual impulse hurl'd,
Clung into shapes, and form'd this fabric of the world.
Then hardens by degrees the tender soil,
And from the mighty mound the seas recoil.
O'er the wide world new various forms arise;
The infant Sun along the brighten'd skies
Begins his course, while Earth with glad amaze
The blazing wonder from below surveys.
The clouds sublime their genial moisture shed,
And the green grove lifts high its leafy head.

The savage beasts o'er desert mountains roam,
Yet few their numbers, and unknown their home.
He next the blest Saturnian ages sung;
How a new race of men from Pyrrha sprung:*
Prometheus' daring theft, and dreadful doom,
Whose growing heart devouring birds consume.
Then names the spring, renown'd for Hylas' fate,
By the sad mariners bewail'd too late;
They call on Hylas with repeated cries,
And Hylas, Hylas, all the lonesome shore replies.
Next he bewails Pasiphæ (hapless dame!)
Who for a bullock felt a brutal flame.
What fury fires thy bosom, frantic queen!
How happy thou, if herds had never been!
The maids, whom Juno, to avenge her wrong,†
Like heifers doom'd to low the vales along,
Ne'er felt the rage of thy detested fire,
Ne'er were polluted with thy foul desire;
Though oft for horns they felt their polish'd brow,
And their soft necks oft fear'd the galling plough.
Ah wretched queen! thou roam'st the mountain-waste,
While, his white limbs on lilies laid to rest,
The half-digested herb again he chews,
Or some fair female of the herd pursues.
'Beset, ye Cretan nymphs, beset the grove,
And trace the wandering footsteps of my love.
Yet let my longing eyes my love behold,
Before some favourite beauty of the fold
Entice him with Gortynian‡ herds to stray,
Where smile the vales in richer pasture gay.'
He sung how golden fruit's resistless grace
Decoy'd the wary virgin from the race.§

* See Ovid. Met. lib. i.

† Their names were Lysippe, Ipponoë, and Cyrianassa. Juno, to be avenged of them for preferring their own beauty to hers, struck them with madness, to such a degree, that they imagined themselves to be heifers.

‡ Gortyna was a city of Crete. See Ovid. Art. Am. lib. i.

§ Atalanta. See Ovid. Metamorph. lib. x.

Then wraps in bark the mourning sisters round,*
And rears the lofty alders from the ground.
He sung, while Gallus by Permessus† stray'd,
A sister of the Nine the hero led
To the Aonian hill; the choir in haste
Left their bright thrones, and hail'd the welcome guest.
Linus arose, for sacred song renown'd,
Whose brow a wreath of flowers and parsley bound;
And 'Take,' he said, 'this pipe, which heretofore
The far famed shepherd of Ascræa‡ bore;
Then heard the mountain-oaks its magic sound,
Leap'd from their hills, and thronging danced around.
On this thou shalt renew the tuneful lay,
And grateful songs to thy Apollo pay,
Whose famed Grynæan§ temple from thy strain
Shall more exalted dignity obtain.'
Why should I sing unhappy Scylla's fate?‖
Sad monument of jealous Circe's hate!
Round her white breast what furious monsters roll,
And to the dashing waves incessant howl:
How from the ships that bore Ulysses' crew¶
Her dogs, the trembling sailors dragg'd, and slew.
Of Philomela's feast why should I sing,**
And what dire chance befel the Thracian king?
Changed to a lapwing by th' avenging god,
He made the barren waste his lone abode,
And oft on soaring pinions hover'd o'er
The lofty palace, then his own no more.
The tuneful god renews each pleasing theme
Which Phœbus sung by blest Eurotas' stream;

* See Ovid. Met. lib. ii.
† A river in Bœotia, arising from Mount Helicon, sacred to the Muses.
‡ Hesiod.
§ Grynium was a maritime town of the Lesser Asia, where were an ancient temple and oracle of Apollo.
‖ See Virgil. Æn. iii.
¶ See Homer Odyss. lib. xii.
** See Ovid. Metamorph. lib. vi.

O

When bless'd Eurotas gently flow'd along,
And bade his laurels learn the lofty song.
Silenus sung; the vocal vales reply,
And heavenly music charms the listening sky.
But now their folds the number'd flocks invite,
The star of evening sheds its trembling light,
And the unwilling Heavens are wrapt in night.

PASTORAL VII.*

MELIBŒUS, CORYDON, THYRSIS

Melibœus.

BENEATH an holm that murmur'd to the breeze
The youthful Daphnis lean'd in rural ease:
With him two gay Arcadian swains reclined,
Who in the neighbouring vale their flocks had join'd,
Thyrsis, whose care it was the goats to keep,
And Corydon, who fed the fleecy sheep;
Both in the flowery prime of youthful days,
Both skill'd in single or responsive lays.
While I with busy hand a shelter form
To guard my myrtles from the future storm,
The husband of my goats had chanced to stray
To find the vagrant out I take my way.
Which Daphnis seeing, cries, 'Dismiss your fear,
Your kids and goats are all in safety here;
And, if no other care require your stay,
Come, and with us unbend the toils of day

* The scene of this pastoral is as follows: Four shepherds, Daphnis in the most distinguished place, Corydon, Thyrsis, and Melibœus, are seen reclining beneath an holm. Sheep and goats intermixed are feeding hard by. At a little distance Mincius fringed with reeds appears winding along. Fields and trees compose the surrounding scene. A venerable oak, with bees swarming around it, is particularly distinguished. The time seems to be the forenoon, of a summer-day.

In this cool shade; at hand your heifers feed,
And of themselves will to the watering speed;
Here fringed with reeds slow Mincius winds along,
And round yon oak the bees soft-murmuring throng.'
What could I do? for I was left alone,
My Phyllis and Alcippe both were gone,
And none remain'd to feed my weaning lambs,
And to restrain them from their bleating dams:
Betwixt the swains a solemn match was set,
To prove their skill, and end a long debate.
Though serious matters claim'd my due regard,
Their pastime to my business I preferr'd.
To sing by turns the Muse inspired the swains,
And Corydon began th' alternate strains.

Corydon.

Ye nymphs of Helicon, my sole desire!
O warm my breast with all my Codrus' fire.
If none can equal Codrus' heavenly lays,
For next to Phœbus he deserves the praise,
No more I ply the tuneful art divine,
My silent pipe shall hang on yonder pine.

Thyrsis.

Arcadian swains, an ivy wreath bestow,
With early honours crown your poet's brow;
Codrus shall chafe, if you my songs commend,
Till burning spite his tortured entrails rend;
Or amulets, to bind my temples, frame,
Lest his invidious praises blast my fame.

Corydon.

A stag's tall horns, and stain'd with savage gore
This bristled visage of a tusky boar,
To thee, O virgin goddess of the chase,
Young Mycon offers for thy former grace.

If like success his future labours crown,
Thine, goddess, then shall be a nobler boon;
In polish'd marble thou shalt shine complete,
And purple sandals shall adorn thy feet.

Thyrsis.

To thee, Priapus,* each returning year,
This bowl of milk, these hallow'd cakes we bear;
Thy care, our garden, is but meanly stored,
And mean oblations all we can afford.
But if our flocks a numerous offspring yield,
And our decaying fold again be fill'd,
Though now in marble thou obscurely shine,
For thee a golden statue we design.

Corydon.

O Galatea, whiter than the swan,
Loveliest of all thy sisters of the main,
Sweeter than Hybla, more than lilies fair;
If aught of Corydon employ thy care,
When shades of night involve the silent sky,
And slumbering in their stalls the oxen lie,
Come to my longing arms, and let me prove
Th' immortal sweets of Galatea's love.

Thyrsis.

As the vile sea-weed scatter'd by the storm,
As he whose face Sardinian herbs deform,†
As burs and brambles that disgrace the plain,
So nauseous, so detested be thy swain;
If when thine absence I am doom'd to bear
The day appears not longer than a year.
Go home, my flocks, ye lengthen out the day;
For shame, ye tardy flocks, for shame, away!

* This deity presided over gardens.

† It was the property of this poisonous herb to distort the features of those who had eaten of it in such a manner, that they seemed to expire in an agony of laughter.

Corydon.

Ye mossy fountains, warbling as ye flow!
And softer than the slumbers ye bestow,
Ye grassy banks! ye trees with verdure crown'd,
Whose leaves a glimmering shade diffuse around!
Grant to my weary flocks a cool retreat,
And screen them from the summer's raging heat;
For now the year in brightest glory shines,
Now reddening clusters deck the bending vines.

Thyrsis.

Here's wood for fuel; here the fire displays
To all around its animating blaze;
Black with continual smoke our posts appear;
Nor dread we more the rigour of the year,
Than the fell wolf the fearful lambkins dreads,
When he the helpless fold by night invades;
Or swelling torrents, headlong as they roll,
The weak resistance of the shatter'd mole.

Corydon.

Now yellow harvests wave on every field,
Now bending boughs the hoary chesnut yield,
Now loaded trees resign their annual store,
And on the ground the mellow fruitage pour;
Jocund, the face of Nature smiles, and gay;
But if the fair Alexis were away,
Inclement drought the hardening soil would drain,
And streams no longer murmur o'er the plain.

Thyrsis.

A languid hue the thirsty fields assume,
Parch'd to the root the flowers resign their bloom,
The faded vines refuse their hills to shade,
Their leafy verdure wither'd and decay'd:
But if my Phyllis on these plains appear,
Again the groves their gayest green shall wear.
Again the clouds their copious moisture lend,
And in the genial rain shall Jove descend.

Corydon.

Alcides' brows the poplar-leaves surround
Apollo's beamy locks with bays are crown'd,
The myrtle, lovely queen of smiles, is thine,
And jolly Bacchus loves the curling vine;
But while my Phyllis loves the hazel-spray,
To hazel yield the myrtle and the bay.

Thyrsis.

The fir, the hills; the ash adorns the woods;
The pine, the gardens; and the poplar, floods.
If thou, my Lycidas, wilt deign to come,
And cheer thy shepherd's solitary home,
The ash so fair in woods, and garden-pine,
Will own their beauty far excell'd by thine.

Melibœus.

So sung the swains, but Thyrsis strove in vain;
Thus far I bear in mind th' alternate strain.
Young Corydon acquired unrivall'd fame,
And still we pay a deference to his name.

PASTORAL VIII.*

DAMON, ALPHESIBŒUS.

REHEARSE we, Pollio, the enchanting strains
Alternate sung by two contending swains.
Charm'd by their songs, the hungry heifers stood
In deep amaze, unmindful of their food;
The listening lynxes laid their rage aside,
The streams were silent, and forgot to glide.

* In this eighth pastoral no particular scene is described. The poet rehearses the songs of two contending swains, Damon and Alphesibœus. The former adopts the soliloquy of a despairing lover: the latter chooses for his subject the magic rites of an enchantress forsaken by her lover, and recalling him by the power of her spells.

O thou, where'er thou lead'st thy conquering host,
Or by Timavus,* or th' Illyrian coast!
When shall my Muse, transported with the theme,
In strains sublime my Pollio's deeds proclaim;
And celebrate thy lays by all admir'd,
Such as of old Sophocles' Muse inspired?
To thee, the patron of my rural songs,
To thee my first, my latest lay belongs.
Then let this humble ivy-wreath enclose,
'Twined with triumphal bays, thy godlike brows.
What time the chill sky brightens with the dawn,
When cattle love to crop the dewy lawn.
Thus Damon to the woodlands wild complain'd,
As 'gainst an olive's lofty trunk he lean'd.

Damon.

Lead on the genial day, O star of morn!
While wretched I, all hopeless and forlorn,
With my last breath my fatal woes deplore,
And call the gods by whom false Nisa swore;
Though they, regardless of a lover's pain,
Heard her repeated vows, and heard in vain.
Begin, my pipe, the sweet Mænalian strain.†
Blest Mænalus! that hears the pastoral song
Still languishing its tuneful groves along!
That hears th' Arcadian god's celestial lay,
Who taught the idly-rustling reeds to play!
That hears the singing pines! that hears the swain
Of love's soft chains melodiously complain!
Begin, my pipe, the sweet Mænalian strain.
Mopsus the willing Nisa now enjoys—
What may not lovers hope from such a choice!

* A river in Italy.

† This intercalary line (as it is called by the commentators), which seems to be intended as a chorus or burden to the song, is here made the last of a triplet, that it may be as independent of the context and the verse in the translation as it is in the original.—Mænalus was a mountain of Arcadia.

Now mares and griffins shall their hate resign,
And the succeeding age shall see them join
In friendship's tie ; now mutual love shall bring
The dog and doe to share the friendly spring.
Scatter thy nuts, O Mopsus, and prepare
The nuptial torch to light the wedded fair.
Lo, Hesper hastens to the western main.
And thine the night of bliss—thine, happy swain!
Begin, my pipe, the sweet Mænalian strain.
  Exult, O Nisa, in thy happy state!
Supremely blest in such a worthy mate;
While you my beard detest, and bushy brow,
And think the gods forget the world below;
While you my flock and rural pipe disdain,
And treat with bitter scorn a faithful swain,
Begin, my pipe, the sweet Mænalian strain.
  When first I saw you by your mother's side,
To where our apples grew I was your guide;
Twelve summers since my birth had roll'd round,
And I could reach the branches from the ground.
How did I gaze!—how perish!—ah how vain
The fond bewitching hopes that sooth'd my pain?
Begin, my pipe, the sweet Mænalian strain.
  Too well I know thee, Love. From Scythian snows,
Or Lybia's burning sands the mischief rose.
Rocks adamantine nursed this foreign bane,
This fell invader of the peaceful plain.
Begin, my pipe, the sweet Mænalian strain.
  Love taught the mother's* murdering hand to kill,
Her children's blood love bade the mother spill.
Was love the cruel cause?† Or did the deed
From fierce unfeeling cruelty proceed?

* Medea.

† This seems to be Virgil's meaning. The translator did not choose to preserve the conceit on the words *puer* and *mater* in his version; as this (in his opinion) would have rendered the passage obscure and unpleasing to an English reader.

Both fill'd her brutal bosom with their bane;
Both urged the deed, while Nature shrunk in vain.
Begin, my pipe, the sweet Mænalian strain.
Now let the fearful lamb the wolf devour;
Let alders blossom with Narcissus' flower;
From barren shrubs let radiant amber flow;
Let rugged oaks with golden fruitage glow;
Let shrieking owls with swans melodious vie;
Let Tityrus the Thracian numbers try,
Out-rival Orpheus in the sylvan reign,
And emulate Arion on the main.
Begin, my pipe, the sweet Mænalian strain.
Let land no more the swelling waves divide;
Earth, be thou whelm'd beneath the boundless tide:
Headlong from yonder promontory's brow
I plunge into the rolling deep below.
Farewell, ye woods! farewell, thou flowery plain!
Hear the last lay of a despairing swain:
And cease, my pipe, the sweet Mænalian strain.
Here Damon ceased. And now, ye tuneful Nine,
Alphesibœus' magic verse subjoin,
To his responsive song your aid we call;
Our power extends not equally to all.

Alphesibœus.

Bring living waters from the silver stream,
With vervain and fat incense feed the flame:
With this soft wreath the sacred altars bind,
To move my cruel Daphnis to be kind,
And with my frenzy to inflame his soul;
Charms are but wanting to complete the whole.
Bring Daphnis home, bring Daphnis to my arms,
O bring my long-lost love, my powerful charms
By powerful charms what prodigies are done!
Charms draw pale Cynthia from her silver throne,

Charms burst the bloated snake, and Circe's* guests
By mighty magic charms were changed to beasts.
Bring Daphnis home, bring Daphnis to my arms,
O bring my long-lost love, my powerful charms.
  Three woollen wreaths, and each of triple dye,
Three times about thy image I apply,
Then thrice I bear it round the sacred shrine;
Uneven numbers please the powers divine.
Bring Daphnis home, bring Daphnis to my arms,
O bring my long-lost love, my powerful charms.
  Haste, let three colours with three knots be join'd,
And say, 'Thy fetters, Venus, thus I bind.'
Bring Daphnis home, bring Daphnis to my arms,
O bring my long-lost love, my powerful charms.
  As this soft clay is harden'd by the flame,
And as this wax is soften'd by the same,
My love, that harden'd Daphnis to disdain,
Shall soften his relenting heart again.
Scatter the salted corn, and place the bays,
And with fat brimstone light the sacred blaze.
Daphnis my burning passion slights with scorn,
And Daphnis in this blazing bay I burn.
Bring Daphnis home, bring Daphnis to my arms,
O bring my long-lost love, my powerful charms
  As when, to find her love, an heifer roams
Through trackless groves, and solitary glooms;
Sick with desire, abandon'd to her woes,
By some lone stream her languid limbs she throws;
There in deep anguish wastes the tedious night,
Nor thoughts of home her late return invite;
Thus may he love, and thus indulge his pain,
While I enhance his torments with disdain.
Bring Daphnis home, bring Daphnis to my arms,
O bring my long-lost love, my powerful charms.

* See Hom. Odyss. lib. x.

These robes beneath the threshold here I leave,
These pledges of his love, O Earth, receive.
Ye dear memorials of our mutual fire,
Of you my faithless Daphnis I require.
Bring Daphnis home, bring Daphnis to my arms,
O bring my long-lost love, my powerful charms.
These deadly poisons, and these magic weeds,
Selected from the store which Pontus breeds,
Sage Mœris gave me; oft I saw him prove
Their sovereign power; by these along the grove
A prowling wolf the dread magician roams;
Now gliding ghosts from the profoundest tombs
Inspired he calls; the rooted corn he wings,
And to strange fields the flying harvest brings.
Bring Daphnis home, bring Daphnis to my arms,
O bring my long-lost love, my powerful charms.
These ashes from the altar take with speed,
And treading backwards cast them o'er your head
Into the running stream, nor turn your eye.
Yet this last spell, though hopeless, let me try.
But nought can move the unrelenting swain,
And spells, and magic verse, and gods are vain.
Bring Daphnis home, bring Daphnis to my arms,
O bring my long-lost love, my powerful charms.
Lo, while I linger, with spontaneous fire
The ashes redden, and the flames aspire!
May this new prodigy auspicious prove!
What fearful hopes my beating bosom move!
Hark! does not Hylax bark?—ye powers supreme,
Can it be real, or do lovers dream?—
He comes, my Daphnis comes! forbear my charms;
My love, my Daphnis flies to bless my longing arms.

IX.*

LYCIDAS, MŒRIS.

Lycidas.

Go you to town, my friend? this beaten way
Conducts us thither.

Mœris.

Ah! the fatal day,
The unexpected day, at last is come,
When a rude alien drives us from our home.
Hence, hence, ye clowns, th' usurper thus commands,
To me you must resign your ancient lands.
Thus helpless and forlorn we yield to fate;
And our rapacious lord to mitigate
This brace of kids a present I design,
Which load with curses, O ye powers divine!

Lycidas.

'Twas said, Menalcas with his tuneful strains
Had saved the grounds of all the neighbouring swains,
From where the hill, that terminates the vale,
In easy risings first begins to swell;

* This and the first eclogue seems to have been written on the same occasion. The time is a still evening The landscape is described at the 97th line of this translation. On one side of the highway is an artificial arbour, where Lycidas invites Mœris to rest a little from the fatigue of his journey: and at a considerable distance appears a sepulchre by the way-side, where the ancient sepulchres were commonly erected.

The critics with one voice seem to condemn this eclogue as unworthy of its author; I know not for what good reason. The many beautiful lines scattered through it would, one might think, be no weak recommendation. But it is by no means to be reckoned a loose collection of incoherent fragments; its principal parts are all strictly connected, and refer to a certain end, and its allusions and images are wholly suited to pastoral life. Its subject, though uncommon, is not improper; for what is more natural, than that two shepherds, when occasionally mentioning the good qualities of their absent friend, particularly his poetical talents, should repeat such fragments of his songs as they recollected.

Far as the blasted beech that mates the sky,
And the clear stream that gently murmurs by.

Mœris.

Such was the voice of fame; but music's charms,
Amid the dreadful clang of warlike arms,
Avail no more than the Chaonian dove,
When down the sky descends the bird of Jove.
And had not the prophetic raven spoke
His dire presages from the hollow oak,
And often warn'd me to avoid debate,
And with a patient mind submit to fate,
Ne'er had thy Mœris seen this fatal hour,
And that melodious swain had been no more.

Lycidas.

What horrid breast such impious thoughts could
breed!
What barbarous hand could make Menalcas bleed!
Could every tender Muse in him destroy,
And from the shepherd's ravish all their joy!
For who but he the lovely nymphs could sing,
Or paint the valleys with the purple spring?
Who shade the fountains from the glare of day?
Who but Menalcas could compose the lay,
Which, as we journey'd to my love's abode,
I softly sung to cheer the lonely road?
'Tityrus, while I am absent, feed the flock,*
And, having fed, conduct them to the brook
(The way is short, and I shall soon return),
But shun the he-goat with the butting horn.'

* These lines, which Virgil has translated literally from Theocritus, may be supposed to be a fragment of the poem mentioned in the preceding verses; or, what is more likely, to be spoken by Lycidas to his servant; something similar to which may be seen Past. 5, v. 20, of this translation.—The original is here remarkably explicit even to a degree of affectation. This the translator has endeavoured to imitate

Mœris.

Or who could finish the imperfect lays
Sung by Menalcas to his Varus' praise?
'If fortune yet shall spare the Mantuan swains,
And save from plundering hands our peaceful plains,
Nor doom us sad Cremona's fate to share
(For ah! a neighbour's woe excites our fear),
Then high as Heaven our Varus' fame shall rise,
The warbling swans shall bear it to the skies.'

Lycidas.

Go on, dear swain, these pleasing songs pursue;
So may thy bees avoid the bitter yew,
So may rich herds thy fruitful fields adorn,
So may thy cows with strutting dugs return.
Even I with poets have obtain'd a name,
The Muse inspires me with poetic flame;
Th' applauding shepherds to my songs attend,
But I suspect my skill, though they commend.
I dare not hope to please a Cinna's ear,
Or sing what Varus might vouchsafe to hear.
Harsh are the sweetest lays that I can bring,
So screams a goose where swans melodious sing.

Mœris.

This I am pondering, if I can rehearse
The lofty numbers of that labour'd verse
'Come, Galatea, leave the rolling seas;
Can rugged rocks and heaving surges please?
Come, taste the pleasures of our sylvan bowers,
Our balmy-breathing gales and fragrant flowers.
See, how our plains rejoice on every side,
How crystal streams through blooming valleys glide:
O'er the cool grot the whitening poplars bend,
And clasping vines their grateful umbrage lend,
Come, beauteous nymph, forsake the briny wave;
Loud on the beach let the wild billows rave.'

Lycidas.

Or what you sung one evening on the plain—
The air but not the words, I yet retain.

Mœris.

'Why, Daphnis, durst thou calculate the skies,
To know when ancient constellations rise?
Lo, Cæsar's star its radiant light displays,
And on the nations sheds propitious rays.
On the glad hills the reddening clusters glow,
And smiling plenty decks the plains below.
Now graff thy pears; the star of Cæsar reigns,
To thy remotest race the fruit remains.'
The rest I have forgot, for length of years
Deadens the sense, and memory impairs.
All things in time submit to sad decay;
Oft have we sung whole summer suns away.
These vanish'd joys must Mœris now deplore,
His voice delights, his numbers charm no more;
Him have the wolves beheld, bewitch'd his song,*
Bewitch'd to silence his melodious tongue.
But your desire Menalcas can fulfil,
All these, and more, he sings with matchless skill.

Lycidas.

These faint excuses which my Mœris frames
But heighten my desire.—And now the streams
In slumber-soothing murmurs softly flow;
And now the sighing breeze hath ceased to blow.
Half of our way is past, for I descry
Bianor's tomb just rising to the eye.†
Here in this leafy arbour ease your toil,
Lay down your kids, and let us sing the while:

* In Italia creditur luporum visus esse noxios; vocemque homini quem priores contemplentur adimere ad præsans.—*Plin. N. H* viii. 22.

† Bianor is said to have founded Mantua.—*Servius.*

We soon shall reach the town; or, lest a storm
Of sudden rain the evening sky deform,
Be yours to cheer the journey with a song,
Eased of your load, which I shall bear along.

Mœris.

No more, my friend; your kind entreaties spare,
And let our journey be our present care;
Let fate restore our absent friend again,
Then gladly I resume the tuneful strain.

PASTORAL X.*

GALLUS.

To my last labour lend thy sacred aid,
O Arethusa; that the cruel maid
With deep remorse may read the mournful song,
For mournful lays to Gallus' love belong.
(What Muse in sympathy will not bestow
Some tender strains to soothe my Gallus' woe?)
So may thy waters pure of briny stain
Traverse the waves of the Sicilian main.
Sing, mournful Muse, of Gallus' luckless love,
While the goats browse along the cliffs above.

* The scene of this pastoral is very accurately delineated. We behold the forlorn Gallus stretched along beneath a solitary cliff, his flocks standing round him, at some distance. A group of deities and swains encircle him, each of whom is particularly described. On one side we see the shepherds with their crooks; next to them the neatherds, known by the clumsiness of their appearance; and next to these Menalcas with his clothes wet, as just come from beating or gathering winter-mast. On the other side we observe Apollo with his usual insignia; Sylvanus crowned with flowers, and brandishing in his hand the long lilies and flowering fennel; and last of all Pan, the god of shepherds, known by his ruddy smiling countenance, and the other peculiarities of his form.

Gallus was a Roman of very considerable rank, a poet of no small estimation, and an intimate friend of Virgil. He loved to distraction one Cytheris (here called Lycoris), who slighted him, and followed Antony into Gaul.

Nor silent is the waste while we complain,
The woods return the long resounding strain.
Whither, ye fountain-nymphs, were ye withdrawn,
To what lone woodland, or what devious lawn,
When Gallus' bosom languish'd with the fire
Of hopeless love, and unallay'd desire?
For neither by th' Aonian spring you stray'd, [shade.
Nor roam'd Parnassus' heights, nor Pindus' hallow'd
The pines of Mænalus were heard to mourn,
And sounds of woe along the groves were borne;
And sympathetic tears the laurel shed,
And humbler shrubs declined their drooping head.
All wept his fate, when to despair resign'd
Beneath a desert cliff he lay reclined.
Lyceus' rocks were hung with many a tear,
And round the swain his flocks forlorn appear.
Nor scorn, celestial bard, a poet's name;
Renown'd Adonis by the lonely stream
Tended his flock.—As thus he lay along,
The swains and awkward neatherds round him throng.
Wet from the winter-mast Menalcas came
All ask, what beauty raised the fatal flame.
The god of verse vouchsafed to join the rest;
He said, 'What frenzy thus torments thy breast?
While she, thy darling, thy Lycoris, scorns
Thy proffer'd love, and for another burns,
With whom o'er winter wastes she wanders far,
'Midst camps, and clashing arms, and boisterous war.'
Sylvanus came, with rural garlands crown'd,
And waved the lilies long, and flowering fennel round.
Next we beheld the gay Arcadian god;
His smiling cheeks with bright vermilion glow'd.
'For ever wilt thou heave the bursting sigh?
Is love regardful of the weeping eye?
Love is not cloy'd with tears; alas! no more
Than bees luxurious with the balmy flower,

Than goats with foliage, than the grassy plain
With silver rills and soft refreshing rain.'
Pan spoke; and thus the youth, with grief opprest;
'Arcadians! here, O hear my last request;
O ye, to whom the sweetest lays belong,
O let my sorrows on your hills be sung:
If your soft flutes shall celebrate my woes,
How will my bones in deepest peace repose!
Ah, had I been with you a country-swain,
And pruned the vine, and fed the bleating train;
Had Phyllis, or some other rural fair,
Or black Amyntas been my darling care;
(Beauteous, though black; what lovelier flower is seen
Than the dark violet on the painted green?)
These in the bower had yielded all their charms,
And sunk with mutual raptures in my arms:
Phyllis had crown'd my head with garlands gay,
Amyntas sung the pleasing hours away.
Here, O Lycoris, purls the limpid spring,
Bloom all the meads, and all the woodlands sing;
Here let me press thee to my panting breast,
Till youth, and joy, and life itself be past.
Banish'd by love, o'er hostile lands I stray,
And mingle in the battle's dread array;
Whilst thou, relentless to my constant flame,
(Ah could I disbelieve the voice of fame!)
Far from thy home, unaided and forlorn,
Far from thy love, thy faithful love, art borne,
On the bleak Alps with chilling blasts to pine,
Or wander waste along the frozen Rhine.
Ye icy paths, O spare her tender form!
O spare those heavenly charms, thou wintry storm!
'Hence let me hasten to some desert-grove,
And soothe with songs my long-unanswer'd love.
I go, in some lone wilderness to suit
Eubœan lays to my Sicilian flute.

Better with beasts of prey to make abode
In the deep cavern, or the darksome wood;
And carve on trees the story of my woe,
Which with the growing bark shall ever grow.
Meanwhile, with woodland-nymphs, a lovely throng,
The winding groves of Mænalus along
I roam at large; or chase the foaming boar;
Or with sagacious hounds the wilds explore,
Careless of cold. And now methinks I bound
O'er rocks and cliffs, and hear the woods resound;
And now with beating heart I seem to wing
The Cretan arrow from the Parthian string—
As if I thus my frenzy could forego,
As if love's god could melt at human woe.
Alas! nor nymphs nor heavenly songs delight—
Farewell, ye groves! the groves no more invite.
No pains, no miseries of man can move
The unrelenting deity of love.
To quench your thirst in Hebrus' frozen flood,
To make the Scythian snows your drear abode;
Or feed your flock on Ethiopian plains,
When Sirius' fiery constellation reigns,
(When deep-imbrown'd the languid herbage lies
And in the elm the vivid verdure dies,)
Were all in vain. Love's unresisted sway
Extends to all, and we must Love obey.'
'Tis done; ye Nine, here ends your poet's strain,
In pity sung to soothe his Gallus' pain
While leaning on a flowery bank I twine
The flexile osiers, and the basket join.
Celestial Nine, your sacred influence bring,
And soothe my Gallus' sorrows while I sing:
Gallus, my much beloved! for whom I feel
The flame of purest friendship rising still:
So by a brook the verdant alders rise,
When fostering zephyrs fan the vernal skies.

Let us be gone: at eve, the shade annoys
With noxious damps, and hurts the singer's voice;
The juniper breathes bitter vapours round,
That kill the springing corn, and blast the ground.
Homeward, my sated goats, now let us hie,
Lo beamy Hesper gilds the western sky.

www.ingramcontent.com/pod-product-compliance
Lightning Source LLC
LaVergne TN
LVHW020223110826
845151LV00003B/804

* 9 7 8 1 4 2 5 5 3 3 1 2 0 *